ENJOYING
ENGLISH

050 - 4217063
Inas
050 - 6861199
Fara 050 - 7740372
Aujat — 050 - 7969700

Books featured

Braithwaite, E.R. *To Sir with Love*
Cook, Kenneth *Frill-Necked Frenzy*
Cormier, Robert *I am the Cheese*
Fisk, Nicholas *On the Flip Side*
Hentoff, Nat *This School Is Driving Me Crazy*
Hines, Barry *A Kestrel for a Knave*
Hinton, S.E. *Rumble Fish*
Holman, Felice *Slake's Limbo*
Jennings, Paul *Uncanny!*
Kata, Elizabeth *A Patch of Blue*
Lord, Gabrielle *Fortress*
Mayne, William *Drift*
Richter, Hans Peter *I Was There*
Sutcliff, Rosemary *Dawn Wind*
Swindells, Robert *Brother in the Land*
Tolkien, J.R.R. *The Hobbit*
Westall, Robert *The Machine-Gunners*
Wyndham, John *The Day of the Triffids*

ENJOYING ENGLISH

BOOK 3   SADLER / HAYLLAR / POWELL

MACMILLAN

First published 1990 by
MACMILLAN EDUCATION AUSTRALIA PTY LTD
107 Moray Street, South Melbourne 3205
Reprinted 1991, 1993 (twice), 1994, 1995, 1996, 1997

Associated companies and representatives
throughout the world

National Library of Australia
cataloguing in publication data

Sadler R.K. (Rex Kevin).
  Enjoying English Book 3

  ISBN 0 7329 0298 3

  I. English language - Rhetoric - Juvenile literature
  2.English language - Composition and excersises -
  Juvenile literature I. Hayllar, T.A.S. (Thomas
  Albert S.), II. Powell, C.J. (Clifford J.) III. Title.

808. '202

Typeset in Palatino by
Superskill Graphics, Singapore
Printed in Malaysia by
Vivar Printing Sdn. Bhd.

CONTENTS

PREFACE

The *Enjoying English* series is a literature-based course for secondary students. It features an extensive selection of passages drawn from high-interest, contemporary novels and non-fiction books. These constitute a base for the development of comprehension skills and additional work on language and writing skills. Because of the quality of these passages, we anticipate that students will be encouraged to read more widely by seeking out these and other similar books from libraries.

The course gives considerable emphasis to poetry and drama. The wide range of poems presented offers an opportunity for students to explore and appreciate the richness of this strand of literature. Many drama extracts and complete scripts are included, as well as creative drama projects and tasks.

The creative writing sections encourage the development of writing skills by the use of writing models and stimulus photographs. Practical language work is incorporated in each unit to reinforce and develop the students' understanding of essential language concepts.

All the material in *Enjoying English* has been thoroughly tested in the classroom to ensure that it offers rich possibilities for valuable learning and enjoyment.

1
FANTASTIC STORIES

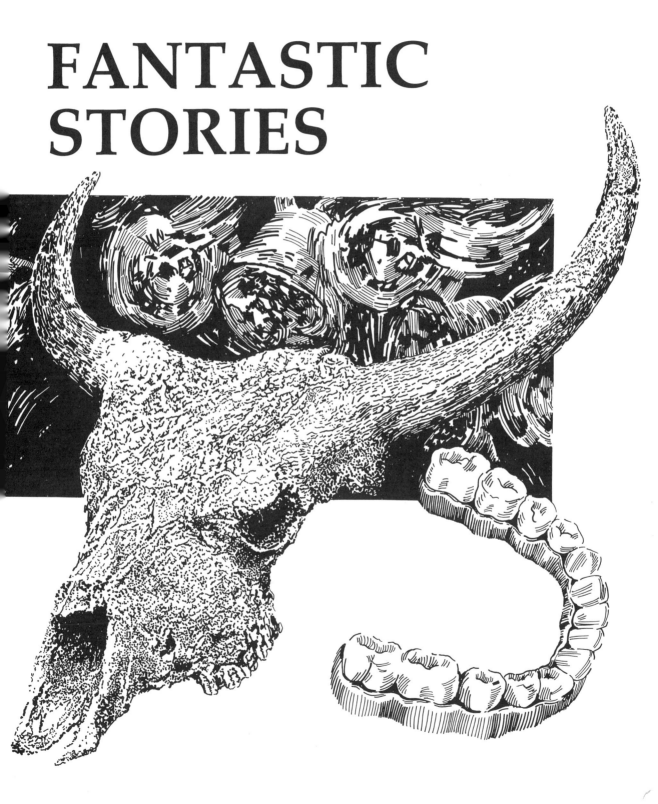

STORIES

A Good Tip for Ghosts

THE WRITER SPEAKS

Wherever I go I am always on the lookout for ideas for stories.

Some of the incidents in my yarns come from things that happened to me as a child. Here is an example.

When I was about eleven or twelve I lived near a rubbish dump called the Dendy Tip (now Dendy Park) in Melbourne. It was wonderful. In the evenings you could go there and throw stones at the crawling rats. There were old prams (with good wheels), dead animals, flies, bits of machinery, rusty cars and an old pond. I once went for a sail in a bath in the pond. The plug popped out and it sank. Boy did I cop it when I got home.

Last year I went to the Warrnambool Tip to dump some junk. I found a good electric sewing machine, an almost new baseball bat, a lawn sprinkler and other great things. My kids were embarrassed and called me a scab. My wife made me take it all back. When I did take it back, another bloke grabbed the sewing machine and put it in his car.

While I was at the tip I thought, 'What a great place for a story. I'll write about a haunted tip.'

You will find some of my experiences in the story 'A Good Tip for Ghosts'.

Paul Jennings

1

Dad was scabbing around in the rubbish.

'How embarrassing,' said Pete, 'It's lucky there's no one else here to see us.'

I looked around the tip. He was right. No one was dumping rubbish except us. There was just Dad, me, and my twin brother Pete. The man driving the bulldozer didn't count. He was probably used to people coming to the tip with junk and then taking a whole pile of stuff back home.

It was a huge tip with a large, muddy pond in the middle. I noticed a steer's skull on a post in the water. There were flies everywhere, buzzing and crawling over the disgusting piles. Thousands of seagulls were following the bulldozer looking for rotten bits of food.

'These country tips are fantastic,' yelled Dad. 'Come and help me get this.' He was trying to dig out an old pram. I looked around and groaned. Another car had just pulled up. It was a real flash one. A Mercedes.

We had just arrived in Allansford the day before. It was a little country town where everybody would know what was going on. Pete and I had to start at a new school the next day. The last thing we wanted was someone to see us digging around in the tip.

A man and a boy got out of the Mercedes. They had a neat little bag of rubbish which the man dropped onto the ground. A cloud of flies rose into the air. 'Let's get out of here,' the man said to the boy. 'This place stinks.'

The boy was about my age but he was twice as big as me. He had red hair and he looked tough. I could see that he was grinning his head off and staring at our car. The back seat of our old bomb was full of Dad's findings. There was a mangled typewriter, a baseball bat, two broken chairs, a torn picture of a green lady lying on a tree branch and a bike with no wheels. I blushed. Dad just could not go to the tip without taking half of it back home with him.

I looked up at the kid with red hair again. He was pointing at Dad and laughing fit to bust. 'Oh no,' groaned Pete. 'Look what he has got now.'

Dad had run over to the bulldozer and held up his hand to stop the driver. He was digging around in front of its blade. He had found an arm sticking out of the junk. It looked like a human arm but it wasn't. It was the arm of one of those shop dummies they put dresses on. Dad pulled and yelled and jiggled until he got the whole thing out. Then he stood there holding it up for all the world to see. A female shop dummy with no clothes on.

It had a wig for hair but apart from that it was stark naked. Its left arm pointed up at the sky. It looked like Dad was standing there with a naked woman. The red-haired kid and his father were both laughing by now. The boy bent down and picked up something from the ground. Then they got into their Mercedes and disappeared through the gate. Pete and I hung our heads with shame. We couldn't bring ourselves to look as Dad dragged the dummy back to the car. I hoped like anything that the red-haired kid didn't go to Allansford School.

'Wonderful,' hooted Dad as he examined the shop dummy. 'Your mother will be pleased. She can use this for making dresses.

'Don't give me that,' yelled Pete. 'You promised Mum that you wouldn't bring anything back from the tip.'

Dad looked a bit sheepish. 'This is different, boys. This isn't junk. This is valuable stuff. Now give me a hand to get this dummy into the car.'

'Not me,' I said.

'Nor me,' added Pete. 'I'm not touching her. She hasn't got any clothes on. It's rude.'

2

There was no room in the back of the car so Dad sat her up in the front. He put the seatbelt on her to stop her falling over. Her lifted-up arm poked through a rust hole in the roof

'Where are we supposed to sit?' I asked. 'There's no room in the back.'

'One on each side of her,' said Dad. 'We'll all sit in the front. There's plenty of room.'

So that's how we went home. Shame. Oh terrible shame. Driving along the road with a naked dummy sitting between us. Every time we passed someone Pete and I ducked down so that they couldn't see us. Dad just laughed. It was all right for him. He wasn't starting at a new school in the morning.

Then it happened. A blue flashing light. A siren. A loud voice saying, 'Pull over, driver.'

It was the police.

A policeman got off his motorbike and walked slowly to the car. He pulled off his gloves and adjusted his sunglasses. Then he leaned in the window. 'What's this naked lady...?' he started off in a cross voice. But then he started laughing. He doubled up, holding his side and pointing to the dummy. 'We had a report that there was a naked woman,' he managed to get out in between gasps. 'But it's only a shop dummy.'

I thought he was never going to stop laughing but finally he said, 'Where did you get all this stuff, sir?'

'The Allansford tip,' answered Dad.

'The locals call it Haunted Tip,' said the policeman with a grin. He seemed to want to stay and talk. He probably was trying to figure out if Dad was a nut case or not. Pete and I just sat there trying not to be seen. 'No one will go there after dark,' he told us. 'They say the ghost of Old Man Chompers walks that tip at night.'

'Old Man Chompers?' said Dad.

'Yes, he was the caretaker of the tip long ago. They say he was minding his two grandchildren there one day. The children disappeared and were never found. The ground collapsed and all the rubbish fell into a huge hole. People think the children

were buried under piles of rubbish. Their bodies were never discovered because the hole filled up with water and formed a lake. Not long after that Old Man Chompers died. People have said that they have seen him walking the tip at night. He pokes at the rubbish, turning things over. He is looking for his lost grandchildren. He moans and groans and calls out for his lost darlings.'

I shivered and looked at Pete. 'You won't catch me going to that tip again,' I said.

'Good,' said the policeman. 'It's a dangerous spot. No place for kids. Anyway — it is said that Old Man Chompers can't leave the tip until he finds his darlings. He has to stay there until he finds them. That's why he wanders the lonely tip at night. He might think that you two would do instead if he caught you there.' Then he said something that made my knees wobble.

'His grandchildren were twins. And Old Man Chompers had poor eyesight. He might mistake you boys for his lost children.' The policeman looked us straight in the eyes and then turned and walked off, chuckling as he went.

3

The next day Pete and I started at Allansford School. It was even worse than we thought it would be. The red-haired kid was waiting at the gate with his tough mates. 'Here they are,' he yelled with glee. 'The twins from the tip.' In a loud voice he started to tell everyone about Dad and the naked shop dummy. Pete and I looked at each other helplessly. We couldn't deny the story. It was true. I could feel tears starting to form behind my eyes. I had to stop them escaping so I blinked real hard. I noticed that Pete was doing the same thing.

It is bad enough starting a new school at the best of times. But when you have to live down something like this it is just terrible. Fortunately the bell went and we had to go inside.

At recess time though, it was even worse. 'I'm the top dog here,' said the red-haired boy. His name was James Gribble. He pushed

Pete in the chest. 'What's your name kid?' he asked roughly.

'Pete.'

Gribble gave a twisted grin. 'This twin is Pete, so this one,' he said, pointing at me, 'must be Repeat. Pete and Repeat, the scabby twins from the tip.' All the kids started to laugh. Some of them weren't laughing too loudly though. I could see that they didn't like Gribble much but they were too scared of him to do anything.

After the laughter died down Gribble went and fetched a shoebox with a small hole in the end. 'I'm the boss here,' he said. 'Every new kid has to take my nerve test. If you pass the nerve test you are okay. If you won't do it I thump you every day until you do.' He held up a clenched fist. The kids all crowded around to see what would happen.

The shoebox had a lid which was tied on with string. Gribble pushed the box into my hand. 'Seeing you like the tip so much, Repeat,' he leered. 'I have brought something back from there for you. One of you two has to have enough nerve to put your hand in there and take out the mystery object that I found at the tip.'

Pete and I looked at the hole in the box. There was just room enough to put a hand inside.

'Go on,' said Gribble. 'Or you get your first thump now.'

I don't mind telling you that I was scared. There was something in the box from the tip. It could be anything. A dead rat. Or even worse; a live rat. Or maybe a loaded mouse trap. My mind thought of the most terrible things. I didn't want to do it but then I noticed one of the kids was nodding to me. A little kid with a kind face. He seemed to be telling me that it was okay.

I looked at Gribble. I have always heard that you should fight a bully when they first pick on you. Then if you fight hard and hurt them they will leave you alone. Even if you lose the fight everyone will respect you and it will be okay. I sighed. Gribble was twice as big as Pete and me put together. And he had tough mates. They would wipe the floor with both of us. Things like teaching the bully a lesson only happen on TV.

Slowly I pushed my hand into the box. At first I couldn't feel anything but then I touched something hard and slimy. It was sort of horseshoe shaped. I shivered. It was revolting. There were rows of little sharp pointed things. Then I felt another one the same. There were two of them. They reminded me of a broken rabbit trap. They felt like they were made of plastic covered in dry mould. I didn't have the faintest idea what I was holding but all sorts of horrible things came into my mind.

Slowly I pulled out my hand and looked. It was a set of old, broken false teeth.

They were chipped and cracked and stained brown. They felt yucky but I smiled at the circle of kids around me. Pete was grinning too. I had passed the nerve test. Or so I thought.

'Okay, Repeat,' said Gribble with a horrible leer. 'You have passed the first bit of the test.' My heart sank. So did Pete's. I didn't realise that there was going to be something else.

Gribble pushed his face up against mine. He had bad breath. 'Now boys,' he growled, 'you have to take the false teeth back where they came from. Back to the tip.' He paused, and then he added, 'At night.'

Pete and I looked at each other. Goose bumps ran up and down our arms. Before we could say anything Gribble told us the next bit. 'And just to make sure that you really go. That you don't just pretend to go. You have to bring something back with you. You have to bring back the steer's skull in the middle of the tip pond. By tomorrow morning. You have to prove that you went to the tip at night by bringing back the skull.'

Pete and I spent the rest of the day worrying. We couldn't concentrate on our school work. I got two out of twenty for my Maths. Pete got four out of twenty. The teacher must have thought that the new kids were real dumb.

That afternoon the boy who had nodded at me in the yard passed me a note. It said:

You had better get the skull. Gribble is real mean. He punched me up every day for a month until I passed his rotten nerve test. Signed, your friend Troy

I passed the note on to Pete. He didn't say anything but he didn't look too good.

After school we walked sadly out of the gate. As we went Gribble yelled at us, 'Have a nice night *my darlings.*'

Neither of us could eat any tea that night. Mum looked at us in a funny way but she didn't say anything. She thought we were just suffering from nerves about the new school. She was right. But only partly. We were also thinking about the ghost of Old Chompers and his lonely search for his lost darlings. I looked at Pete and he looked at me. It was like staring in a mirror. It reminded me that Old Chompers' lost grandchildren were twins too.

'We could pretend to be sick tomorrow,' I said to Pete after tea.

'It wouldn't work,' he answered. 'Mum never gets fooled by that one. Anyway, we would have to go back to school sooner or later.'

'We could tell Dad and...'

'Oh sure,' put in Pete before I could finish. 'And he will tell the teachers and everyone in the school will call us dobbers.'

'What about throwing the false teeth in the bin and getting a steer's skull from somewhere else?' I yelled. 'Gribble would never know that we hadn't really been to the tip.'

Pete looked at me as if I was a bit crazy. 'Great,' he answered in a cross voice. 'And where are you going to get a steer's skull at this time of night? It can't be any old steer's skull you know. It has to have white horns and horrible teeth. No—we will have to do it. We will take the false teeth back to the tip and bring the steer's skull back with us. There's nothing to be scared of really. Ghosts aren't true. There aren't any ghosts. People just think they see them when they are scared.'

I nodded my head without saying anything. I was scared already. And I didn't even want to *think* that I saw a ghost. But I knew Pete was right. We would have to go. It was the only way.

4

That night after Mum and Dad had gone to bed we snuck out of the window and headed off for the tip. We walked slowly along the dusty road which wound through the moonlit paddocks. Pete carried a rope with a hook on the end for getting the skull out of the middle of the pond. I carried a torch in one hand and the false teeth in the other.

They felt all slimy and horrible. I sure was looking forward to getting rid of them.

There was not a soul to be seen. The crickets were chirping their heads off and now and then an owl would hoot. Cows sat silently in the dry grass on the other side of the barbed-wire fences. I was really scared but for some reason the cows made me feel a little better. I don't know why this was because if anything happened the cows weren't going to help. Basically a cow is just a cow.

The further we got from home the more my knees started to wobble. I kept thinking that every shadow hid something evil and terrible. The inside of my stomach wall felt like a frog was scribbling on it with four pencils.

Our first problem started when we reached the tip. It had a high wire fence around it with barbed wire on the top. And the gates were locked. A gentle wind was blowing and the papers stuck to the fence flapped and sighed.

'How are we going to get in?' I asked Pete. Secretly I was hoping we would have to go home.

'Climb over,' he said.

We threw over the rope with the hook on it and clambered up the high wire fence. The wire was saggy and it started to sway from side to side with our weight. We ended up perched on the top trying to get our legs over the barbed wire. Suddenly the whole fence lurched over and sent us crashing onto the ground on the inside. Then the fence sprang back up again with the rope on the other side.

'Ouch, ow, ooh...that hurt,' I yelled. I rubbed my aching head.

'Quiet,' whispered Pete fiercely. 'You're making enough noise to wake the dead.'

His words sent a chill up my spine. 'I wish you hadn't said that,' I whispered back.

Pete looked up at the fence. We were trapped inside. 'We will never get back over that,' he said. I could tell that he was thinking the same thing as me. What fools we were. What were we doing in a lonely tip in the middle of the night? There was no one to help us. There was not another soul there. Or was there?

A little way off, behind some old rusting car bodies, I thought I heard a noise. Pete was looking in the same direction. I was too

We both screeched the same word at exactly the same moment. 'Run.'

And did we run. We tore through the waist-high rubbish. Scrambling. Screaming. Scrabbling. Not noticing the waves of silent rats slithering out of our way. Not feeling the scratches of dumped junk. Not daring to turn and snatch a stare at the horrible spectre who hobbled behind us.

Finally, with bursting lungs, we crawled into the back of an old car. It had no doors or windows so we crouched low, not breathing, not looking, not even hoping.

Why had we come to this awful place? Fools, fools, fools. Suddenly the thought of Gribble and the steer's skull and the false teeth seemed stupid. I would have fought a thousand Gribbles rather than be here. Trapped in a tip with a ghost.

I could feel Pete trembling beside me. And I could hear the voice of someone else. A creaking, croaking cry. 'My darlings...my darlings...my darlings...my darlings.'

terrified to move. I wanted to run but my legs just wouldn't work. I opened my mouth to scream but nothing came out. Pete stood staring as if he was bolted to the ground.

It was a rustling, tapping noise. It sounded like someone digging around in the junk, turning things over. It was coming in our direction. I just stood there pretending to be a dead tree or a post. I wished the moon would go in and stop shining on my white face. The tapping grew louder. It was coming closer.

And then we saw it. Or him. Or whatever it was. An old man, with a battered hat. He was poking the ground with a bent stick. He was rustling in the rubbish. He came on slowly. He was limping. He was bent and seemed to be holding his old, dirty trousers up with one hand. He came towards us. With a terrible shuffle.

Pete and I both noticed it at the same time. His feet weren't touching the ground. He was moving across the rubbish about thirty centimetres above the surface.

It was the ghost of Old Man Chompers.

5

I knew it. I just knew it. The ghost of Old Man Chompers had seen us. He thought we were his lost darlings. His dead grandchildren. He was coming to get us. Then he would be able to leave this place. And take us with him. To that great ghost tip in the sky.

I thought of Mum and Dad. I thought of my nice warm bed. I would never see them again. Our parents would never know what had happened to us. Never know that we had come to our end in the bowels of the Allansford Tip.

'At last, at last...my darlings...at last.' The wailing voice was nearby. He knew where we were. Without a word we bolted out of the car. We fled blindly across the festering tip until we reached the pond. The deep black pond, filled with floating foulness.

And behind, slowly hobbling above the bile, came the searching figure of Old Chompers. We were trapped against the edge of the pond.

In panic we looked around for escape. Mountains of junk loomed over us on either side. To the back was the pond and to the front...we dared not look.

'Quick,' yelled Pete. 'Help me with this.' He was pulling at an old rusty bath. Dragging it towards the water.

'It won't float,' I gasped. 'Look at the plughole. The water will get in. It'll sink.'

Pete bent down and scratched up a dollop of wet clay from the edge of the water. He jammed it into the plughole. 'Come on,' he panted. 'Hurry.'

The bath was heavy but terror made us strong. We launched it out into the murky water. Then we scrambled in. Just in time. The bath rocked dangerously from side to side but slowly it floated away from the approaching horror.

We paddled frantically with our hands until the bath reached the middle of the pond. Then we stopped and stared at Old Chompers. He hobbled to the edge of the water. He staggered towards us. He was walking on the water. His hands outstretched. 'My darlings,' he groaned. 'My long-lost darlings.' Pete and I clung to the sides of the bath with frozen fingers.

The moon went in and everything was black.

Suddenly there was a pop. The clay plug shot into the air followed by a spout of water. Brown wetness swirled in the bath. We were sinking. In a flash we found ourselves swimming in the filthy water. We both headed for the shore, splashing and shouting and struggling. Pete was a better swimmer than me. He disappeared into the gloom.

My jumper soaked up water and dragged me down. I went under. I came up again and spat out the lumpy brown liquid. I knew I would drown unless I could find something to grab on to. The bath was gone.

Then my hand touched something. It was a post with something on the end. I grabbed onto it and kicked towards the shore. As my feet touched the bottom I realised that the post had horns. Then I saw that it had a face. A staring dead face with sharp teeth. It was the horrible leering steer's skull.

I screamed and crawled over to where Pete lay on the shore.

We were both soaked to the skin. We were cold and exhausted. We were too tired to move.

The ghost of Old Man Chompers crept across the water with outstretched hands. His face was wrinkled like a bowl of hard, cold custard. His mouth was as a black hole

formed in the custard by a vanished golf ball. He chuckled as he looked at me.

In my left hand I still had the false teeth. All the time I had been running I had held onto them. I had no other weapon so I held them out in front of me. My fingers were shaking so much that it made them chatter.

As the ghost of Old Man Chompers jumped at me I screamed and screamed and tried to push him off with the teeth.

He grabbed the false teeth from my quivering fingers and shoved them into his mouth. 'At last,' he said. 'I've found them. My darlings. My darlings.' He opened and closed his mouth with joy, making sucking noises as he did it.

After a bit of this he pulled out a ghostly apple from his pocket and started to chomp on it. 'Wonderful,' he cackled. 'Wonderful. You don't know what it was like without my darlings...I owe you boys a big favour for bringing these back.'

We both lay there looking at the grinning ghost. Suddenly he didn't seem so scary Pete found his voice first. 'You mean,' he said. 'That your darlings are your false teeth? Not your long-lost grandchildren?'

The ghost started to cackle even more. 'Them,' he said. 'Them brats. What would I want them for? I told 'em not to play around here. Told 'em it was dangerous. No I was lookin' for these.' He smacked his lips again and showed the cracked, brown teeth. 'Couldn't leave without these. Been lookin' for 'em for years. Now I can go. Now I can leave this rotten dump and join all the others.' As he said this he started to fade away. I knew that we would never see him again.

'Wait,' yelled Pete. 'Don't go. Come back.'

Chompers stopped fading and looked at Pete. 'What?' he said. 'What do yer want?' I could see that he was in a hurry. He didn't want to hang around the tip for any longer than he had to.

Pete looked the ghost straight in the eye. 'You said that you owe us a big favour for bringing your teeth back. Well we want to be paid back. We want one favour before you go.'

'Well,' said Old Chompers with a chipped smile. 'What is it?'

6

Old Chompers wasn't the only one who didn't want to hang around that tip. He showed us a hole in the fence and we ran back down that road as fast as we could go. When we got back to Allansford we climbed up a certain tree and looked in a certain window.

Gribble was fast asleep in bed. He had a big smile on his face. He had fallen asleep thinking about how smart he was making those dumb twins go to the tip in the middle of the night.

Suddenly he was awakened by a noise. It sounded like a person tapping with a stick. It was coming towards his window. Then he heard a croaky voice. 'My darling,' it said. 'At last I've found my darling.'

Gribble was terrified. He wanted to scream but nothing would come out.

A terrible figure floated through the wall. He had a face which was wrinkled like a bowl of hard, cold custard. His mouth was as a black hole formed in the custard by a vanished golf ball. And in that black hole was a pair of cracked old false teeth.

The ghost chuckled as he held the horrible skull over Gribble's head. 'I think you wanted this,' he said as he dropped his load on Gribble's face.

'That was from Pete,' he screeched. 'And this,' he yelled picking it up again, 'is a Repeat.'

Gribble didn't feel the steer's skull the second time. Nor did he see the ghost fade away. He had fainted.

The next day at school though, James Gribble was very nice to me and Pete. I had never met a more polite boy. And there is one thing I can tell you for a fact—he never mentioned anything about being the top dog ever again.

from Uncanny! by Paul Jennings

Reading for Meaning

1 How do the boys feel about their father 'scabbing around in the rubbish'?

2 Why does the boy telling the story groan when another car comes to the tip?

3 'Pete and I hung our heads in shame.' Why do the two boys feel ashamed?

4 Why is the ride home from the tip embarrassing for the boys?

5 According to the policeman, why does the ghost of Old Man Chompers walk the tip at night?

6 'Then he said something that made my knees wobble.' What does the policeman say to cause this?

7 What makes the two boys feel close to tears when they arrive at their new school?

8 At recess, how does Gribble make all the kids laugh at the boys?

9 What is the 'nerve test' that Gribble has prepared for them?

10 What must the boys do to pass the second part of the nerve test?

11 How do the boys feel as they make their way towards the tip that night?

12 What causes the 'rustling, tapping noise' that terrifies the boys?

13 How do the boys escape across the pond as 'the searching figure of Old Chompers' approaches?

14 'Suddenly there was a pop.' What happens to the boys in the middle of the pond?

15 How do the boys make the ghost of Old Man Chompers very happy?

16 How does the ghost explain his presence at the tip for many years?

17 Explain the favour the ghost does for the boys.

18 'A terrible figure floated through the wall.' What is the ghost's face and mouth compared to?

19 Why does Gribble faint?

20 How does Gribble's attitude towards the two boys change?

21 The plot of this story turns on the meaning of 'my darlings'. Explain how this is the case.

22 Did you find this story entertaining? Why or why not?

Charles

An amazing child is the central character of this unusual story.

[handwritten notes, left margin:] sually questions 2,3 contextual (based on the text). Reasoning question. Opinion based.

[handwritten notes, right margin:]
1 - reject ✓
2 - walk or behave with aggresive pride
3 - loud and harsh ✓
4 - disrespectful ✓

The day my son Laurie started kinder- garten he renounced corduroy overalls with bibs and began wearing blue jeans with a belt; I watched him go off the first morning with the older girl next door, seeing clearly that an era of my life was ended, my sweet-voiced nursery-school tot replaced by a long-trousered, swaggering character who forgot to stop at the corner and wave good-bye to me.

He came home the same way, the front door slamming open, his cap on the floor, and the voice suddenly become raucous shouting, 'Isn't anybody *here*?'

At lunch he spoke insolently to his father, spilled his baby sister's milk, and remarked that his teacher said we were not to take the name of the Lord in vain.

'How *was* school today?' I asked, elaborately casual.

'All right,' he said.

'Did you learn anything?' his father asked.

Laurie regarded his father coldly. 'I didn't learn nothing,' he said.

'Anything,' I said. 'Didn't learn anything.'

'The teacher spanked a boy, though,' Laurie said, addressing his bread and butter. 'For being fresh,' he added, with his mouth full.

5. prvent from using or enjoying something.

6. special right granted to a person

'What did he do?' I asked. 'Who was it?'

Laurie thought. 'It was Charles,' he said. 'He was fresh. The teacher spanked him and made him stand in a corner. He was awfully fresh.'

'What did he do?' I asked again, but Laurie slid off his chair, took a cookie, and left, while his father was still saying, 'See here, young man.'

The next day Laurie remarked at lunch, as soon as he sat down, 'Well, Charles was bad again today.' He grinned enormously and said, 'Today Charles hit the teacher.'

'Good heavens,' I said, mindful of the Lord's name, 'I suppose he got spanked again?'

'He sure did,' Laurie said. 'Look up,' he said to his father.

'What?' his father said, looking up.

'Look down,' Laurie said. 'Look at my thumb. Gee, you're dumb.' He began to laugh insanely.

'Why did Charles hit the teacher?' I asked quickly.

'Because she tried to make him colour with red crayons,' Laurie said. 'Charles wanted to colour with green crayons so he hit the teacher and she spanked him and said nobody play with Charles but everybody did.'

The third day—it was Wednesday of the first week—Charles bounced a see-saw on to the head of a little girl and made her bleed, and the teacher made him stay inside all during recess. Thursday Charles had to stand in a corner during story-time because he kept pounding his feet on the floor. Friday Charles was deprived of blackboard privileges because he threw chalk.

On Saturday I remarked to my husband, 'Do you think kindergarten is too unsettling for Laurie? All this toughness, and bad grammar, and this Charles boy sounds like such a bad influence.'

'It'll be all right,' my husband said reassuringly. 'Bound to be people like Charles in the world. Might as well meet them now as later.'

On Monday Laurie came home late, full of news. 'Charles,' he shouted as he came up the hill; I was waiting anxiously on the front steps. 'Charles,' Laurie yelled all the way up the hill, 'Charles was bad again.'

'Come right in,' I said, as soon as he came close enough. 'Lunch is waiting.'

'You know what Charles did?' he demanded, following me through the door. 'Charles yelled so in school they sent a boy in from first grade to tell the teacher she had to make Charles keep quiet, and so Charles

7. occuring at the same time ✓

had to stay after school. And so all the children stayed to watch him.'

'What did he do?' I asked.

'He just sat there,' Laurie said, climbing into his chair at the table. 'Hi, Pop, y'old dust mop.'

'Charles had to stay after school today,' I told my husband. 'Everyone stayed with him.'

'What does this Charles look like?' my husband asked Laurie. 'What's his other name?'

'He's bigger than me,' Laurie said. 'And he doesn't have any rubbers and he doesn't ever wear a jacket.'

Monday night was the first Parent—Teachers meeting, and only the fact that the baby had a cold kept me from going; I wanted passionately✓ to meet Charles's mother. On Tuesday Laurie remarked suddenly, 'Our teacher had a friend come to see her in school today.'

'Charles's mother?' my husband and I asked simultaneously. ✓

'Naaah,' Laurie said scornfully. 'It was a man who came and made us do exercises, we had to touch our toes. Look.' He climbed down from his chair and squatted down and touched his toes. 'Like this,' he said. He got solemnly back into his chair and said, picking up his fork, 'Charles didn't even *do* exercises.'

'That's fine,' I said heartily. 'Didn't Charles want to do exercises?'

'Naaah,' Laurie said. 'Charles was so fresh to the teacher's friend he wasn't *let* do exercises.'

'Fresh again?' I said.

'He kicked the teacher's friend,' Laurie said. 'The teacher's friend told Charles to touch his toes like I just did and Charles kicked him.'

'What are they going to do about Charles, do you suppose?' Laurie's father asked him.

Laurie shrugged elaborately. 'Throw him out of school, I guess,' he said.

Wednesday and Thursday were routine; Charles yelled during story hour and hit a boy in the stomach and made him cry. On Friday Charles stayed after school again and so did all the other children.

With the third week of kindergarten Charles was an institution in our family; the baby was being a Charles when she cried all afternoon; Laurie did a Charles when he filled his wagon full of mud and pulled it through the kitchen; even my husband, when he caught his elbow in the telephone cord and pulled telephone, ashtray, and a bowl of flowers off the table, said, after the first minute, 'Looks like Charles.'

8. a home in which people with special need are cared for.

During the third and fourth weeks it looked like a reformation in Charles; Laurie reported grimly✓ at lunch on Thursday of the third week, 'Charles was so good today the teacher gave him an apple.'

'What?' I said, and my husband added warily, 'You mean Charles?'

'Charles,' Laurie said. 'He gave the crayons around and he picked up the books afterward and the teacher said he was her helper.'

'What happened?' I asked incredulously. ✓

'He was her helper, that's all,' Laurie said, and shrugged.

'Can this be true, about Charles?' I asked my husband that night. 'Can something like this happen?'

9. a person who belives people's motives are usually bad or selfish

'Wait and see,' my husband said cynically. 'When you've got a Charles to deal with, this may mean he's only plotting.'

He seemed to be wrong. For over a week Charles was the teacher's helper; each day he handed things out and he picked things up; no one had to stay after school.

'The PTA meeting's next week again,' I told my husband one evening. 'I'm going to find Charles's mother there.'

'Ask her what happened to Charles,' my husband said. 'I'd like to know.'

'I'd like to know myself,' I said.

On Friday of that week things were back to normal. 'You know what Charles did today?' Laurie demanded at the lunch table, in a voice slightly awed. 'He told a little girl to say a word and she said it and the teacher washed her mouth out with soap and Charles laughed.'

'What word?' his father asked unwisely, and Laurie said, 'I'll have to whisper it to you, it's so bad.' He got down off his chair and went around to his father. His father bent his head down and Laurie whispered joyfully. His father's eyes widened.

'Did Charles tell the little girl to say *that*?' he asked respectfully.

'She said it *twice*,' Laurie said. 'Charles told her to say it *twice*.'

'What happened to Charles?' my husband asked.

'Nothing,' Laurie said. 'He was passing out the crayons.'

Monday morning Charles abandoned the little girl and said the evil word himself three or four times, getting his mouth washed out with soap each time. He also threw chalk.

My husband came to the door with me that evening as I set out for the PTA meeting. 'Invite her over for a cup of tea after the meeting,' he said. 'I want to get a look at her.'

'If only she's there,' I said prayerfully.

'She'll be there,' my husband said. 'I don't see how they could hold a PTA meeting without Charles's mother.'

At the meeting I sat restlessly, scanning each comfortable matronly face, trying to determine which one hid the secret of

10. looking pale.

Charles. None of them looked to me haggard enough. No one stood up in the meeting and apologised for the way her son had been acting. No one mentioned Charles.

After the meeting I identified and sought out Laurie's kindergarten teacher. She had a plate with a cup of tea and a piece of chocolate cake; I had a plate with a cup of tea and a piece of marshmallow cake. We manoeuvred up to one another cautiously, and smiled.

'I've been so anxious to meet you,' I said. 'I'm Laurie's mother.'

'We're all so interested in Laurie,' she said.

'Well, he certainly likes kindergarten,' I said. 'He talks about it all the time.'

'We had a little trouble adjusting, the first week or so,' she said primly, 'but now he's a fine little helper. With occasional lapses, of course.'

'Laurie usually adjusts very quickly,' I said. 'I suppose this time it's Charles's influence.'

'Charles?'

'Yes,' I said, laughing, 'you must have your hands full in that kindergarten, with Charles.'

'Charles?' she said. 'We don't have any Charles in the kindergarten.'

from *The Lottery* by Shirley Jackson

Reading for Meaning

1 On the day Laurie starts kindergarten, what changes in him are noticed by his mother?

2 When Laurie returns home, what does he have to say about his first day at kindergarten?

3 How does Laurie bring Charles into the conversation?

4 What joke does Laurie play on his father?

5 Explain why Charles can be described as a violent boy at kindergarten?

6 Why does Laurie's mother feel that kindergarten might be too unsettling for him.

7 What is her husband's attitude to Charles?

8 'On Monday Laurie came home late...' Why is Laurie late?

9 How is Laurie disrespectful to his father at the table?

10 How does Charles treat the man who comes to make the kindergarten children do exercises?

11 'Wednesday and Thursday were routine.' What kinds of 'routine' violence does Charles practise on these days?

12 Explain how Charles becomes 'an institution' in Laurie's family.

13 Explain the change that comes over Charles during his third and fourth weeks at kindergarten.

14 'On Friday of that week things were back to normal.' What happens to create this normality?

15 How does Charles craftily escape punishment for telling a little girl to swear?

16 'Monday morning Charles abandoned the little girl...' Why would this Monday morning have been a terrible one for the teacher?

17 At the PTA meeting, why don't any of the parents look like Charles's mother?

18 What is the surprise ending of this story?

19 Explain why you think Laurie behaves as he does throughout the story.

20 What do you think is unusual about this story?

POETRY

REAL-LIFE POEMS

Something Has Got to Be Said

something has got to be said
about all these squashed animals on the road
how the guts get squeezed out of them
like gory toothpaste from furry tubes
how gobs of bleeding meat
get flattened into a stain
covered by a tatty fur mat

I mean the pressed cats of all colours
the slouched hulks of possums
pelts still weirdly rich and the fists still curled
like babies' when they're sleeping
& I mean the scrawny sprawl of native hens
still on the run with necks stretched out
toward the ditch never reached

once there were two swans
flanking the banked curve of the highway
black monuments with heads flung back
and wings fanned out
looking so much like graveyard statuary
it gave you the creeps
to pass between them

somehow the wallabies
are usually off on the side of the road
it must be the final leap
dead or alive of the long springing haunches
that carries them over at last
to crash among the beer cans
and bottle glass

it's just as well too
because you wouldn't want to drive over such a bulk
of dead weight
swelling out already the belly distended
you'd be lucky to clear it
and you'd rather not hear that wet mucky smack
bad enough just to imagine it

eventually everyone gets
the thunk of a bird who swung too low
the plump of a rabbit whose dodging didn't work
or what is even worse the crunch of a bandicoot
they are so brittle born senile
poor little stripey-rumped ditherers
their corpses are plentiful

thank god for the crows
and other carrion eaters who clean up the roads
it's all under control
you tell yourself nothing really gets wasted in this world
meanwhile you drive like through a minefield
because you hate the feel
of meat sliding under the wheels

Edith Speer

Questions

1 In the first verse, what are the 'squashed animals' compared to?

2 What does the poet mean by 'pressed cats'?

3 What has happened to the native hens?

4 Why does it give the poet 'the creeps' to pass between the two dead swans?

5 Why are the wallabies 'usually off on the side of the road'?

6 What seems horrifying about their final landing place?

7 How is the reader's sense of hearing appealed to in the sixth verse?

8 Why does the poet say 'thank God for the crows'?

9 Why is the drive along the road 'like through a minefield'?

10 How does the poet achieve her purpose of shocking the reader?

Money Moans

Money I haven't got enough
Money I'll never have enough
Money is what I want, I want
Money so that I don't have to worry about

Money When you have lots of
Money you can make lots more
Money by doing nothing but letting your
Money work for you by making

Money breeds
Money leads to
Money leads to
Money leads to worrying about

Money makes holes in trouser pockets
Money makes guns and nuclear rockets
Money makes hospitals and tanks
Money makes funeral parlours and banks
Money makes people go off the rails
Money fill coffers, coffins and jails

I lie awake at night
Worrying about   *money*
A taxperson somewhere
Spends all the days
Making lots of   *money*
Finding new ways
To keep me awake at night
Worrying about   *money*

Mone mone money
All I do is moan
about money.

Roger McGough

Questions

1 What complaint does the poet begin with?

2 Why does the poet want lots of money?

3 In the fourth verse, what point do you think the poet is making when he lists some of the things money is used for?

4 In the fifth verse, what effect does money have on the poet's life?

5 In the last verse, how does the poet link 'moan' with money?

6 In 'Money Moans', what is the poet's message to the reader?

7 Do you think the title 'Money Moans' is suitable? Why or why not?

8 Using this poem as your model, write your own poem on a topic of special importance to you (for example: Time, Love, Friends, School).

Old Mister Roberts

Old Mister Roberts lives on the corner
next to the sweetshop. Tall and dusty,
very slow-moving; walks with a cane.
Thin dry face, all stretched and bony,
straight pinched nose with bristly whiskers,
not much hair, but bushy eyebrows,
small blue eyes as bright as flames.

Old Mister Roberts goes out walking;
raises his hat if you say Good Morning,
shakes his stick if you call him names.
Always wears an old red waistcoat,
jacket patched with leather elbows,
wears no collar when it's sunny,
wears a trilby when it rains.

Old Mister Roberts was a sailor:
round the world with coal and timber
—probably sailed the Spanish Main.
Sometimes, in the park in Summer,
you can meet him when he's walking;
then he'll sit and tell you stories,
dreaming that he's young again.

Tony Charles

Questions

1 What actions of Old Mister Roberts show that he is <u>frail</u>?   *weak*

2 In the <u>first verse</u>, what do you discover about his <u>physical appearance</u>?
All the rest of his face looks old but his eyes still look young and full of life

3 How are his eyes in contrast to the rest of his face?
When someone says good Morning he raises his hat as a reply.

4 How does Old Mister Roberts display the polite side of his nature?
Whenever a person calls him names he shakes his stick

5 How does he display the angry side of his nature?
He dosen't give up his old things easily

6 'Always wears an old red waistcoat'. What does this suggest about Old Mister Roberts' attitude to life?
Sailor. Because sailors always come across adventures

7 What words in the third verse suggest that his past life may have been full of adventure?
He wants to be young again.

8 What is special about the stories Old Mister Roberts might tell you in the park?
Old age is just a stage of life and all will one day come to a stage like

9 What do you think was the poet's purpose in writing this poem?
Because when your old you wish to be young again. And it is a old Mister Roberts

10 After reading this poem, why do you think a feeling of sadness is sometimes associated with old age?
times sad to old ones trying so hard to be young again

thin
dry
face
as bright
flames

A1. He walks slowly and need the help of cane to move.

A2. He is tall, has a thin dry face, he's bony, straight pinched nose with bristly whiskers, bushy eyebrows and small blues.

Breakdancers

Our stage is plaza, shopping mall, pedestrian zone,
or the arcades outside the stores on closing day.
Evenings especially, outside Woolworth's or the C and A,
we flock together, man, to rap and break the night away.

The streets are ours as well as yours, and so you stop
and watch in wonder as we strut our breaks. In groups
of five or six we switch our stuff and hip the hop—
we need no classy club to spread our twirls and loops.

And so you see us tumble, shadow-box, do double somersaults
and spin on headstands, handstands, double-jointed tops:
our ghetto-blasters scratch the beat, we pop our joints
to R and B and Rock, with one-hand flips and flops.

They call us breakers, smurfers, scratchers, robot hips.
We do our solo turns—the flopping fish, the head-walk and
the nerveless, boneless pantomime that—though we dance
alone—makes unseen partners take us by the hand.

We are the blacks, hispanics, rejects and the out-of-work.
Our youth is useless in society today. Our energy, for sure,
can not be channelled into army, factory, production line—
and so we break, till bottoms, hands and feet are sore.

But we are young, athletic, acrobatic, tai-chi punks,
we have the look, the caps, the sneakers and the gloves,
the knee-caps, bottom-bumpers, headbands—all the gear
to help us flip and jerk the way the public loves.

They stand and watch us do our turns, and maybe drop
a coin or two into our common pot. We need the dough, to buy
our Adidas or Pumas, Nike Golfs, or ten-feet moquette spreads
we lay on any concourse corner for a natural high.

We must be fit, and fast, and funny too. We take no drugs, no smokes.
These rippling spines and fluid limbs are trained and taut and neat
so we can break and strut instead of steal and fight—
and speak the universal language of the hip-hop street!

James Kirkup

Questions

1 What setting is described in the first verse?

2 What does the second verse reveal about the breakdancers' attitude to life?

3 What does the third verse tell us about what breakdancers do?

4 Why do 'unseen partners' appear to be at work in breakdancing?

5 Who are the breakdancers?

6 Why do they dance?

7 Why does the public love to watch the breakdancers?

8 Why do the breakdancers need their public?

9 Why do the breakdancers 'take no drugs, no smokes'?

10 Do you think this poem successfully conveys what it is like to be a breakdancer? Give reasons for your opinion.

Hairstyle

What about my hairstyle?
On my head I carry
a phosphorescent porcupine —
but it's mine it's mine
and if you don't like my head
you can drop dead.

What about my hairstyle?
On my head I bear a mane
of flaming dreadlocks
sometimes hidden by the red gold and green
but flaming all the same
with I-rie pride of Africa.
Know what I mean?

What about my hairstyle?
On my head I wear
a Mohican rainbow
that makes me glow.
I know some eyebrows go
up in despair
but it's my hair it's my hair.

What about my hairstyle?
On my head I show a crown
Of incandescent candy floss.
Who cares if some people frown
and say, 'Young people are lost'.
At least me Mum doesn't get on me back;
she says, 'I suppose you're only young once'.

What about my hairstyle?
On my head I have whispers
of braided beads.
Me Mum says she wouldn't have the patience —
but these beads are in no hurry
I tell them my needs
they listen to the song inside of me.

John Agard

Cycling Down the Street to Meet My Friend John

On my bike and down our street,
Swinging round the bend,
Whizzing past the Library,
Going to meet my friend.

Silver flash of spinning spokes,
Whirr of oily chain,
Bump of tyre on railway line
Just before the train.

The road bends sharp at Pinfold Lane
Like a broken arm,
Brush the branches of the trees
Skirting Batty's Farm.

Tread and gasp and strain and bend
Climbing Gallows' Slope,
Flying down the other side
Like an antelope.

Swanking into Johnnie's street,
Cycling hands on hips,
Past O'Connors corner shop
That always smells of chips.

Bump the door of his back-yard
Where we always play,
Lean my bike and knock the door,
'Can John come out to play?'

Gareth Owen

WRITING

FILM AND VIDEO REVIEWS

WHAT IS A FILM REVIEW?

A film reviewer critically examines a film for the benefit of the intending film-goer. First, the reviewer provides such information about the film as its title, the names of the main actors, its rating and often the theatres at which the film is showing. A good reviewer will then go on to describe what he or she believes to be the film's main strength. Often this is concerned with the film's characterisation. The reviewer discusses how suitably cast the actors are, and often presents the audience's reaction to one or more of the characters.

At the heart of any film is its theme or central idea, and the film reviewer evaluates this in terms of whether the storyline or plot of the film does justice to the theme. In doing so, the reviewer gives us a general idea of the plot, (although the climax or ending is never revealed for obvious reasons.)

Sometimes in a review the focus has to be on the setting, especially if special effects make a spectacular contribution to the entertainment value of the film. This is the case in the Indiana Jones movies.

Finally, the reviewer makes his or her judgement, weighing up the good and bad features of the film and making a recommendation to the film-goer, (such as 'Highly recommended for teenagers'.)

Let's look at a film review to see how this works in practice.

Indestructible Indy

Special effects do a magnificent job

By Mr Showbiz MATT WHITE

There are several hundred names in the screen credits which unroll after the showing of *Indiana Jones and the Last Crusade* and I'm sure I saw one for 'Senior Char Lady'.

Be that as it may—the point is that apart from the six principal players comprising **Harrison Ford, Sean Connery, Denholm Elliott, Alison Doody, John Rhys-Davies** and **Julian Glover**, the special effects credits are endless.

And every one of them is well deserved.

More than ever, in this last of a trilogy of daring-do by the indestructible Indiana Jones, whose real name we now discover is Henry Jones Jnr (Indiana was his boyhood dog's name!), the special effects are magnificent.

Stunt work by an army of fearless stuntpersons also accounts for some of the best moments in a film story that would be rather dreary without their breath-taking action.

This third Indiana Jones movie is a hoot and the addition of Sean Connery, a dab hand at tongue-in-cheek thrills, as Harrison Ford's dad, is a delightful addition, blowing a little originality along a well-worn adventure trail.

And a chuckle-worthy hoot it should be, having cost something like $50 million, but in spite of the million dollars a giggle, one feels Indiana's trail in and out of merry mayhem is overdue for a last ride into the sunset.

But this doesn't mean you'll be bored by this latest saga.

There isn't time for that. Just hanging in to stay with the pace of the action is like clinging to the safety bar of a rollercoaster. No chance of attention wandering from what's directly ahead.

There are some wonderful one-liners that will crack any

Indiana Jones and his dad on the quest for the Holy Grail

audience up as the plot hurries at breakneck speed to its obvious conclusion.

Indiana Jones and the Last Crusade begins with Indiana as a teenager, played with much gusto by River Phoenix, rescuing a valuable antique from grave robbers and being chased over mountains and train roofs to his home.

There, we hear — but don't see — his dad, Professor Henry Jones, as he mutters comment while perusing some massive tome on anthropology or whatever.

In fact, we don't come face to face with Poppa Connery until Indy is grown up and hell-bent on rescuing his dad from Nazis in an Austrian castle hideout where they are demanding he lead them to where the Holy Grail is hidden.

Elusive

Now, as any lad and lass who has given books about knights on noble quests more than a casual glance knows, that elusive chalice from which Jesus is said to have taken his last sip has been hidden for centuries.

The Nazis want it to prove they're a super race and they're getting a lot of help from an attractive anthropologist named Elsa Schneider who, unbeknown to her colleagues, wants the Holy Grail for herself.

Meanwhile, she has a love affair with Indy who later suspects he was second to his father for that favour when he asks how his dad knew she was not a nice lady.

'She talks in her sleep,' growls his dad, and the expression of dawning disgust on Indy's face is a joy to behold.

The conclusion is obvious from the start and it's enough to say now that the road to victory is thick with suspenseful episodes.

This brings me back to the folk who made the riveting action scenes.

Steven Spielberg has done a splendid job of directing these sequences, but my accolades go to special effects supervisors **George Gibbs** and **Michael McAlister**.

They created an array of machinery ranging from mechanical rats and pre-World War II armoured vehicles to speedboats being chewed to pieces by a ship's propeller.

Then there are the stunt artists **Vic Armstrong** and **Gabe Cronelly** who substituted for the cast in dangerous scenes involving runaway vehicles and explosives.

It all adds up to a lot of fun. But enough is enough, and I trust that Steven Spielberg will keep his word and ensure, as he does in this third Indy picture, that its hero keeps riding into the sunset.

from *The Daily Mirror*

LAST CRUSADE   HOYTS 6 EASTGARDENS
WARRINGAH MALL
HOYTS 6 WARRAWONG   BONDI JUNCTION

Questions

1 What is eye-catching about the title of the review?

2 What is the title of the film being reviewed?

3 Who is the film reviewer?

4 In the reviewer's opinion, what is the most magnificent aspect of the film?

5 'This third Indiana Jones movie is a hoot...' Say what this means in your own words.

6 Why does the reviewer think the actor Sean Connery is a 'delightful addition'?

7 How does the reviewer suggest that the Indiana Jones series has lost some of its appeal?

8 What will prevent viewers being bored by the Indiana Jones saga?

9 At what point in the review is the story (or plot) of the film outlined?

10 What group is presented as the enemy in the film?

11 Around what famous object does the plot revolve?

12 How were the film's cast members protected from dangerous situations?

13 What point is the reviewer making in the last paragraph of the review?

14 Look at the cinema ad that follows the review. What rating has the film been given?

15 Would this review make you want to go and see *Indiana Jones and the Last Crusade*? Why or why not?

WRITING YOUR OWN REVIEW

Here is a review of a film that is available on video. Notice that after the title there is a rating given in brackets. The rating system used is **G** (for general exhibition), **PG** (parental guidance recommended), **M** (for mature audiences), and **R** (restricted to persons 18 years and over).

Other information in this review includes: the year the film was made; the category (comedy, drama, adventure, etc.); the names of the two main actors and the director; the running time; and the name of the company that made the film. Then follows a brief summary of the story, comments on the acting and a conclusion about the film's worth. Finally, the video is assessed. Five stars means 'outstanding', four stars means 'excellent', three stars means 'very good', two stars means 'average' and one star means 'below average'.

Big (PG)

1988. Comedy. Tom Hanks, Elizabeth Perkins. D: Penny Marshall. 100 mins. CBS/ Fox

A 12-year-old boy, who makes a wish to be big, wakes up one morning to find he has been transformed into a 35-year-old man. Complications arise when he shoots swiftly up the corporate ladder of a toy company and falls for a female executive.

Hanks gives his best performance yet as Josh, the boy who ages 23 years overnight. He is well supported by Perkins and the young lad who plays his neighbour and classmate. Director Marshall, of *Laverne & Shirley* fame, handles her task with ease to produce the best of the current crop of body-swapping films that are all the rage at the moment.

Now write your own review of a video you have watched recently. Copy the video review card into your workbook and fill in all the details about the video. You can then use the information on your card to help you write the review.

VIDEO REVIEW CARD

Title: Lizzie Mcguire Movies

Rating: Excellent   Year: 2003

Main actors: Hilary Duff

Category: Comedy

Director:

Running time: 2½ hr   Film company: Walt Disney

1 Why is the title appropriate? Because its about her.

2 Why did you like/dislike the main character(s)? I like the main character because she fits the role purfectly.

3 Which minor characters impressed you? Why? Gordo, because he was so funny.

4 Who was the best actor or actress? Why? Hilary Duff because her acting takes my breath away.

5 How did the conflict between characters first show itself? It started when she spoilt her graduation and her rivals never let her forget it.

6 Briefly describe the setting and comment on its effectiveness. Its about Rome

7 What special effects were impressive? The part where the show one of the monuments of Rome.

8 Did the plot (or storyline) hold your interest? Why or why not? Yes, because it was something different.

9 What was the theme (or main idea)? Dreams can come true

10 Did the ending leave you satisfied? Why or why not? Yes because it was an unexpected ending which kept me on my toes.

Assessment (number of stars): ★★★★

16·9·03
C·W

LANGUAGE

LANGUAGE IN ACTION

Let's think about four very important parts of speech: nouns, adjectives, verbs and adverbs.

NOUNS

Nouns are the words that are used to name people, animals, places, things, feelings and qualities. Here are some examples of nouns.

people: hitch-hiker, conjurer, bricklayer, teacher, passenger
animals: rat, horse, pigs, cows, rabbits
places: tip, kindergarten, London, school, Scotland
things: skull, car, rubbish, fingers, motorcycle
feelings: fear, annoyance, amazement, anger, joy
qualities: trouble, ugliness, beauty, skilfulness, sleekness

Nouns and Meanings

For each of the following meanings, supply a noun from the box.

pedestrian 11	school 9	thigh 3	excitement 6
Jupiter 20	telephone 18	consciousness 19	Mercedes 7
relaxation 13	Rome 2	criminal 8	rat 14
teeth 10	recipe 17	strength 5	rubbish 4
driver 1	accelerator 3	aquarium 16	accuracy 12

1 A person who controls a car

2 The capital city of Italy

3 The part of the leg above the knee

4 Worthless or waste material

5 Power and endurance

6 A thrilling feeling

7 The name of a luxury German car

8 A person who commits a crime

9 A place where students are taught

10 Bone-like objects embedded in the jaws

11 A person who travels on foot

12 The quality of being exact

13 A feeling of ease and calm

14 The pedal on a car that controls speed

15 A long-tailed rodent

16 A place where fish are kept

17 Directions for preparing food

18 An instrument of communication

19 A state of awareness

20 The largest of the planets

ADJECTIVES

We often need additional information about nouns, and it is adjectives that supply us with this information. Adjectives describe nouns by referring to their size, shape, colour or other characteristics. For example, from 'A Good Tip for Ghosts' we have this description of Old Chompers, the ghost of the tip. The adjectives are in heavy type.

OLD CHOMPERS

A **terrible** figure floated through the wall. He had a face which was wrinkled like a bowl of **hard**, **cold** custard. His mouth was as a **black** hole formed in the custard by a **vanished** golf ball. And in that **black** hole was a pair of **cracked old** false teeth.

from 'A Good Tip for Ghosts' by Paul Jennings

Adjectives in Action

In the following passage from Conan Doyle's Sherlock Holmes story 'The Hound of the Baskervilles', the ferocious dog that dominates the story is described in ghastly detail by the use of appropriate adjectives. However, a number of important adjectives have been removed and placed in the box. Your task is to rewrite the passage correctly, inserting the adjectives from the box as you go. Note that some letters have been given to help you.

delirious	enormous	coal-black	open
hellish	smouldering	dark	appalling
mortal	savage	flickering	disordered

THE HOUND APPEARS!

A hound it was, an enormous. c.oa\.....-b.la..k.... hound but not such a hound as m.arta.... eyes have ever seen. Fire burst from its o.pen.... mouth, its eyes glowed with a s.avage... glare, its muzzle and hackles and dewlap were outlined in f.lickering flame. Never in the delirous.. dream of a disordered brain could anything more smouldering more a.palling., more hellish.. be conceived than that d.ar.k...k form and savage face which broke upon us out of the wall of fog.

from 'The Hound of the Baskervilles' by Sir Arthur Conan Doyle

Description are made descriptive by the use of adjectives of size, shape, colar characteristic

VERBS

Verbs express action. They are *doing, being* and *having* words. A verb can be just a single word or it can consist of several words. Here are examples of verbs taken from the stories at the beginning of this unit. The verbs are shown in heavy type.

- A cloud of flies **rose** into the air. 'Wonderful,' **hooted** Dad...
- 'Your mother **will be pleased**.'
- The day my son Laurie **started** kindergarten he **renounced** corduroy overalls...
- I **was waiting** anxiously on the front steps.

Verb Opposites

For each of the following verbs there is a verb (one word only) that has the opposite meaning. Give the missing verbs. Note that an example and clues are provided.

1	begin	finish	11	lengthen	shorten
2	give	take	12	forget	remeber ..
3	lose	find	13	appear	disappear
4	float	sink	14	prevent	allow ....
5	join	seperate .	15	admit	deny ... —
6	succeed	fail	16	lead	follow ...
7	create	destroy ..	17	enter	leave ....
8	save	spend ...	18	arrive	depart ...
9	teach	learn	19	expand	contract ..
10	send	recieve ..	20	tighten	loosen ..

ADVERBS

(Just as adjectives tell us more about nouns, adverbs tell us more about verbs.) They tell *how*, *when*, *where*, or *why* the action of the verb takes place. For example:

• The police officer signalled **vigorously** to the driver.

Note that the adverb 'vigorously' tells us more about the verb by telling us *how* the police officer signalled.

An adverb can also be used to change the structure of a sentence in order to focus the reader's attention on *how, when* or *where* or *why* an action was performed. For example:

• The boys crept **cautiously** through the tip.

Now let us change the structure of the sentence by putting the adverb first. This has the effect of focussing the reader's attention on *how* the boys crept.

• **Cautiously** the boys crept through the tip.

Beginning Sentences with Adverbs

Rewrite each of the following the sentences so that it begins with the adverb.

1 She waited anxiously for the survivors to appear.
Anxiously she waited for the survivors to appear

2 In the tip, rubbish was strewn everywhere.
Everywhere rubbish was strewn in the tip

3 The police officer came strolling slowly towards us.
Slowly the...police...officer...came...~~that~~...strolling toward us.

4 My father often collected huge piles of rubbish.
Often ...my...father...collected...huge...piles...of...rubbish

5 He walked sadly away from the school gate.
Sadly ...he...walked...away...from...the...school...gate.

6 He placed the watch carefully on the leather tray.
Carefully ...he...placed...the...watch...on...the...leather tray

7 'Here they are,' he yelled gleefully.
Gleefully ...he...yelled..'Here...they...are'......

8 The car up ahead suddenly accelerated.
Suddenly ...the car...up...ahead...accelerated...

Word Families

Given one word in each word family, fill in the others correctly under their headings. The first one has been done for you.

	Noun	Adjective	Verb	Adverb
a	success	successful	succeed	successfully
b	quiteness	quiet	quiten	quietly
c	amazement	amazingg	amaze	amazingly
d	haste	hasty	hasten	hastily
e	fright	frightful	frighten	frightfully
f	equality	equal	equalise	equally
g	beauty	beautiful	beautify	beautifully
h	attractiveness	attractive	attract	attractively
i	terror	terrible	terrify	terribly
j	satisfaction	satisfactory	satisfy	satisfactorily

GETTING IT RIGHT

COMPARISONS

Comparisons Involving Two

When an adjective is used to compare one person or thing to another, we can either add 'er' to the adjective or use the word 'more'. For example:

- Laurie is **tall**.
  Laurie is the **taller** of the two students.

- Pete was **cautious**.
  Pete was the **more cautious** of the two boys.

(If the adjective is a short word, add 'er'; if it is a long word, use 'more'.)

Comparisons Involving More Than Two

Adjectives can also be used to compare one person or thing with more than two others. Such adjectives end in 'est' or use, the word 'most'. For example:

- My car is the **largest** of the three vintage cars.
- This park is the **most beautiful** in the district.

(If the adjective is a short word, add 'est'; if it is a long word, use 'most'.)

Exceptions

Here are some important adjectives that do not obey the rules.

- **good** better best
- **bad** worse worst
- **little** less least

Getting Comparisons Right

Complete each of the following sentences by inserting in the space provided the correct form of the adjective in brackets.

1 The rubbish tip is the .... place in our suburb.   (dirty)

2 Of the two of us, Pete was the .... when it came to getting away from the ghost.   (fast)

3 Old Chompers lifted the .... end of the rope.   (thin)

4 Laurie was easily the .... pupil in the class.   (bad)

5 The younger policeman was the .... of the two.   (friendly)

6 Her exam results are .... than mine.   (good)

7 The hitch-hiker's hands were much .... than the driver's.   (skilful)

8 The brain is the .... computer ever created.   (wonderful)

DRAMA

Decline of the Roman Umpire

by Bill Condon

> **CHARACTERS**
>
> **Cheapus Dirt**
> **Gladdus Dirt**
> **Dodo the Mind Reader**
> **a chariot driver**
> **a beggar**
> **Typhus the Tentmaker**
> **Saliva**
> **Senator Alka Seltzer**
> **Tupperware the Unbreakable**
> **Trainer — Miss Herculaneum the Cranium**
> **a large and volatile crowd**

The play is set in ancient Rome and all players, unless otherwise specified, wear togas. As the curtain rises Cheapus Dirt and his wife Gladdus enter. Gladdus is wearing a blindfold.

Cheapus   At last we're here.

Gladdus   Great. Now take this blindfold off me.

Cheapus   Not so fast, Gladdus. First you have to try to guess where we are.

Gladdus   We're in Bath of course. We always spend our holidays in Bath because your cousin Tiberius can get us in for free.

Cheapus   Are you implying that I'm mean with money?

Gladdus   Why on earth would I imply that, Cheapus? Just because I am the only woman in all of Rome who had to give her wedding ring back seconds after her marriage.

Cheapus   I explained that, Gladdus—hiring a ring was a very sensible idea.

Gladdus   And then you had the hide to charge the guests admission to the wedding reception.

Cheapus   Don't exaggerate, dear. I didn't charge them to come in, only to come out.

Gladdus   Take off this blindfold, Cheapus. For your sake I hope we're not in the same old place—I always feel so drained after going to Bath.

(He removes the blindfold.)

Cheapus   I knew you were dirty on Bath, so I brought you somewhere you've never been before.

Gladdus   Wow! This is exciting. Where are we?

Cheapus   You mean you don't recognise it from the postcards? You don't recognise one of the foremost tourist attractions in the country? Go on, take a guess.

Gladdus   Gee! This is one of the four most tourist attractions?

Cheapus   You betcha.

Gladdus   What are the other three most?

Cheapus   Just take a guess, Gladdus.

Gladdus   Hmm, I really don't know, but if I must take a stab at it—I have got a slight leaning towards Pizza.

Cheapus   Pizza! Come on, Gladdus. Would I take you to some crummy Pizza joint for our annual holidays? Try again.

Gladdus   Cheapus, I've been travelling for six hours, I'm tired and I think I'm coming down with chariot lag. Where are we?!

Cheapus   Surprise! Surprise! We're in good old Pompeii!

Gladdus   Pompeii! Sun and fun capital of the Roman empire?!

Cheapus   You know me, sweetie, nothing but the very best.

Gladdus   But Pompeii is so expensive. Only rich chariot-setters can afford it.

Cheapus   I know, I know. Let's just say I managed to cut a few corners here and there.

Gladdus   Which corners?

Cheapus   I put the chariot fare on your father's account.

Gladdus   How dare you!

Cheapus   But you'll be pleased to know I paid for all the accomodation myself.

Gladdus   You did? Oh, well that's different.

Cheapus   Of course it's not the Julius Caesar Hilton you understand.

Gladdus   That's okay, honey. Any moderately priced villa will be fine.

Cheapus   How about a moderately priced tent?

Gladdus   A tent? You know I hate camping.

Cheapus   Not just a tent—a tent with a view!

Gladdus   What kind of a view?

Cheapus   Do the words panoramic and breathtaking mean anything to you?

Gladdus   Oh Cheapus—it's that good?

Cheapus   Like I said—nothing but the best.

Gladdus   Whereabouts is this tent?

Cheapus   On the slopes of Mount Vesuvius!

Gladdus   But Cheapus, isn't Mount Vesuvius an active volcano?

Cheapus   Exactly! That's why I picked it. See, honey, if Vesuvius erupts we'll have a close-up view—and at no extra charge!

Gladdus   I am impressed.

Cheapus   Me too. But then I've always said I'm not just a tiger in a toga. I've got intelligence, Gladdus—intelligence with a capital...??? um...ah, forget it.

Gladdus   Oh, Cheapus, I'm so happy.

Cheapus   Great. Great. What time is it, my love?

Gladdus   I don't know. I had to put my sundial in for repairs. It needed new batteries.

Cheapus   I'd better find out. We have to be at the amphitheatre by four o'sundial.

(Just then a woman enters on her hands and knees.)

Gladdus   Quick, Cheapus, get on your hands and knees.

(He does this, as does Gladdus.)

Cheapus   All right, Gladdus, I'm on my hands and knees, now would you mind telling me why?

Gladdus   When in Rome, do as the Romans do.

Cheapus   We're in Pompeii, not Rome!

(They get to their feet. The woman remains on all fours. She is searching for something.)

Gladdus   Sorry. I forgot.

Cheapus   Never mind. I'll ask this young woman —

Dodo   It's three o'sundial. You'll have to hurry if you want to make it to the amphitheatre.

Cheapus   Amazing! You knew the question before I asked it.

Dodo   That's my job. I'm Dodo the Mind Reader.

Gladdus   Dodo, do you mind if I ask —

Dodo   You want to know why I'm crawling around like this, right?

Gladdus   Yes.

Dodo   I lost my best and dearest friend. Will you help me look for him? You will? Thanks.

(They both start crawling around with Dodo.)

Cheapus   What's his name?

Dodo   Octavius. And the answer to your next question is: No, there's no reward.

Gladdus   Shame on you, Cheapus.

Dodo   Here, Octavius. Here, fella.

Gladdus   Come to mummy, Octavius.

Cheapus   By the way, Dodo—

Dodo   You want to know what we're looking for?

Cheapus   It might help.

Dodo   My asp of course.

Gladdus   An asp? What's an asp?

Cheapus   I have no idea, but there seems to be a snake coming your way, Dodo.

Gladdus   A snake!!

Dodo   It's okay, its okay. I've got you, Octavius...oops, I mean, you've got me, Octavius...aargghh!

(She crawls off stage to die.)

Gladdus   Oh, Cheapus, do you think she's all right?

Cheapus   No, honey, I don't—I'm afraid Dodo is extinct.

Gladdus   I think snake's are so low. Let's get out of here.

Cheapus   We can't go yet, I have to get to the amphitheatre. Have you noticed there's never a chariot around when you need one?

(At that moment a chariot enters. The design of the chariot is left to the director's discretion.)

Driver   Whoa! Whoa there, horsies! Pompeii Chariot Cabs at your service. All aboard who's going aboard.

Cheapus   Take us to the amphitheatre driver, and step on it.

Driver   Step on what, sir?

Cheapus   Just take us to the amphitheatre. I'm in a hurry.

Driver   Sorry, sir. All roads lead to Rome.

Gladdus   That's ridiculous. We just came from Rome, we don't want to go back there.

Driver   I agree entirely. It's a stupid road system we have here in Pompeii. Between you and me, I don't think the person who designed it was a roads scholar.

Cheapus   Isn't there another way to get to the amphitheatre?

Driver   Yes, but I can't tell you. I've taken a solemn vow never to tell another living soul.

Gladdus   We'll pay you handsomely.

Driver   Handsomely?! No one has ever called me that before! Very well, I'll tell you. You take six steps to the right.

(Cheapus and Gladdus pace out six steps.)

Driver   Turn around three times and you're there!

(As they finish turning around a crowd enters.)

Cheapus We're here!

Gladdus Thanks, driver.

Driver Thank you. Wait till I tell my wife someone thinks I'm handsomely! Giddyup, horsies!

(The chariot exits.)

Cheapus I didn't think we were going to make it in time, Gladdus.

Gladdus In time for what?

Cheapus I have to umpire at the Pompeii Gladiators Grand Final. I did a deal with Typhus the Tent Maker.

Gladdus What kind of deal?

Cheapus Typhus gave me free tents on Mount Vesuvius and in return I'm going to make sure his son wins the grand final.

Gladdus That's cheating. You said you'd reformed.

Cheapus Well, I have, almost. Rome wasn't built in a day you know.

Beggar Excuse me, magnificent and wondrous one.

Gladdus Hello there.

Cheapus He means me, Gladdus. What can I do for you?

Beggar I was wondering if you wouldn't mind lending me your ears.

Cheapus You're sick! Scrammus! Really, Gladdus, that Mark Antony had no right to ask for ears in the first place. Now everyone wants them!

(Typhus steps forward with his son, Saliva.)

Typhus Greetings, Cheapus, Mrs Cheapus.

Gladdus It's Mrs Dirt actually, Gladdus Dirt.

Typhus Oh you poor thing. Not to worry, a bit of dirt doesn't hurt, that's what I say. Cheapus, Gladdus, I'd like you to meet my son—my son whose name is...don't tell me, I've got it right on the tip of my tongue...um.... I give up.

Saliva My name's Saliva.

Typhus That's it! I knew I had it on the tip of my tongue.

Cheapus Nice to meet you, Saliva.

Saliva Just call me Spit.

Typhus Spit just won the semi-final. He beat Timidus the Fragile in a split decision.

Saliva Yeah. Timidus was just about to slay me when Dad split him in two.

(The crowd all boo.)

Typhus The crowd think I cheated. I can't understand it.

Gladdus I don't like this, Cheapus. If you let Spit win the crowd will tear you to bits.

Typhus Sure, but he's getting two free tents remember.

Cheapus That's hardly enough to risk my life for.

Typhus Then I'll throw in some free advice.

Cheapus That's more like it.

(A loud rumbling noise is heard. This could be made by the crowd.)

Typhus   Horrible Hercules! What was that strange rumbling noise?

(Senator Alka Seltzer steps forward.)

Senator   Do excuse me. I think it was my rumbly tum-tum. It's a big problem but I'm hopeful of discovering an elixir to cure it.
Gladdus   And what's your name, sir?
Senator   Senator Alka Seltzer. But you can call me Al.
Typhus   Time for your big speech, Al.

(The Senator steps forward and stands on a box.)

Senator   Friends, Romans, countrymen, lend me your ears!
Cheapus   Another one who wants ears! What do they do with them?
Senator   As I was saying, we are gathered here today to witness the Pompeii Gladiators Grand Final, proudly brought to you by our sponsors, the Three-Coins-in-a-Fountain Restaurant. Don't forget now, when you eat at the Three-Coins-in-a-Fountain you're eating the food of the emperors — so if they come home unexpectedly, watch out! Now let's bring on the contestants.
Typhus   Here he is, Al, my boy, the future champion of the world...um...er...
Saliva   Saliva, Dad.
Typhus   That's it! Introducing, in the red corner, weighing in at 392.5 lira, hailing out of Pompeii, the Vesuvian Vulture — Saliva the Savage!

(The crowd boos. Another great rumble is heard.)

Cheapus   What was that rumbling sound?
Typhus   Only one man could make that noise!
Cheapus   Who?
Typhus   That's the footsteps of —

(Tupperware enters.)

Tupperware   Me! I'm Tupperware the Unbreakable!

(His trainer steps out of the crowd.)

Trainer   And I'm his trainer, Miss Herculaneum the Cranium. Where's the umpire?
Cheapus   That's me, Cheapus the Just: unbiased, unbribeable and unethical.
Trainer   Good. Because if there's any cheating by the umpire I will personally tear him apart limb by limb, boil him in oil and feed him to my pet lion!
Typhus   Ha! Don't let her scare you, Cheapus. I've seen her lion — it's a pussy cat.
Senator   All right, you boys, I want to see a good clean dirty fight here; no cringing in the corners, no begging for mercy. We've got a lot of talent scouts from the Colosseum here today, so let's give them what they came to see. I'm talking about fire and brimstone, blood and guts, violence, carnage! And fellas — don't forget to smile. You have a nice day now.
Cheapus   Let the contest begin.
Saliva   This is the end of you, Tupperware.

Saliva the savage

Tupperware   Oh yeah?!

(Tupperware grabs Saliva in a headlock. Immediately Cheapus blows a whistle and separates them.)

Cheapus   Foul play. Tupperware is fined two points. Lose another three points and you'll be back to fighting with P-plates.
Trainer   What do you mean, foul play? My boy was winning fair and square.
Cheapus   He happens to be using a Yale headlock.
Trainer   What's wrong with that?
Cheapus   His opponent hasn't got the key to it. On your marks, get set — wrestle!

(They start again and Tupperware gets Saliva in an armlock. Once again Cheapus blows his whistle and separates them.)

Cheapus   Half-time everyone!
Trainer   It can't be half-time yet.
Cheapus   Well I say it is. In fact, I think it's time we had a little entertainment. Hit it, Gladdus.
Gladdus   Entertainment?
Cheapus   Stall! Stall!
Gladdus   Right! You sir, pick a piece of papyrus, any piece of papyrus —
Senator   This is highly irregular.
Trainer   It's cheating!
Gladdus   I'd like a volunteer from the audience. I'd like to saw them in half so it would be best if they had no plans for the weekend.
Trainer   This is trickery!
Senator   Treachery!
Tupperware   We wuz robbed!

(The crowd boo.)

Senator What do you have to say for yourself, Cheapus?

(Another loud rumble is heard.)

Cheapus Oops, excuse me—must have been something I ate.
Senator I'll let the blood-thirsty, ravenous mob decide your fate—best of luck. What shall we do with him?

(The crowd give the thumbs down sign and yell.)

Crowd The lions! The lions! Feed him to the lions!
Senator It seems unanimous. Cheapus Dirt, have you any last words?
Cheapus Yes. Is anyone interested in buying a couple of tents? They've got a top view.
Senator Away with him!
Gladdus Please, sir. Could I have a few moments alone with my husband first?
Senator Yes I think you should. He needs cheering up.
Gladdus Well, Cheapus, this is a fine mess you've got us into.
Cheapus Us?! I'm the one who's going to be eaten by the lions, Gladdus.
Gladdus Yes, but who's going to have to clean up after you? Me of course. Some holiday!
Cheapus Don't worry, my darling. We'll meet again, I don't know where, I don't know when, but I know we'll meet again, some sunny day.
Gladdus Jeepers! Cheapus! You must have been bitten by the love bug.
Cheapus Why?
Gladdus Because what you just said was so Roman-tick. I can't leave you now. Senator, if he's thrown to the lions I'm going with him.
Senator Splendid! A double bill. Take them away.

(The loudest rumble yet is heard.)

Cheapus It wasn't me that time.

Typhus   Look! There seems to be smoke coming from Mount Vesuvius.
Gladdus   It might be Indians sending us a message.
Senators   Indians?!
Cheapus   Pay no attention, Gladdus has always been ahead of her time.
Tupperware   There's flames shooting up in the air.
Trainer   And lava cascading down the mountainside.
Saliva   It's coming straight towards us.
Senator   Friends, Romans, countrymen—let's get the heck out of here!

(There is a mad panic as everyone scrambles off stage. Only Gladdus and Cheapus remain.)

Gladdus   Quickly, Cheapus! Let's scrammus!
Cheapus   Sorry, Gladdus. This is a once-in-a-lifetime opportunity.
Gladdus   What do you mean?
Cheapus   Put it this way: do you know how much you can get for souvenir lava?
Gladdus   You're going to sell lava?
Cheapus   That's just a spin-off; first of all I'm going to sell tickets to the eruption! There's a fortune to be made here!
Gladdus   What a brain! What a brain!
Cheapus   Well don't just stand there, Gladdus—
Gladdus   Volcano seats! Ringside volcano seats! Discount prices!
Cheapus   Step right up folks—ringside volcano seats—get 'em while they're hot!

(Black out.)

Questions

1 Where is the play's setting?

2 As the play opens we find Cheapus Dirt living up to his name in several ways. What are some of his actions that indicate he is 'cheapus'?

3 Why does Cheapus choose the slopes of Mount Vesuvius for his tent holiday?

4 What special quality does Dodo possess?

5 What are several ways in which she displays this quality?

6 How does the saying 'All roads lead to Rome' create difficulties for Cheapus, Gladdus and the chariot driver?

7 How does the name 'Saliva' lead to a humorous exchange among the characters?

8 How does Senator Alka Seltzer live up to his name?

9 Why does the crowd give Cheapus the thumbs down sign?

10 How does Cheapus turn the eruption of Vesuvius to his advantage?

11 What do you like best about this play?

12 How is the humour in this play created?

2
SURVIVAL

NOVELS

The Rumble

Rusty-James runs his own gang and has a reputation for toughness. His hero and model is his older brother, the Motorcycle Boy. The following 'rumble' (gang fight) shows much about their character.

Across the field was Biff and his gang. I counted them, just like the Motorcycle Boy taught me to. Know everything you can about the enemy. There was six. Even enough. I was getting so high on excitement I couldn't stand still.

'Rusty-James!'

It was Biff, coming across the lot to meet me. Oh, man, I couldn't wait. I was going to stomp him good. It seemed like my fists ached to be pounding something. 'I'm here!' I called.

'Not for long, you punk,' Biff said. He was close enough for me to see him clearly. My eyes get supersharp before a fight. Everything gets supersharp before a fight — like with a little effort I could fly. During a fight, though, I almost go blind; everything turns red.

Biff was sixteen, but not any bigger than me; husky; his arms hung off his shoulders like an ape's. He had a pug-ugly face and wiry blond hair. He was dancing around worse than I was.

'He's been poppin' pills,' Smokey said behind me.

Now, I hate fighting hopped-up people. They're crazy. You get crazy enough in a fight without being doped up. You fight some cat who's been washing down bennies with sneaky pete and they can't tell if you kill 'em. Your only advantage is a little more control. I never do dope, as a rule. Dope ruined the gangs.

Biff looked high. The light from the street-lamps was bouncing off his eyes in a way that made him look crazy.

'I hear you're lookin' for me,' I said. 'Here I am.'

I've done this lots of times before. I'd get in a fight about once a week. I hadn't lost a fight in almost two years. But Biff was a little tougher than the usual kid. If the gang wars had still been going on he would have been leader of the Devilhawks. He didn't like anybody to forget that, either. You can't take it for granted you're going to stomp some snotty-nosed seventh-grader, so when you go up against somebody like Biff Wilcox you think about it.

We started in on the warm up, cussing each other out, name-calling, threats. This was according to the rules. I don't know who made up the rules.

'Come on,' I said finally. I like to get down to business. 'Take a swing at me.'

'Take a swing at you?' Biff's hand went to his back pocket and came out flashing silver. 'I'm gonna cut you to ribbons.'

I didn't have a knife with me. Most people didn't knife-fight these days. I usually carried a switchblade, but I got caught with it at school and they took it away from me and I hadn't gotten around to getting another one. Biff should of told me it was going to be knife-fighting. God that made me mad! People don't pay attention to the rules any more.

Biff's friends were cheering and screaming and my friends were grumbling, and I said, 'Anybody lend me a blade?' I still thought I could win — Biff wouldn't have pulled a knife if he thought he could win in a fair fight. All I had to do was equal things up.

Nobody had a knife. That's what comes of not gang-fighting. People are never prepared.

Somebody said, 'Here's a bike chain,' and I held back my hand for it, never taking my eyes off Biff.

Just like I expected, he tried to make the most of that moment, lunging at me. I was quick enough, though, grabbing the chain, dodging the knife, and sticking out my foot to trip him. He just stumbled, and whirled around, jabbing at me. I sucked in my gut and wrapped the chain around his neck, jerking him to the ground. All I wanted to do was get the knife away from him. I'd kill him later. First things first. I jumped on top of him, caught his arm as he swung the knife at me, and for what seemed like hours we wrestled for that knife. I took a risk I thought was worth taking and tried holding his knife hand with one arm, and used the other to smash his face. It worked, he loosened his hold on the knife long enough for me to get it away from him. It fell a few feet away from us, far enough away that I didn't bother trying to reach for it, which was good. If I had gotten a hold of it, I'd have killed Biff. As it was, I was pounding his brains out. If he'd give up on that damned knife he might of stood a chance; he was older than me, and just as tough. But he didn't come there to fight fair, so instead of fighting back, he'd just keep trying to get away and crawl over to the knife. Gradually I started to calm down, the red tinge to everything went away, I could hear every-one screaming and yelling. I looked at Biff. His whole face was bloody and swollen.

'You give?' I sat back on his gut and waited. I wouldn't trust him as far as I could throw him. He didn't say anything, just lay there breathing heavy, watching me out of the one eye that wasn't swollen shut. Everybody was quiet. I could feel his gang tensed, ready, like a dog pack about to be set loose. One word from Biff would do it. I glanced over to Smokey. He was ready. My gang would fight, even if they weren't crazy about the idea.

Then a voice I knew said, 'Hey, what's this? I thought we signed a treaty.' The Motorcycle Boy was back. People cleared a path for him. Everybody was quiet.

I got to my feet. Biff rolled over and lay a few feet away from me, swearing.

'I thought we'd stopped this cowboys and Indians crap,' said the Motorcycle Boy.

I heard Biff dragging himself to his feet, but didn't pay any attention. Usually I'm not that stupid, but I couldn't take my eyes off the Motorcycle Boy. I'd thought he was gone for good. I was almost sure he was gone for good.

'Look out!' somebody screamed. I whipped around and felt the knife slide down my side, cold. It was meant to split me open from throat to gut, but I had moved just in time. It didn't hurt. You can't feel a knife cut, at first.

Biff stood a few feet away from me, laugh-ing like a maniac. He was wiping blood off the blade on his already-splattered T-shirt. 'You are one dead cat, Rusty-James.' His voice was thick and funny-sounding, because of his swollen nose. He wasn't dancing around any more, and you could tell by the way he moved he was hurtin'. But at least he was on his feet, and I wouldn't be much longer. I was cold, and everything looked watery around the edges. I'd been knife cut before, I knew what it felt like to be bleeding bad.

The Motorcycle Boy stepped out, grabbed Biff's wrist and snapped it backwards. You could hear it crack like a matchstick. It was broke, sure enough.

The Motorcycle Boy picked up Biff's switchblade, and looked at the blood running down over the handle. Everybody was frozen. They knew what he had said about gang-fighting being over with.

'I think,' he said thoughtfully, 'that the show is over.'

from *Rumble Fish* by S.E. Hinton

Reading for Meaning

1 'I counted them...' Why does Rusty-James do this?

2 How does Rusty-James feel as Biff comes across the lot to meet him?

3 What change takes place in Rusty-James before a fight?

4 In what way does Biff resemble an ape?

5 How does Rusty-James feel about fighting people who have been taking pills?

6 How does Rusty-James know that Biff is 'high'?

7 What happens in the 'warm up'?

8 Why doesn't Rusty-James have a switchblade with him?

9 What contrast is there between the behaviour of Biff's friends and those of Rusty-James?

10 'I still thought I could win...' Why does Rusty-James think this?

11 What does Rusty-James do with the bike chain?

12 'I took a risk I thought was worth taking...' What risk does Rusty-James take?

13 What does Biff do 'instead of fighting back'?

14 'People cleared a path for him. Everybody was quiet.' Why do you think everybody reacts to the Motorcycle Boy's presence in this way?

15 Why is Biff able to knife Rusty-James?

16 How does Biff react to having knifed Rusty-James?

17 What feelings does Rusty-James experience after being 'knife cut'?

18 How does the Motorcycle Boy punish Biff?

19 What comments would you make about Biff's character?

20 What comments would you make about the Motorcycle Boy's character?

Attacked by a Savage Dog

An innocent walk through a pleasant wood turns into a desperate struggle for survival for Adam and his father.

As they entered the wooded area, he saw his father glance backward. Adam followed the glance—still nobody there.

'Everything all right, Dad?' he asked, lips trembling.

'Just fine, Adam, just fine,' his father said in his own voice.

So they plunged into the woods, tripping sometimes over tree limbs knocked down during winter storms, crashing through brush as if they were on safari in Africa, and after a while Adam began to enjoy himself.

'Hey, Dad, this is kind of fun,' Adam said.

His father, breathing hard, tousled Adam's hair. 'Not as bad as I thought it would be,' he said.

Adam felt a sense of camaraderie. And that was when they encountered the dog, like an apparition from nowhere, ugly, unidentifiable, a piglike snout, glittering eyes, and yellowed teeth.

'This is ridiculous,' his father said now.

Adam knew what his father meant by ridiculous. Here they were being frightened and intimidated and held at bay by, of all things, a dog. Not an armed robber. Not a wild animal. But a dog. Adam felt, in fact, that he and his father might have been running away from a greater danger behind them. But that danger evaporated in the presence of the dog. The dog looked capable of attack and violence, the low growl in its throat menacing, deadly.

'Let's back up a little,' his father said.

But the movement brought a loud growl from the animal. The boy's heart began to beat wildly.

'Look, Adam. We've got to do something about this.'

'But what, Dad?' Adam asked, feeling his chin trembling.

'First, I want you to get out of here.'

'I want to stay with you, Dad.'

'Look, the dog will probably let one of us go. Here's what to do. I'll take a small step forward—you take a big one backward. That might confuse him. Then take another one while I make a slight movement. But go slow. Don't upset the beast. Just walk backward. Keep going...'

'Where will I go?'

'I heard traffic a while ago. The highway runs to our left.' His father was talking softly, barely moving his lips. 'Make it to the highway and flag down a car.'

'But what about you, Dad?'

'I think I can handle it alone. I'll try moving back,' he said.

'I want to stay with you, Dad.' Actually he wanted to get away, he was terrified of the dog, but he felt as though he'd be betraying his father if he left.

'You'll be helping most by going, Adam,' his father said, finality in his voice. 'Now, do it slowly...'

Adam retreated reluctantly, backing up slowly, not daring to glance at the dog, keeping his eyes on the ground, hoping he wouldn't trip and find himself on the ground, the dog rushing at him. He heard his father muttering, 'A dog, for crissakes.' The dog didn't move. Adam glanced up, the dog's ferocious eyes were on his father.

Adam took one more step—and the dog

attacked, the growl reaching a siren's howl as the animal leaped towards his father. His father stepped aside, one arm outstretched, the dog's teeth ripping the sleeve of his father's jacket. The teeth caught on the jacket for a moment, long enough for his father to fling the animal away, changing its course for an instant. In that instant, his father cried for Adam to run, but Adam was frozen with horror to the spot. His father crouched low, close to the ground, meeting the dog at its level. But Adam saw that his father's right hand was searching the ground for a weapon, a stone or a stick. The dog, too, was crouched, body sloped forward, chin almost touching the ground. Adam's father slowly rose from the crouched position; he held a tree limb in his hand. The limb was about an inch thick. He thrust it towards the dog, as if offering the animal a gift. For the first time, the animal seemed confused, the glittering eyes wavering in their intensity. Then without warning, the dog leaped again—but this time at the limb, grasping it with its teeth. His father grabbed the limb with both hands and swung it as the dog

closed its jaws around it. He swung furiously, the dog hanging on frantically. Suddenly his father let go of the limb, allowed it to soar away from him, the dog still gripping it in its teeth. Thrown off balance and spinning dizzily in the air, the dog fell awkwardly to the ground, howling now, scurrying to its feet. Adam's father grabbed another branch, and another. He held tree limbs in each hand now. He looked like a lion tamer in a movie.

'Come on, you bastard,' his father yelled at the dog.

Adam had never heard his father swear like that before, although he said 'hell' and 'damn' once in a while. The sound coming from the dog was not a growl anymore but a kind of cry, a moan, as if it had been injured. And then, as suddenly as it had appeared, it departed, pawing the ground one moment and then turning away the next, thrashing through bushes and thicket.

from *I am the Cheese* by Robert Cormier

Reading for Meaning

1 'Everything all right, Dad?' What causes Adam to ask this question?

2 Why does it seem as if Adam and his father are 'on safari in Africa'?

3 What comments would you make about the dog's physical appearance?

4 Why does Adam's father say 'This is ridiculous'?

5 How does the dog react when Adam and his father move back a little?

6 How does Adam's father hope to confuse the dog?

7 Where does Adam's father want Adam to go? Why?

8 'I want to stay with you, Dad.' Why does Adam feel he has to stay with his father?

9 What sound is heard as the dog attacks?

10 'The teeth caught on the jacket for a moment...' How does this help Adam's father?

11 '...his father cried for Adam to run...' Why doesn't Adam run?

12 'For the first time, the animal seemed confused...' What causes this?

13 What does Adam's father do once the dog closes its jaws on the limb?

14 Why does Adam's father look 'like a lion tamer in a movie'?

15 What evidence can you find to show that the dog, by the end of the story, was no longer a threat to Adam and his father?

16 What has this incident revealed to you about the character of Adam's father?

17 What has this incident revealed to you about the character of Adam?

18 What comments would you make about the relationship between Adam and his father?

The Deadly Pit

An ordeal of terror begins for teacher Sally Jones and her small band of students when they are kidnapped from their school by a gang of ruthless killers, all of whom are wearing grotesque masks. However, the instinct of the teacher and children for survival soon turns the hunted into the destroyers.

'killing was a game that two could play...'

Jim nudged his brother. Sonny turned.
  'What do you want?'
'Go in and get them.'
  'What? Now?'
  'Yes, now. Flush them out. I want to see her running. Then I'll get her.
  Sonny looked at his brother and seemed about to say something, but the torch-light that fell on the older man's face warned him against it. He shrugged.
  'Okay. I'll go in.' He picked up the shotgun that was standing against a tree and started walking carefully up the incline. Then he turned.
  'Hey, how am I supposed to see? Give us the torch.'

'Get going. I'll need it. I'm going to do a little spotlighting. Spotlighting with a shotgun.' And he laughed, an ugly sound that reached the ears of the listeners in the cave.

Sonny made his way carefully through the dark scrub, leaning forward to keep his balance, straining his eyes to keep the little light that streamed out of the cave mouth in his vision. He swore softly and viciously as a sharp twig caught the corner of his eye. He stood still, momentarily blinded as his other eye closed in sympathy with the damaged one. He didn't like what he was doing; often, he hadn't liked the things he had done with Jim. But he didn't seem to be able to say no. It wasn't until this trip that he had realised that it was fear of his brother that kept him obedient. The thought angered him and he increased his speed, scrambling up the slope. This is it, he thought to himself. This is it. I'll get out of it after this. Hunting school kids...There's more things in life than that. He straightened up and looked ahead. There, not more than fifteen yards away, was the cave that Jim had told him about. A pale yellow glow was streaming from its narrow mouth. Sonny stood and watched for a few minutes. Then he called.

'Okay. The fun and games are over. All of you get. Get out now, do you hear?' Nothing. No one stirred. No one answered. Sonny yelled again, his demands flying around the still, cold valley.

'Out. Come out.'

Twenty yards away in the cave, the small group sat in tense expectation, hunched around the fire, stones and makeshift spears clenched in their hands. The echoes of Sonny's demands died out, and they sat in stiff silence.

Come on, prayed Sally, just a little further. Come on. Come on.

Outside, Sonny was quickly and venomously furious... They were making a mug of him. Jim would be laughing to himself back there.

'Get out now, you bunch of little brats!'

he roared and then started to run up the slope, crushing the leaves and brush underfoot. Then in bewilderment, he felt himself falling. The earth opened under his striding feet and hurled him into agony.

He screamed in horror and disbelief as two of Derek's stiff shafts, fire-hardened and deadly, pierced his thigh and rib-cage. He threw back his head and bellowed, then screamed in fresh pain as his body slipped further, the spear points tearing through flesh, forcing his body to contract together, his head to jerk down. The tip of Leanne Pearce's bladed spear drove through his right eyeball, into his cortex. Sonny retched and died.

In the cave the children leapt about, yelling and whistling.

'We got him. We got him. The spear pit got him! Our spears!'

Sally joined with them, wild triumph soaring through her body. Her exhaustion was forgotten. She felt nothing but this wild surge of mad joy. Sid and Derek were doing a crazy dance around the fire. Marilyn and Narelle hugged each other. Even Sue seemed happier. Tommy opened his eyes and looked bewilderedly around. Sid ran to him, kneeling beside him.

'We got him, Tom. We got one of them in our spear pit. I'll bet he's as dead as anything.' Tommy nodded briefly and his eyes closed again.

Sally raised her hands and the cheers and whistles ceased. 'Now we must be quiet. We must listen. We've got one, now we must get the other one. We must be ready.'

The children had quietened down, but the triumph shone in their eyes. Derek clambered back to his perch above the entrance and sat, smiling, his arm around the boulder, cuddling it. Sid took up his position at the doorway, with Sally standing close behind him. The others stood or crouched near the fire, their weapons in their hands, smiling and waiting.

from *Fortress* by Gabrielle Lord

Reading for Meaning

1 Why does Jim want Sonny to 'flush them out'?

2 Why does Jim refuse to give Sonny the torch?

3 How is Sonny able to know where the cave is, even though it is dark?

4 What causes Sonny to swear?

5 Why has Sonny always obeyed his brother?

6 What is Sonny's attitude to 'hunting school kids'?

7 What does Sonny do as he draws near the cave?

8 'Out. Come out.' What are the children doing inside the cave?

9 What does Sally want Sonny to do?

10 How does Sonny feel when the children and Sally don't come out of the cave?

11 What happens to Sonny after he starts to run up the slope?

12 What are Sally's feelings after Sonny has been killed?

13 How do Marilyn and Narelle react to Sonny's death?

14 What is Sally's plan?

15 After the children have quietened down, what does Derek do?

16 'The others stood or crouched near the fire, their weapons in their hands, smiling and waiting.' Why do you think the children are smiling?

17 What did you learn about Sally's character from your reading of this passage?

18 Do you think the children and Sally were justified in killing Sonny? Why or why not?

POETRY

Lebanese Kids

Fuad, just fourteen has a light moustache.
He has already moved between his country here
and his country there, three times, and has lost
the subtleties of both his tongues.
He has brought a geography project
to safety in the office: very proud
of his mountain village cut from cardboard,
glued to a tray. He has stopped to talk
to Mina, from the same hills, the same war.
This was my home, he shows the girl;
my school, my uncle an important man
lived here, two storeys, but a shell
knocked off some of the rooms. This is the way
it used to look, and see this road,
it is the road that goes to your village.
At the crossroads, see, here, was a tree —
I used to play in it, my brother too,
but they knocked it down with a tank
and the women took it for firewood then.
Today, there's a checkpoint there.

Fuad, fled from shells, talking to Mina,
from his mountains, outside my office,
has recovered during daytime from the war.
At night, he crawls still to his parents' bed,
and clings, screams and clings and cries to sleep.

John Griffin

Questions

1 Why do you think the poet has called his poem 'Lebanese Kids'? What other title could you give this poem?

2 What evidence can you find to suggest that the poet is a teacher?

3 What are Fuad's feelings about 'his mountain village cut from cardboard'?

4 What had happened to the home of Fuad's uncle?

5 What had happened to the tree in which Fuad used to play?

6 What do you think the poet is trying to show about Fuad's life in these lines: 'Fuad, fled from shells, talking to Mina,/from his mountains, outside my office'?

7 At night, how does Fuad react when he remembers the war?

8 What is the difference between Fuad's past life and his present one?

9 What are your feelings towards Fuad?

10 What is the poet's message to the reader in 'Lebanese Kids'?

Race

This girl will run against the odds.
Her child's heart lost control of counts
It oozed, not pumped; it gave no promises
Of seeping into adulthood or
Anything like that.

She went for her operation
In her nurse's uniform, with
Her Ladybird book of Florence Nightingale and
Her grandma's real nurse watch
Measuring last moments.
How well we played that game, my girl and I.

Someone took me inside the tent where
She was held between air and nothing
On webs as fine as breath, cradled
In nothing but the flow of oxygen and blood,
Nothing more, nothing to say the heart of her still lives.
Nothing in all that silence save
The slow sucked gasp she gave
And the screen to chart her passage back to life.

Now she practises sprint starts
And each burst is a birth,
A charge of sap and strength that
Flows in the living swing of her hair
And in the mysterious machinery of her limbs.

Berlie Doherty (For Janna)

Questions

1 Why do you think the poem is called 'Race'?

2 What words in the first verse make you aware of the girl's heart problems?

3 What evidence can you find in the second verse to show that the girl is quite young?

4 What was happening inside the tent?

5 What do the words 'slow sucked gasp' reveal about the girl's breathing?

6 What evidence can you find to show that the poet was the girl's parent?

7 What words in the last verse reveal that the operation was successful?

8 The poem describes three stages in the girl's life. What are these three stages?

9 In 'Race', what is the poet trying to show the reader?

10 Do you think 'Race' is a good poem? Why or why not?

Ward F 4

There is no weather in my room,
a white cube, bare
except for a bedside chest; one chair.
The window behind my bed
looks blind on a blind wall,
but I cannot turn my head.

No sky; no sun;
one lamp with hard green shade
is my daylight
and nightlight.
(No flowers, please, nowhere
to put them but on the floor.)
I face the brown door, stare
at the black knob, waiting...

Nurses come and go
brisk, kind under crackling starch.
They give me pills, injections
with cheerful remarks about the weather.
But there is no weather in my room.

For twelve months I have not seen a
or a patch of grass.
I think I could walk again
if I saw grass.
I shut my eyes.

I can see more with my eyes shut—
heather, a bright stream,
the flash of a bird.

Autumn, Winter have wasted away;
today is the first day of Spring;
and nurse says the sun is shining...
My splints are off;
my limbs feel supple
and I'm running over grass
where the willow lets down her yellow hair.

Toffee-brown chestnut buds unclose
fingers soft as silver-fox.
There's movement among branches: a speckled thrush
swings and sings, frilling the needled larch
with promised green.
Blossom and cloud pile high, higher as I pass.
I am free; the grass is warm,
yielding to my feet...

The door opens and the doctor comes in
returning me to the white cube.
He talks of tests and treatment,
makes no promises.
Improvement is slow.

Visitors come and go
bringing rain on their coats
or a bunch of flowers—
only they bring the weather into my room.
But when they've gone
I'm more alone than before
waiting, watching the door.
The clock ticks on.

Phoebe Hesketh

Questions

1 Do you think the title 'Ward F 4' is a good one for this poem? Why or why not?

2 'There is no weather in my room'. Why is the room itself so depressing?

3 What impression do you have of the nurses?

4 How many different colours can you find in the poem? What comment would you make about the poet's use of colours?

5 What are some of the scenes from nature that are described in the poem?

6 Why do you think nature is so important to the patient?

7 How do the visitors 'bring the weather' into the hospital room?

8 'The clock ticks on'. Why do you think the poet finishes the poem with these words?

9 How would you describe the patient's feelings in this poem?

10 What are your feelings towards the patient by the end of the poem?

Cross-Country

On and on
Through the snow we run
Puffing and panting
It's not much fun
Over the fence
And into the stream
Mouths obscured by commas of steam
Plimsolls soaked
Shorts splattered with mud
Freezing to death
'For our own good'!
Plodding along
Mile after mile
Under the gate over the stile
Legs like jelly
Feet like lead
Wet hair slapping
Against the forehead
Defying the cold
For just under an hour
Before burning to death
In a scalding hot shower!

Ray Mather

The Children's Fall-Out Shelter

Deep in their underground shelter
Three people sit in the dark.
Remembering how when they were children
The world was lit by a spark.

They were placed in underground shelters
By parents who did not survive.
They were packed into underground shelters
Like bees packed into a hive.

Tom had wanted to be a farmer
But the earth was bare as a stone

Bill had wanted to be a hermit
But found no place to be alone

Susan had wanted to travel
But the earth was covered in flame

So they sat in their underground shelter
Wondering who was to blame.

Now deep in their underground shelter
Three old people sit in the dark,
Recalling stories of the fire-flood
And of the fire-proof Ark.

Deep in their underground shelter,
Safe from poison and from flames,
They shape coffins out of the cradles
Upon which were written their names.

Brian Patten

Questions

1 Why is 'The Children's Fall-Out Shelter' a suitable title?

2 'The world was lit by a spark'. What is the poet referring to?

3 In what way are the children in their underground shelters similar to 'bees packed into a hive'?

4 Why wasn't Tom able to become a farmer?

5 Why couldn't Bill be a hermit?

6 What prevented Susan from travelling?

7 What did the three children think about as they sat in the shelter?

8 Why is the shelter described as a 'fire-proof Ark'?

9 Explain what is happening in the last verse.

10 What is the poet's message to the reader?

Dobbo's First Swimming Lesson

Dobbo's fists
spiked me to the playground wall
nailed me to the railings.

The plastic ball
he kicked against my skinny legs
on winter playtimes

Bounced a stinging red-hot bruise
across the icy tarmac.

The day we started swimming
we all jumped in
laughed and splashed, sank beneath
the funny tasting water.

Shivering in a corner
Dobbo crouched, stuck to the side
sobbing like my baby brother
when all the lights go out.

David Harmer

WRITING

THE WRITER'S POINT OF VIEW

FIRST PERSON

Some writers use what is called the **first person** approach to writing. That is, the narrator of the story tells the story personally and uses words such as 'I', 'me' and 'my' as he or she describes what is happening for the reader. In *The Pigman*, author Paul Zindel has his two main characters, John and Lorraine, telling the story in the first person. In this extract, John is telling the story.

I GOT ELECTED THE BATHROOM BOMBER

Now, I don't like school, which you might say is one of the factors that got us involved with this old guy we nicknamed the Pigman. Actually, I hate school, but then again most of the time I hate everything.

    I used to really hate school when I first started at Franklin High. I hated it so much the first year they called me the Bathroom Bomber. Other kids got elected G.O. President and class secretary and lab-squad captain, but I got elected the Bathroom Bomber. They called me that because I used to set off bombs in the bathroom. I set off twenty-three bombs before I didn't feel like doing it any more.

The reason I never got caught was because I used to take a tin can (that's a firecracker, as if you didn't know) and mould a piece of clay round it so it'd hold a candle attached to the fuse. One of those skinny little birthday candles. Then I'd light the thing, and it'd take about eight minutes before the fuse got lit. I always put the bombs in the first floor boys' john right behind one of the porcelain unmentionables where nobody could see it. Then I'd go off to my next class. No matter where I was in the building I could hear the blast.

If I got all involved, I'd forget I had lit the bomb, and then even I'd be surprised when it went off. Of course, I was never as surprised as the poor guys who were in the boys' john on the first floor sneaking a cigarette, because the boys' john is right next to the Dean's office and a whole flock of gestapo would race in there and blame them. Sure they didn't do it, but it's pretty hard to say you're innocent when you're caught with a lungful of rich, mellow tobacco smoke. When the Dean catches you smoking, it really may be hazardous to your health. I smoke one with a recessed filter myself.

from *The Pigman* by Paul Zindel

SECOND PERSON

Writers of novels do not often use the **second person** in their storytelling. They prefer to use first or third person, or sometimes a combination of both. The second person approach is characterised by words such as 'you' and 'your'. The use of second person tends to occur in instruction manuals, recipe books and sometimes in short stories. Notice the effectiveness of Elizabeth Mansutti's use of the second person in her short story 'Okay, Doris Day!'.

SIXTEEN

You were sixteen and just out of hospital after twelve weeks. Weeks of rheumatic fever, of daily nose bleeds, watching your pale blood pour, then drip into the stainless steel bowl. Weeks of blood tests that found the sister searching for veins big enough to get a needleful, and pain. Pain, with every movement setting off the minute, burning knives that twisted and turned in all the joints of your body. You would grit your teeth against the pain and forbid the tears to flow. You had found small comfort in the fact that over the weeks the number of painful joints became less and you would avoid moving so that you didn't discover the day's villains until the doctor came and made you move.

from *Okay, Doris Day!* by Elizabeth Mansutti

THIRD PERSON

When writers use the **third person** in their writing, it gives them flexibility in dealing with the actions, words, thoughts and feelings of the characters they are describing. The third person narrator is an 'observer', able to reveal what is going on in the minds of all the characters in the story. The third person narrator can also describe the different events and settings of the story more comfortably than the first person narrator.

The third person approach is characterised by words such as 'he', 'she', 'it' and 'they'. In the following passage from *My Darling, My Hamburger*, Paul Zindel has chosen to write in the third person.

SEAN LOVES LIZ

Life was one huge pathetic waste as far as Sean was concerned.

Until Liz.

He had first noticed her in the halls at school a year ago. She had been around before that, but she used to have her hair cut short, and she kept very much to herself. It was just after summer vacation when she showed up in his chemistry class. A few of the boys had pushed to date her, but they had no luck. Then he had asked her out, and she had turned him down. 'I'm sorry,' she had said, as though she were refusing to donate to some charity.

He had told her off. *'Who the hell do you think you are?'* He remembered how shocked she looked when he said that. Before he fell asleep that night he could still see her. Her voice had sounded so snobbish, but her eyes haunted him like those of a wounded fawn. The thought crossed his mind that maybe she was as depressed and disgusted with living on this planet as he was—that the tone of her voice was a defence, like the endless defences he had erected between himself and the world. And that was the moment he decided to handle her as if she was a frightened animal.

The next day he asked her out again and she refused. This time he was the one who said 'I'm sorry'. And the next day he asked her again. Every day for two weeks he asked her out. He checked the attendance book in her register class for her telephone number, and on weekends he called her house. Finally she started to smile when he passed her in the halls. Then one day she said Yes.

'What?' he asked.

'Yes,' she repeated.

They had gone to a picnic on the first date, but all they did was talk—and laugh. He remembered feeling like a creature from outer space who after a million years of banishment from his home planet had at last found another exile. Two foreign spirits trapped under human skins were finally able to breathe.

from *My Darling, My Hamburger* by Paul Zindel

YOUR TURN TO WRITE

First Person

Write a story that begins: 'Suddenly I was changed into a...' Then go on to describe some of the problems and adventures in your new life. Here is a list of identities for you to choose from.

- bulldozer
- ice block
- motor car
- mad computer

- school desk
- baseball bat
- teacher
- film star

- baby
- pilot
- dentist
- explorer

- mosquito
- spider
- snake
- dinosaur

Second Person

Using the second person, describe how to do or make something. For example: a treehouse, a surfboard, a cake, a new invention, a television game show.

Third Person

Write a story about the following cartoon, with yourself acting as the third person narrator. You may like to imagine that the two people in the cartoon are astronauts from another planet who have suddenly come upon an abandoned shopping trolley while they have been exploring planet Earth. The astronauts have no idea what they have found. What happens next?

27.9.03 - C.W

LANGUAGE

Rules for word forms:
nouns - ending - ing , tion, sion
adj - ending - le , able , ing
adv - end in - ly

WORD FORMS

Creating Correct Word Forms ✓

The following sentences are based on events in the novel *I am the Cheese*. Use the correct word form of the words in the brackets to complete the sentences. The first one has been done to help you.

1 Adam retreated reluctantly (reluctant), backing up slowly. (slow).

2 The wooded area seemed enjoyable *(adj)* ✓ (enjoy) to Adam, before the menacing *(adj)* ✓ (menace) dog appeared.

3 At first Adam was frightening *(adj)* ✗ (frighten) by the dangerous *(adj)* ✓ (danger) animal.

4 Adam's father swung furiously *(adv)* (furious), the dog hanging on frantically *(adv)* (frantic).

5 When the situation was desperate *(adj)* ✓ (despair), Adam's father acted courageous ✓ (courage).

6 Adam's heart began to beat wildly *(adv)* ✓ (wild) after the dog had growled loudly *(adv)* ✓ (loud) at him.

7 The horrifying *(adj)* ✓ (horrify) situation could have been disastrous ✓ (disaster) for Adam and his father.

8 Even though Adam was dependable *(adj)* ✗ (depend) on his father, he showed he was reliable *(adj)* ✗ (rely) in a crisis.

9 The story had a memorial *(adj)* ✗ (memory) ending when Adam's father successfully *(adv)* ✓ (successful) put the dog to flight.

10 *I am the Cheese* is a fascinating ✓ (fascinate) and exciting *(adj)* ✓. (excite) novel.

Using Word Forms

Complete each sentence by selecting the appropriate word from the box. Each word is to be used only once.

necessary	necessity	necessitate	necessarily	unnecessary

1 This isn't .... *necessarily* ✓ true.

2 Buying a house would *necessarily* ✗ obtaining a loan from the bank.

3 He has the *necessitate* ✗ skills for the job.

4 A knowledge of the road rules is a *necessity* ✓ for a car driver.

5 It is *unnecessary* ✓ to wake her yet.

prosper	prosperous	prosperity	prospered	prosperously

✔

1 She is a *prosperous* ✓ businesswoman.

2 The farmer lived *prosperously* ✓ for more than thirty years.

3 They wish you happiness and *prosperity* ✓.

4 The accountant's business has *prospered* ✓ during the last decade.

5 Cheats never *prosper* ✓.

calculated	calculations	calculator	calculus	miscalculated

1 Because he *miscalculated* ✓ the turn, the racing driver crashed into the fence.

2 The gambler took a *calculated* ✓ risk.

3 She used a *calculator* ✓ to work out the square root of seventeen.

4 *Calculations* ✗ is a branch of mathematics.

5 His *calculus* ✗ are rarely accurate.

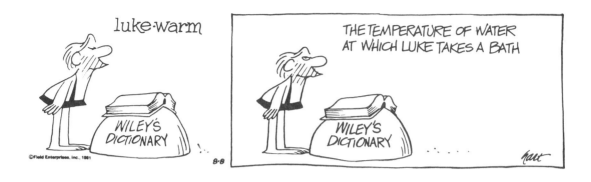

Plural Forms

Singular means 'one' and **plural** means 'more than one'. Most nouns have a singular and a plural form. For example:

Singular: horse   baby   monkey   woman
Plural: horses   babies   monkeys   women

For each of the following phrases, write down the correct plural form of the words in brackets.

1 an album of *photoes* . (photo)

2 multiple *injuries*. (injury)

3 overseas *countries* (country)

4 a flock of *geese* .... (goose)

5 a box of *peaches* (peach)

6 polluted *beaches* (beach)

7 a city of *churches* (church)

8 drinking *glasses* (glass)

9 a pack of *wolfs* ... (wolf)

10 two front *teeth* . (tooth)

11 a bag of *cherries* (cherry)

12 a class of *children* (child)

13 a chorus of *echos* ... (echo)

14 a parade of *heros* ... (hero)

15 a set of *dominoes* (domino)

16 a team of *oxen* . (ox)

17 autumn *leaves* ... (leaf)

18 a set of *knifes* . (knife)

19 a kilo of *potatoes* (potato)

20 tinned *tomatoes* (tomato)

From Plural to Singular

Rewrite the following sentences changing the plural nouns in heavy type into their singular forms. You may also need to make other minor changes. For example:

The **factories** had large **chimneys**. (plural)
The **factory** had a large **chimney**. (singular)

1 The **men** forced the **donkeys** to make difficult **journeys**.
man   _donkey_   _journey_

2 The **ladies** and **gentlemen** clapped loudly.
lady   _a gentleman_

3 **Foxes** lived in the **bushes**.
Fox   _bush_

4 The **women** possessed **diaries**.
woman   _diary_

5 The **calves** ate the **loaves** of bread.
calf   _loaf_

6 On the **shelves** were **bunches** of grapes.
shelf   _bunch_

7 The **armies** conquered the neighbouring **countries**.
army   _country_

8 There are **stories** written about erupting **volcanoes**.
story   _volcanoe_

9 The **radii** of the **circles** were easy to calculate.
radious

10 Finding the **oases** saved the **travellers' lives**.
Oasis   _traveller_

Using Prefixes to Create Opposites

For each of the following words, add the prefix _un_, _in_, _im_, _ir_, _il_ or _dis_ to create a word that is opposite in meaning.

1 selfish	9 controllable	17 credible
2 attentive	10 responsible	18 appear
3 certain	11 polite	19 mature
4 pure	12 relevant	20 agree
5 legal	13 happy	21 regular
6 competent	14 literate	22 probable
7 possible	15 mortal	23 formal
8 honourable	16 known	24 friendly

GETTING IT RIGHT

VERB TENSES

Look closely at the following verb table.

Present Tense	Past Tense	Past Tense (have/had)
I awake	I awoke	I have/had awakened
I become	I became	I have/had become
I begin	I began	I have/had begun
I bite	I bit	I have/had bitten
I blow	I blew	I have/had blown
I break	I broke	I have/had broken
I choose	I chose	I have/had chosen
I do	I did	I have/had done
I draw	I drew	I have/had drawn
I drink	I drank	I have/had drunk
I drive	I drove	I have/had driven
I eat	I ate	I have/had eaten
I fall	I fell	I have/had fallen
I fly	I flew	I have/had flown
I forget	I forgot	I have/had forgotten
I give	I gave	I have/had given
I go	I went	I have/had gone
I grow	I grew	I have/had grown
I hide	I hid	I have/had hidden
I keep	I kept	I have/had kept
I know	I knew	I have/had known
I lose	I lost	I have/had lost
I make	I made	I have/had made
I ride	I rode	I have/had ridden
I ring	I rang	I have/had rung
I shake	I shook	I have/had shaken
I sing	I sang	I have/had sung
I speak	I spoke	I have/had spoken
I swim	I swam	I have/had swum
I tear	I tore	I have/had torn
I write	I wrote	I have/had written

VERB TENSION

Using the Correct Verb Forms

For each of the following sentences, insert the correct words from the brackets into the spaces provided. You may need to refer to the verb table.

1 He abruptly .... (tore, tear) up the letter, which I had just .... (wrote, written).

2 The travellers .... (drunk, drank) their coffee after they had .... (eaten, ate).

3 The teacher .... (break, broke) the vase which he had .... (chose, chosen) for the classroom.

4 The student .... (begin, began) to understand what the artist had .... (drew, drawn).

5 The phone .... (rang, rung) before he had .... (awoke, awakened).

6 The thieves had .... (forgot, forgotten) where they had .... (hid, hidden) the loot.

7 The champion .... (knew, know) she had .... (lose, lost).

8 Before the teacher .... (drove, driven) into the school grounds, the principal had .... (speak, spoken) to the students.

9 The tree .... (shook, shake) as the wind .... (blew, blow).

10 The child .... (keep, kept) the present that she had been .... (gave, given).

DRAMA

THE SKILL OF MAKING CONVERSATION

Picture the scene. Suzanne and Tony are on their first date. They've been to a movie and now they're sitting in a coffee shop and have ordered cheese fingers and a cappuccino. So far they have been getting on well, but now the feared moment has arrived. Now they actually have to talk, to hold a conversation! How will they handle this moment of crisis?

It's not unusual for people to be nervous about having to converse or make 'small talk'. Often they are shy, or afraid that the other person will find them boring. Sometimes they are afraid that one of those terrifying 'moments of silence' will occur and they will sit there, not knowing what to say, hoping that the world ends shortly to cover the embarrassment they feel. Some people have even been known to carry little lists of 'topics-to-talk-about' in their pocket so that they can sneak a look when the conversation dries up.

Learning to converse is a skill. It can be practised and learned. This section gives you the opportunity to practise the skill in a 'safe' and perhaps humorous setting.

THE ELEMENTS OF CONVERSATION

1 The Greeting
In our society we have a number of standard ways of greeting another person. If we don't know the person we usually introduce ourselves first, and then either ask the other person his or her name, or just wait for it to be given. For example:

Sue: Hi, I'm Sue. I don't think we've met before.
Tony: I'm Tony. Er, I'm new here. My family just moved from the country a week ago.

If we already know the other person we don't bother to give our name, or to seek their name. Usually the greeting is something like 'Hi, how are you going?' or 'G'day, what's new?'.

2 The Body of the Conversation
The main section of a conversation is made up of two parts — **asking questions** and **giving information** about yourself.

Usually a conversation gets underway, after the greeting, because someone asks a question. For example:

- 'What did you do on the weekend?'
- 'What sort of week have you had?'
- 'Where have you moved from?'

This enables the other person to begin giving information about themselves. The best questions are ones that require the other person to explain something, rather than questions that can be answered by a simple 'yes' or 'no'. Questions beginning with 'what' are often good conversation starters. Usually it is important not to ask more than three or four questions in a row, or it may begin to feel like an interrogation rather than a conversation.

After one person has asked one or two questions, there comes a point where the other person asks return questions. If he or she doesn't ask, it is still important for the first person to talk about what happened over the weekend, or whatever seems appropriate. In this way, questions and information flow back and forth and a conversation is created.

It is important to note that you can 'pick up' information given by someone when they answer a question and pursue that as a topic. For example, in response to 'Where have you moved from?' a person might answer 'We were living on a farm in the country where we grew wheat and raised sheep. But the market's been bad, and my father's health is shot, so we had to move.' It would then be appropriate to ask questions about life on the farm, what the person enjoyed on the farm, how the person felt about moving, and so on. When people give you information about themselves you can usually assume that it is safe to talk further about it.

3 The Conclusion

When a conversation finally 'dries up' or someone has to go, we have a number of standard conclusions. Often we just say something like 'Well, I've enjoyed talking to you. I have to go now but I hope we can get a chance to talk further', or something similar.

PRACTISING CONVERSATIONS

The eight characters described on the pages 80–81 are all from the same school class. Read through each description carefully, then read through the list of situations opposite.

In pairs, choose the two characters you find most interesting and match them with an appropriate situation. Develop the conversation that could take place between the two characters, keeping in mind the elements of conversation (the greeting, the body of the conversation and the conclusion). You could prepare a script of the conversation or you may prefer to improvise.

Practise your conversation until you feel ready to act it out for the rest of the class.

THE SITUATIONS

1 _____ has just had an argument with her parents over poor school marks. She is walking along the street towards the shops when she meets _____. They start a conversation.

2 _____ has just heard that the family can't afford to go on holidays this year. With the cost of living so high, the family has to tighten its belt and so some sacrifices have to be made. _____ is talking about the situation with _____.

3 _____ is excited because his favourite team won on the weekend. He was there (along with thousands of others) to see the win and to celebrate afterwards. He is talking about the weekend with _____.

4 _____ has just broken up with her boyfriend. They had been going together for a year and she is hurt. She is talking about this to _____.

5 _____ attended a rock concert with some of the gang over the weekend. Actually it was a bit of a disappointment considering the cost and the quality of the performance. _____ is talking with _____, who didn't go to the concert.

6 _____ is excited because an uncle has sent her a hundred dollars for her birthday. She has some ideas but isn't quite sure what to do with it. She is talking about it with _____.

7 _____'s younger brother has just been diagnosed as having a serious illness. The whole family is in shock and _____, who is close to her brother, is worried. She is talking with _____.

8 A new girl in another class has caught _____'s eye. He thinks she may be interested in him, too. He wants to get to know her, and is talking to _____ about his hopes.

9 _____ has just got a new 10-speed racing bike, one he's been saving for since last year. He's looking forward to taking a long ride on the weekend and is talking to _____ about his plans.

10 _____'s family is going to have to move because his father has been transferred to another state. He is not looking forward to the move, but is realistic enough to know that it has to happen. He is talking with _____ about it.

THE CHARACTERS

Tracey loves nothing better than riding her BMX bike. She has won many trophies and hopes to compete in interstate competitions soon. Her father is the local Anglican minister and she is active in the church youth group. She hopes to go overseas as an exchange student for a year if the opportunity presents itself.

Grace is from a wealthy family so she has the latest clothes, always top name brands. Even so, she is generous and a good friend. She has taken an interest in politics and would like to study law when she finishes school. At the moment she is looking forward to a skiing holiday.

Carleen loves music and plays the piano. She enjoys bushwalking, and works part-time at a dry cleaners to earn some money. She hopes to go into a career involving classical music after doing some more study.

Patrick spends most of his spare time at the beach. His main interests are fishing and surfing. Most of the girls think he is 'cute'. He is learning to shape surfboards and is planning a surfing holiday around Australia with some mates.

Theresa's parents separated three years ago. She lives with her mother, but they are constantly arguing. She plays hockey and has interests in drama and singing. She is planning to travel overseas when she finishes school and currently works at a service station after school.

Chris is the third child in a family of six children. He follows the local football team and 'gets by' at school without being brilliant at anything. His older brother is a builder and he thinks he would like to work with him, but at the moment he is a bit 'lost' about where he is going or what he is doing.

Tony is a bit shy, especially with girls. He has two older brothers and has to work hard in the family business, which is a milk bar. He studies hard and is quite good at maths. He would like to go into the Air Force as a pilot.

Gary is mad keen on motorbikes. He has his own bike and enjoys racing, especially if it involves some jumping or crossing rugged country. School is a bit of a drag except for the opportunity to meet with his friends.

3
LET'S LAUGH

HUMOUR

Rolling Pumpkins

Sam promised to take two large pumpkins to school for the Hallowe'en celebrations. However, he soon learned that two pumpkins are not easy to juggle on a bumping bus.

'Hey now,' the driver said as he drew back. 'What is this? I'm not a relative of yours.'

In despair, Sam opened his mouth, le'ting the bus pass fall at his feet.

'The bus pass.' Sam nodded anxiously towards the floor while just managing to keep the pumpkin in his left arm from falling. But that motion loosened his grip on the other pumpkin, which landed on the driver's lap.

'I had my bus pass in my teeth,' Sam explained.

The driver, staring at Sam stonily, lifted the pumpkin from his lap and stuck it under Sam's right arm. 'You keep that,' he said. 'We are not allowed to take food from the passengers.'

Slowly, carefully, Sam lowered himself, a pumpkin clutched to each side, until he was close enough to the floor to make a try at getting the bus pass between two fingers. The bus started up, jouncing one of the pumpkins loose. Sam, straightening suddenly to go after the pumpkin rolling down the aisle, banged his elbow against the change box, howled in pain, and howled again on seeing the second pumpkin follow the other to the back of the bus.

'Hey,' the bus driver said, 'aren't you the kid who had roller skates on yesterday?'

Sam kept his eye on the pumpkins, now stuck in a thicket of passengers' feet. 'That was me. I'm not gonna do that any more. I almost rolled under the bus when I got off.'

'O my God!' the driver cried as he stopped short at a red light. 'Off! Off! Get those pumpkins and get off this bus. I don't take drunks and I don't take boys who get themselves and everybody else in trouble.'

'You can't kick me off,' Sam protested. 'I have a bus pass.'

'I decide who gets on this bus,' the driver said and his voice rasped and rose. 'And I decide who stays on this bus. Out!'

A large red-faced man picked up the pumpkins, brought them to the front of the bus, inserted them under Sam's arms, and said to the bus driver, 'You're not serious? The boy didn't do anything.'

Sam, his book bag around his neck, his bus pass in his teeth, a pumpkin twice as big as his head in one arm, and a second pumpkin in the other, was just barely able to open the door. Leaving it open, he pressed the elevator button with his nose, saw the elevator was going up past his floor, and walked slowly over to the stairs. Once on the street, he walked carefully to the bus corner and waited, hunched over, with his book bag nearly touching the ground. As his bus pulled up, he sighed with relief and slowly, ever so carefully, went up the stairs and leaned over the change box towards the bus driver.

'Fare, young man,' the driver said.

'Bssss pssss.' Sam's face was now very close to the driver's.

'Yeah,' Sam agreed. 'I didn't do anything. Show me where it says pumpkins aren't allowed to ride a bus.'

'Now look here,' the driver said over Sam's head to the large man, 'this maniac almost made me cut his legs off yesterday. I want him to learn a lesson. Maybe next time he'll come on the bus without pumpkins, without roller skates, without driving me crazy.'

'Now look here yourself' — the large man's face seemed to swell — 'you've got no right to throw this kid off. Suppose it was your kid?'

'I don't have any children, thank God.' The driver opened the door, and Sam, hugging the pumpkins to his chest, jumped down.

'You don't have to get off, you know,' the red-faced man shouted after him.'

'That's OK,' Sam shouted back. 'I'll remember his number, and I'll sue him.'

'You are not allowed on this bus — *for ever!*' The driver was really shouting now.

'And you a grown man,' an elderly woman seated just behind the driver spoke accusingly into his ear.

'I have a good mind to order *everybody* off this bus,' the driver muttered.

As the bus drove off, Sam frowned, put the pumpkins on the ground, and searched his pockets wildly. 'Damn,' he said, 'I never picked the bus pass off the floor.'

from *This School Is Driving Me Crazy* by Nat Hentoff

Reading for Meaning

1 Why is Sam barely able to open the door?

2 How does he try to signal the elevator to stop at his floor?

3 Why does Sam wait 'hunched over' for the bus?

4 What is the bus driver's reaction when Sam leans over to say 'Bssss pssss'?

5 What happens while Sam tries to keep the left pumpkin from falling?

6 What is the driver's comment as he returns Sam's pumpkin?

7 How does Sam manage to lose both pumpkins?

8 'Off! Off!' Why does the driver refuse to allow Sam to stay on the bus?

9 How does the large red-faced man help?

10 What lesson does the driver want Sam to learn?

11 How does Sam threaten the bus driver?

12 What ban does the driver place on Sam?

13 Why do you think the bus passengers are on Sam's side?

14 How do we know the driver is fed up with all the passengers?

15 How is Sam finally the loser in this bus experience?

16 Is your sympathy with Sam or with the driver? Give a reason for your answer.

You Can't Love an Ostrich

An ostrich deprived of its egg can become a very aggressive bird, as Kenneth Cook discovers in the following story from his collection entitled *Frill-Necked Frenzy*.

The ostrich is an evil bird. It has eyes that reflect its nature—beady, mean and pitiless. The only expressions it has are loathing and contempt for all living things in general and for me in particular. It also has a kick like a camel and can break rocks with its beak.

I only ever encountered one ostrich, but it scarred my soul so badly that I would sooner face a koala in its rage than confront an ostrich again.

Strangely enough, the Parks and Wildlife officer who led me into the claws of a koala also placed me face to face with an ostrich.

She was Dr Mary Anne Locher, a very pleasant lady socially, but absolute hell to work with because of her belief that animals are definitely more valuable than people.

I ran into her in the South Australian Museum a couple of years after the affair of the killer koala and, as my scars had healed, I didn't turn and run as I should have done as soon as I saw her. She's a short, fat, round, attractive lady with pretty little ears that stick out through her fluffy brown hair. She isn't much younger than I am and that fools you because there is a general illusion that mature people have some prudence.

This is quite wrong. There is no correlation between age and caution. I demonstrated this quite clearly by accepting Mary Anne's invitation to go and find an ostrich egg.

'But are there ostriches in Australia,' I asked, 'except in zoos?'

'Oh dear, yes,' said Mary Anne. 'Plenty. Dozens of people brought them out here early this century and tried to farm them for their feathers. That didn't work and the ostriches were turned loose. You'll find them in lots of places.'

It transpired that one of those places was the Coorong, east of Adelaide; a splendid tract of sand, sea inlets and fascinating scrub. Waterbirds love the Coorong and the place abounds in pelicans and just about every other lovely winged creature that you can think of.

Naturally, this is one of the few places where the South Australian government allows people to go shooting for sport. Only foxes and rabbits are supposed to be shot, but the South Australian government is demonstrating unusual naiveté in supposing that shooters restrict themselves to vermin.

Mary Anne proposed to haul me off to the Coorong to find an ostrich egg.

'Why do you want an ostrich egg?' I asked.

'I'm doing a thesis on the relationship between the emu and the ostrich and I want to catch an ostrich egg and an emu egg in exactly the same conditions.'

'You're not trying for another doctorate?'

'Yes I am,' said Mary Anne defensively.

'Why?' I asked.

'You can't have too many degrees these days,' she told me. After all, she was an academic, a class I detest, but she was one of the rare, better sort who are socially acceptable. That's what I thought then.

So I found myself driving through the Coorong with Mary Anne in her Mitsubishi four-wheel-drive station wagon.

'There goes one,' said Mary Anne. To our right, I saw a large ostrich racing across the sand, feathers puffed like a black and white ballet dress in poor condition. The creature looked like a raddled old dancer in her cups, fleeing an outraged audience on long, skinny legs.

'How do you propose to get near a thing that moves as fast as that?' I asked.

'I don't,' said Mary Anne. 'What we do is follow the tracks until we find an egg. Come on.'

She hopped out of the station wagon and began rummaging in the back. Presently she emerged with a net bag and what looked like a large, single-barrelled shotgun.

'What's that?' I asked.

'A net bag to carry the egg in,' said Mary Anne. 'I'd rather not handle it much.'

'No, I mean the other thing.'

'That's a tranquilliser gun,' said Mary Anne.

'What do you want that for? You don't have to tranquillise eggs, do you?'

'Of course not. It's just that ostriches can be pretty aggressive, particularly if you interfere with their eggs.'

That was when I knew it was time to go home but, as usual, the knowledge came too late. I could hardly stun Mary Anne and drive off in her car. I wish I had.

Mary Anne slipped the net bag into the pocket of the blue overalls she was wearing, slung the gun over her shoulder and stumped off. I followed. We soon crossed the ostrich's tracks. They were as big as dinner plates and so deeply embedded in the sand that they indicated a very heavy bird indeed. I began to imagine such prints appearing in due course on various sections of my anatomy.

'Will that gun thing of yours stop one of these creatures?' I asked nervously.

'Oh, yes,' she said, 'puts them to sleep in a few seconds. Doesn't hurt them in the least, either.'

I wasn't all that worried about the ostrich being hurt. I was more concerned with how much hurting it could do in the few seconds before it fell asleep. I longed for my old .303.

After about two hours of carefully walking back along the ostrich tracks, largely going round in circles, we found an ostrich nest. In it was an ostrich egg the size and shape of a small football. The colour was not unlike that of an emu egg.

Mary Anne knelt down beside the egg and felt it gently.

'Lovely specimen,' she said. 'I'd say it was near hatching, too.'

She took a stethoscope from the pocket of her overalls and applied it to the egg. 'Yes, you can hear its heart beating very strongly. There's a fully formed chick in there. Just what I wanted. Taking it back won't do any harm at all.'

She took out her net and handed it to me.

'Just hold that open while I put the egg in it.'

Picking up the egg was something of an effort for Mary Anne. I was astonished at its weight when it went into the net.

'I'll carry this for you if you like,' I said.

'No, I'd better do it. It's best to be very careful. You take the gun.'

She handed me the gun, took the egg, and we set out for the car. Mary Anne, walking slowly, was holding the net awkwardly out from her body with both hands so the egg wouldn't bang against her legs, and I drifted about twenty metres ahead of her.

There was a hideous droning sound like a bullroarer being blown by an asthmatic camel and a huge ostrich burst out of the scrub twenty metres ahead of me.

Its head must have been more than three metres from the ground and its body, feathers puffed in rage, was enormous. Its eyes were fierce and seeking blood, its deadly-looking beak was open and that horrible noise seemed to be spewing from its vitals up through its long, quivering neck. Its mighty claws were tearing the ground and sending up clouds of dust, and it was almost on me.

I threw my hands in front of my face and squealed as I do when I'm in danger. But the brute wasn't after me; it blasted past lashing my arms with its feathers and hurtled down on Mary Anne.

She had more warning than I, with time to turn and start running. She was a sprightly creature, despite her rotundity, and made surprisingly good time, but she was no match for the ostrich. It ran down on her with the obvious intention of trampling her to death after pecking out her brains. Even as she ran, Mary Anne kept that wretched egg held out in front of her so that it wouldn't be damaged. Scientists are a dedicated lot.

Some millions of years before, the grace of God had planted a huge, easy-to-climb boulder in Mary Anne's path and she went up it like a possum. The ostrich reached the rock just as she did and struck at her back with its beak, missed and chipped off a piece of stone as big as my head. I shuddered to think what that blow would have done to Mary Anne's back. But she clambered to the top of the rock four metres above the ground, still holding the egg, and lay there panting while the ostrich did a frustrated war dance, raising clouds of dust with its claws and chipping great hunks of rock off the boulder with its beak. Its stamping feet made a primeval drum accompaniment to the furious, droning gobbling. It was an angry bird.

I looked around for a convenient tree, but the ostrich showed no interest in me. Apparently all it wanted to do was disembowel Mary Anne and get its egg back. Mary Anne scrambled to her feet, examined the egg carefully, then called to me, 'Put a dart into that creature!'

I remembered the tranquilliser gun on my shoulder, unslung it and tried to work out the mechanism. I couldn't.

'How do you use it?' I called.

'Pull back the bolt until it catches, then aim it and pull the trigger.' I could hardly hear her over the ostrich's awful din.

I found the bolt and pulled it back. It seemed simple enough. Raising the gun to my shoulder, I tried to line the sights up on the ostrich. The damn thing was leaping about so much it was like trying to shoot a ping-pong ball in play.

'You'd better get in closer,' called Mary Anne. I wasn't too keen on that. My meaner self was telling me that all I had to do was run back to the car and go for help. Mary Anne was not in immediate danger. However, it did strike me that, at the rate the ostrich was pecking and kicking the boulder, it would soon reduce it to a heap of rubble, with Mary Anne going the same way soon after. I am by nature far from heroic but, as the ostrich's attention was firmly fixed on Mary Anne, I thought it reasonably safe to go a few metres nearer to make sure of hitting my target.

I approached within about ten metres of the ostrich after making sure that an easily climbed tree was nearby.

I lined up the sights on that frantic feathered form, the muzzle of my weapon weaving constantly to keep up with its movements.

'Put it in its thigh!' called Mary Anne.

I felt I would be lucky even at point-blank range to hit the thing at all, much less pick on a precise part of its anatomy. However, I tried. I probably spent five minutes following the ostrich's movements, concentrating on the thigh. Eventually I squeezed the trigger.

It was an airgun and there was not much noise, but it kicked with surprising violence.

The tranquilliser dart sped straight and true.

Into Mary Anne's forearm.

'You — —'screamed Mary Anne, using a series of words I wouldn't have expected to hear from an academic.

She whipped the dart out of her forearm as soon as it went in, but enough of the tranquilliser had been injected to have appalling effects. Her knees started to buckle almost immediately. She called to me, 'Get me out of this, you — —' once more displaying a remarkable vocabulary. Then she was rolling around on her back on the top of the rock, making strange noises that mingled with the strange noises of the ostrich.

My first impulse was to get the hell out of there. But on reflection, my reputation would have suffered if it were made public that I had left my scientific hostess to the mercies of a mad ostrich, having first shot her with a tranquilliser gun.

Mary Anne was rolling around on top of the rock so violently that it was obvious she would shortly roll off into the beak and claws of the ostrich.

I recocked the tranquilliser gun and tried another shot, but of course there was no dart in the breech.

There was nothing for it but heroics, which are not my style at all.

Swinging the gun like a club, I threw my bulk towards the rock at what I hoped was a run but what was more like a lumbering trot.

The ostrich turned its head towards me and then kicked backwards with its right leg. One of its claws caught my shirt and tore it off my body. I threw the tranquilliser gun at the bird's head and happily hit it. The ostrich was momentarily disconcerted and I went clambering up the face of the boulder.

I heard that hideous beak crash into the stone just below my heels and then I was lying panting on the top, clutching at Mary Anne, trying to stop her rolling over the side.

She was making the most extraordinary sounds and it took me some seconds to work out that she was laughing her head off. Almost within striking distance of a lethal ostrich, Mary Anne was rolling around, convulsed with roars of laughter.

The effects of the tranquilliser that had penetrated her bloodstream had rendered her in effect rolling drunk.

I had no idea what to do, so contented myself with making soothing noises and stopping her from falling into the ostrich's maw.

The egg, I noticed, was safely at one end of the boulder, still intact.

It was an impasse. I could do nothing but hang on to Mary Anne. The ostrich showed no signs of ever going away. There was no reason the situation should not be maintained until I died of fatigue, hunger, thirst, embarrassment, or all four.

Then Mary Anne suddenly fell asleep.

At first I thought she had died, but as I feverishly felt for her pulse, she started to snore loudly. I let her lie there, stood up and looked down at the ostrich.

It was still beating the life out of the earth with its feet and tearing away at the boulder like a jackhammer.

I picked up the egg, still in the net, and wondered.

If I tossed the egg down to the ostrich, would it be mollified and go away? On the other hand, if I tossed the egg down, might it break and kill the chick inside, thus provoking the ostrich to an even greater murderous rage?

I was standing there dithering, egg in hand, when a voice behind me snapped, 'What the hell do you think you're doing?'

Mary Anne, sober, self-possessed and alert, was sitting up glaring at me.

'You're all right!' I said cheerfully.

'Of course I'm all right,' said Mary Anne. 'You didn't get enough of that stuff into me to do more than make me a bit silly for a few minutes. What are you doing to that egg?'

'I thought of giving it back to its mother in the hope she'd go away.'

'That's a male ostrich,' said Mary Anne, ever the pedant.

'You mean she didn't even lay this egg?'

'It would be biologically unusual,' said Mary Anne.

I wasn't really interested in a scientific discussion.

'Assuming it's a he, and I'm damned if I know how you can tell, it's obvious he has a strong paternal interest in this egg. Why don't we give it to him?' After all, it's his if it's anybody's.'

'Over my dead body,' said Mary Anne, taking the egg from my hands. I forbore from commenting that I thought this highly likely.

'Give me the gun,' she said. 'I'll knock the brute out.' She emphasised 'I'll', implying that I wouldn't be able to. Experience, of course, gave her some justification. She pulled a tranquilliser dart from her overalls pocket.

I pointed to the ground where the gun was being battered by the flailing feet of the ostrich.

'I threw it at him, getting up here to help you,' I said defensively.

Mary Anne snorted.

'Then you'd better go down there and get it,' she said, 'or we'll be here forever.'

I looked down at the ostrich whose energies showed no sign of flagging, and shook my head firmly.

'No way, Mary Anne.' I am not a forceful man, but on some occasions I can express determination. This was one of them.

Mary Anne recognised my position, stood up and thought.

'I tell you what,' she said after a minute or so. 'You take the egg, slide down the other side of the rock and run like hell. The ostrich will follow you. I'll grab the gun and pick him off before he gets you. How about it?'

'No, Mary Anne,' I said firmly.

'Then what the hell?' said Mary Anne, whose language showed a deplorable tendency to sink to gutter level under tension. This seemed to be a characteristic of academics.

'*You* take the egg and run, and *I'll* grab the gun and pick him off before he gets you,' I said. 'How about it?'

Mary Anne looked at me evenly.

'I wouldn't trust you to shoot a toy duck in a bath,' she said. Under the circumstances, she had a point.

We both sulked for about ten minutes, my

gaze fixed on the ostrich which, by now, had eroded a substantial part of the boulder.

If we just stayed there, it seemed to me it was only a matter of time before both of us fell under the terrible impact of beak and claws.

'Oh, all right,' I said petulantly. 'Give me the bloody egg.'

'Be careful with it,' said Mary Anne.

'Oh, shut up,' I said, no longer feeling very polite to Mary Anne.

I slid down the side of the boulder, clutching the egg and not caring whether I cracked it or not, and bolted towards the car. I didn't look back but I heard the droning gobble halt briefly and start again, louder than ever. Then I heard the pounding of huge, clawed feet gaining on me.

Meanwhile Mary Anne had slid down the rock, grabbed the gun, shoved in a dart of which she had a huge supply, then started firing as she ran after us.

I heard the darts whizzing past my head. It became obvious that if I didn't fall in the ostrich's path from exhaustion, I would soon be tranquillised into immobility and easily slaughtered. At least, I thought, that should be painless.

The thud of ostrich feet was shaking the ground around me. I could feel its hot breath on my neck. Its gobbling was stunning my mind. I was breathless and exhausted. I turned at bay and as the brute rushed up to finish me off I flung the egg at it.

The shell shattered against its legs. I stopped and looked down. There, tangled in the net, was an ostrich chick, alive and kicking, if slightly bemused. It was quite big. There seemed to be a lot more ostrich chick than there had been egg.

The chick struggled out of the net and ran away into the scrub... was the father) went... instead of gobbling.

I stood there sobbing. Ma... angrily, brandishing the gun.

'What have you done with my... said, staring at the bits of shell arou... net.

'Let's go home, Mary Anne,' I said wearily.

When, oh when, will I learn *never* to have anything to do with an academic?

from *Frill-Necked Frenzy* by Kenneth Cook

Reading for Understanding

1 How does the writer describe the eyes of an ostrich?

2 Why would you have to be wary of an ostrich's legs and beak?

3 Why is Dr Mary Anne Locher 'absolute hell to work with'?

4 Why are there ostriches in some wild places in Australia?

5 Why does Mary Anne want to find an ostrich egg?

6 What comparison does the writer use to describe how their first large ostrich looked as it raced across the sand?

7 What does the ostrich egg they found look like?

8 '...a huge ostrich burst out of the scrub...' What sound accompanies the sound of the ostrich?

9 How does Mary Anne escape the ostrich?

10 What happens when the writer fires the dart at the ostrich?

11 What actions does the writer take to save Mary Anne from falling off the rock into the beak and claws of the ostrich?

12 In what condition does the writer find Mary Anne after she has been shot by the tranquilliser dart?

13 What plan of escape do the writer and Mary Anne finally agree on?

14 What does the writer do as the ostrich rushes up to finish him off?

15 How does the ostrich react when the chick runs off into the scrub?

16 What lesson does the writer learn from his experience with the egg?

17 Why is the title of the story appropriate?

18 What makes this piece of writing so amusing?

ctacular Failures

baton-twirling troupe and a sunbather are just
failures featured in *The Return of Heroic Failures*.

Let's Laugh

93

Its father (I presumed it
after it, clucking now

Anne ran up

egg?' she
the

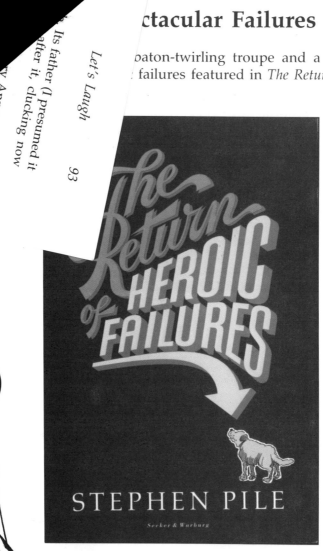

The Least Satisfactory Robot

Seeking greater efficiency, the Kavio Restaurant in Leith bought Donic, a robot programmed as a wine waiter. In the summer of 1980, they dressed it in a black hat and bow tie, fitted the batteries and turned on.

Showing a natural flair for the work, this advanced machine ran amok, smashed the furniture, poured wine all over the carpet and frightened the diners until its lights went out, its voice box packed up and its head dropped off in a customer's lap. When asked to account for this outstanding performance, the robot's manufacturer said that he had given the operating instructions to the restaurant's disc-jockey.

The Least Successful Baton Twirling

Noted for the height, range and drama of their twirls, members of the Ventura Baton Twirling Troupe surprised even themselves on one occasion in the late 1960s.

During an Independence Day march, one of their batons hit a power cable, blacked out the area, started a grass fire and put the local radio station off the air. 'They were on form,' the mayor said.

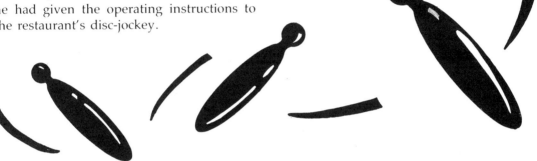

The Least Successful Sunbather

In 1983, a Californian sunbather decided to acquire the perfect tan. Hearing that a better-quality ray was available above the urban smog, he attached 42 helium balloons to his deckchair, which was itself tethered to the earth by means of a long rope.

He was supposed to rise 6,000 feet and there bask in the ultra-violet possibilities. However, he did much better than this when his rope snapped and the deckchair rose, untrammelled, to a height of 15,000 feet, where a passing airline pilot reported him as a UFO sighting.

Prepared for all possibilities, he pulled out an air pistol and shot the balloons one by one. His deckchair demolished a power cable, blacking out the whole area, and he arrived back on earth much paler than when he left.

The Least Successful Weather Forecast

At the end of a bravura weather forecast in October 1987, Mr Michael Fish told British televiewers that 'a woman rang to say she'd heard there was a hurricane on the way. Well, don't worry. There isn't.' Brushing aside this fanciful amateur forecast with a chuckle, the immortal Fish predicted 'sea breezes' and a 'showery airflow'.

In no time Britain was hit by 120 mph winds that ripped up 300 miles of power cables, plunged a quarter of the country into darkness, blocked 200 roads with fallen branches, felled 25 per cent of the trees in Kent and stopped all rail traffic in the south of England for twenty-four hours. An ambulance at Hayling Island was hit by a yacht floating across the road and the Meteorological Office said it was the worst hurricane since 1703.

A spokesman for Mr Fish later said: 'It is really all a question of detail.'

Reading for Meaning

The Least Satisfactory Robot

1 Who was Donic? *a robot programmed as a wine waiter seeking great effeciency*

2 Why did the restaurant buy Donic? *it seemed to have a natural flair*

3 In what three ways did the robot run amok? *smashed the furniture, poured wine over the carpet, frightened the diners until it's light went.*

4 How did it fall apart? *it's head dropped on a customers lap*

5 How did the robot's manufacturer explain its performance? *he explained the instructions to the disc jockey*

6 Did you find this incident humorous? Why? *No. It was kind of predictable, espicially the part where the robot misses he ccu*

The Least Successful Sunbather

1 What decision was made by a Californian sunbather in 1983? *he planed to have the perfect tan*

2 What did the sunbather believe lay above the urban smog? *he believed there was better-quality ray.*

3 What preparations did the sunbather make for his excursion? *he attached 42 ballons to his chair and the chair was attached to something.*

4 What did the sunbather expect to do? *he expected to rise 6000 feet and bask in the ultra violent possibilties*

5 What actually happened? *the rope which held the chair snapped and he rose to a height of 15000*

6 How did a passing airline pilot react to his presence? *as a UFO*

7 How did the sunbather arrange his descent? *since he was prepared for everything he pulled out an air pistol and shot the ballons.*

8 What were the two results that followed his descent? *his chair demolished a power cable blacking the whole area and he came back paler than before.*

The Least Successful Baton Twirling

1 What aspects of their baton twirling were the Ventura Troupe noted for? *height, range, and drama of their twirls.*

2 What results followed when one of their batons hit a power cable? *it blacked out the area, the grass was on fire, and put the local radio stations off the air.*

3 What was the mayor's comment? *"They were on form."*

The Least Successful Weather Forecast

1 What startling warning was telephoned to Mr Michael Fish? *there was a hurricane on the way*

2 What did Mr Michael Fish think of the warning? *He brushed it away and ignored the warning*

3 What were the two main items in his own forecast? *sea breezes and showery airflow*

4 What were the results of the 120 mph winds of the hurricane. *it ripped up 300 miles of cable, plunged quater of the country into darkness blac, 200 hundred roads with fallen branches felled 25% of the trees in kent, stopped all rail traffic in London for 24h and an ambulance was hi by yatch.*

5 What happened at Hayling Island? *a yatch was hit an ambulance*

6 What is amusing about the comment in the last paragraph?

POETRY

POEMS TO MAKE YOU LAUGH

Where's Your Homework?

As soon as I got home last night, Sir
I finished off my English homework first.
Put it on the kitchen table but my baby sister
found it. Chewed it and slavered all over it, Sir.
So I took it into the bath to check it through
like you asked us to do, Sir.
But reaching for the sponge
I dropped it in the bath.
It was so soggy that
I had to put the hair drier on it.
I burnt it to a crisp. Bone dry the paper was, Sir.
So I had a brainwave. I smeared Suntan lotion
on it to soften it up.
Left it for ten minutes
and the pages started to turn brown.

This morning I looked inside
and all the writing was smudged, Sir.
Could I have a new exercise book, please?

David Jackson

Questions

1 a Who asks the question in the title?
   b Who answers the question in the poem?

2 How did the baby sister ruin the homework?

3 Why was the bath the wrong place to check the homework?

4 'I burnt it to a crisp'. Why did this happen to the homework?

5 What was the student's brainwave?

6 Why do you think the last three lines of the poem have been made into a separate verse?

7 The poem's last line seems to explain all that has gone before. Why is this?

8 Did you think this poem was humorous?

Dog-Gone

There's a phantom dog in the city.
He never can be found.
We only know he's been here,
By the messages left around.

No one ever admits it
No one cleans it up.
But everybody steps right in.
This mess of a miscreant pup.

It always seems to happen,
Whenever you buy new shoes.
It squelches over the edges,
And packs hard into the grooves!

No matter how hard you scrape them,
Along the pavement side.
The smell goes with you all the day,
Like something nasty died!

Joggers, walkers, victims all,
Shout 'It's a disgrace!'
Somewhere sits the phantom pooch,
With a smirk across his face.

Russell Adams

The Trouble with My Sister

My little sister was truly awful,
She was really shocking,
She put the budgie in the fridge
And slugs in Mummy's stocking.

She was really awful,
But it was a load of fun
When she stole old Uncle Wilbur's
Double-barrelled gun.

She aimed it at a pork pie
And blew it into bits.
She aimed it at a hamster
That was having fits.

She leapt up on the telly,
She pirouetted on the cat,
She gargled with some jelly
And spat in Grandad's hat.

She ran down the hallway,
She ran across the road,
She dug up lots of little worms
And caught a squirming toad.

She put them in a large pot
And she began to stir,
She added a pint of bat's blood
And some rabbit fur.

She leapt upon the Hoover,
Around the room she went.
Once she had a turned-up nose
But now her nose is bent.

I like my little sister,
There is really just one hitch.
I think my little sister
Has become a little witch.

Brian Patten

The Unincredible Hulk-in-Law

Being the Incredible Hulk's
scrawny stepbrother ain't easy.
Sticky-fisted toddlers
pick fights with me
in misadventure playgrounds.

On beaches
seven-stone weaklings
kick sand in my eyes
vandalise my pies
and thrash me with candyfloss.

They all tell their friends
how they licked the Hulk...
(...well not the Hulk exactly,
but an incredibly unincredible relative).

Bullied by Brownies
mugged by nuns
without a doubt
the fun's gone out
of having a TV star in the family.

Think I'll marry
Wonderwoman's asthmatic second cousin
and start a commune in Arkansas
for out-of-work, weedy
super heroes-in-law.

Roger McGough

Questions

1 Why isn't it easy being the Incredible Hulk's stepbrother?

2 How is the stepbrother assaulted on beaches?

3 What is unusual about the idea of being thrashed with candyfloss?

4 Why does the poet describe himself as 'an incredibly unincredible relative'?

5 'Bullied by Brownies/mugged by nuns'. What is the poet saying to us about the character and strength of the stepbrother?

6 Why has the fun gone out of 'having a TV star in the family'?

7 Why do you think the stepbrother decides to marry 'Wonderwoman's asthmatic second cousin'?

8 How does the poem end on a humorous note?

9 What examples of exaggeration can you find in this poem?

10 What do you think is this poem's most entertaining feature?

Billy Dreamer's Fantastic Friends

The Incredible Hulk came to tea,
Robin was with him too,
Batman stayed at home that night
Because his bat had flu.

Superman called to say hello
And Spiderman spun us a joke.
Dynamite Sue was supposed to come
But she went up in smoke.

The Invisible Man might have called,
But as I wasn't sure,
I left an empty chair and bun
Beside the kitchen door.

They signed my autograph book,
But I dropped it in the fire,
Now whenever I tell my friends
They say I'm a terrible liar.

But incredible people *do* call round
('Specially when I'm alone),
And if they don't, and I get bored,
I call them on the phone.

Brian Patten

Questions

1 Do you think the title of this poem is suitable? Why?

2 How does the first verse make us think of the name 'Batman' in a new way?

3 'And Spiderman spun us a joke', Why is 'spun' an appropriate word to use here?

4 How do we learn that Dynamite Sue was well named?

5 Why wasn't Billy sure about the visit of the Invisible Man?

6 Why kind of hospitality did Billy extend to the Invisible Man, just in case he did call?

7 Why was it impossible for Billy to prove that his fantastic friends had visited him.

8 How do his friends respond when he tells them about his visitors?

9 What have you learned about the character of Billy from your reading of this poem?

10 Did you enjoy this poem? Why or why not?

WRITING

THE TALL STORY

The form of humorous writing called the **tall story** is based on exaggeration. A tall story often describes someone or something whose size, habits, courage (or other characteristics) are tremendously exaggerated. Notice, for example, the exaggeration in each stage of Crooked Mick's babyhood.

CROOKED MICK

Crooked Mick was born, so the old-timers say, when the Darling River was a possum pad and the Jenolan Caves were wombat holes. He grew fast, and by the time he was three weeks old he had become so large and heavy that his father had to erect a windlass to haul him out of his cot.

   He was not yet a weaner when his first adventure befell him. He crawled out of the hut one day while his mother was boiling a wash-copper full of milk for his mid-day meal. For six months his distraught parents searched for him in every likely place on the Speewah. When they found him he was being suckled by a giant wombat; and he was so far from home that from where he was lying he could watch the tea-pickers at work in China.

from *The Childhood and Youth of Crooked Mick* by Bill Wannan

Now let's look at a tall story in more detail. The questions that follow the story are designed to direct your attention to some of the ways in which exaggeration contributes to its humour.

The Story of the World's Worst Whinger

I first met this bloke—the World's Worst Whinger—in a shearing shed in Queensland during the Depression. I asked him an innocent question: 'How would you be?' Well, he dropped the sheep he was shearing, spat, and fixed me with a pair of bitter eyes and he says: 'How would I be? How would you expect me to be?' Get a load of me, will you? Dags on every inch of me hide; drinking me own sweat; swallowing dirt with every breath I breathe; shearing sheep that should have been dogs' meat years ago; working for the lousiest boss in Australia; frightened to leave because the old woman's looking for me in Brisbane with a maintenance order. How would I be? I haven't tasted beer for weeks and the last glass I had was knocked over by some clumsy coot before I finished it.'

He must have been a whinger, all right.

The world's worst, like I told you. Next time I met him he was in an army camp in Melbourne. 'How would you be?' I asked him. 'How would I be? Get a load of this outfit. Look at me flamin' hat. Size nine and a half and I take six and a half. Get an eyeful of these strides—you could hide a blasted brewery horse in the seat of them and still

have room for me. And get on to these boots, will yer? There's enough leather in 'em to make a full set of harness. And some idiot brasshat told me this was a man's outfit. How would I be? How would you *expect* me to be?'

Is this story true?

True? Well most of my stories are true but this one, you might say it's truer than true. I met him next in Tobruk. He was sitting on a box, tin hat over one eye, cigarette butt dangling from his bottom lip, rifle leaning on one knee, cleaning his finger nails with his bayonet. I should have known better but I asked him: 'How would you be, Dig?' He swallowed his cigarette butt and stared at me with a malevolent eye. 'How would I be? How would I be? How would you expect me to be? Shot at by every Fritz in Africa; eating sand with every meal; flies in me eyes: frightened to go to sleep; expecting to die in this Godforsaken place. And you ask me *how would I be?*'

Did you ever meet him again?

No, he was killed in Tobruk, as a matter of fact.

Well, one thing, he wouldn't do any more whingeing poor devil.

You know, I dreamt about him the other night.

Yeh?

Yeh. I dreamt I died and went to Heaven. It was as clear as on a television screen. I saw him there in my dream and I asked: 'How would you be?' He eyed me with an angelic expression and he says; 'How would I be?' Get an eyeful of this nightgown, will yer? A man trips over it fifty times a day and takes ten minutes to lift it to scratch his knee. And take a gander at my right wing, feathers falling out of it, a man must be moulting. Cast your eyes over this halo; only me big ears keep the rotten thing on me skull. And just take a Captain Cook at this harp, five strings missing and there's band practice in five minutes. *How would I be? you ask. How would you expect a man to bloody well be?*'

from *The Yarns of Billy Borker* by Frank Hardy

Questions

1 What example of exaggeration can you find in the story's title?

2 What question is used by the writer to begin the tall story?

3 In the first paragraph, what do you find to be the most humorous piece of exaggeration?

4 What humorous exaggeration is used by the whinger concerning his army 'strides' (trousers)?

5 Do you think the whinger really does have something to whinge about when he is at Tobruk during World War II? Give reasons for your answer.

6 What is the setting of the story's last paragraph?

7 How does the whinger exaggerate about his 'nightgown'?

8 What is the whinger's last whinge?

9 What makes this story a 'tall story'?

10 How is the humour in this story created?

WRITING YOUR OWN TALL STORY

Choose one of the following topics and write your own tall story. You may like to adopt some of the techniques used in 'The Story of the World's Worst Whinger'.

Topics
- The World's Worst Student
- The World's Worst Teacher
- The World's Worst Doctor
- The World's Worst Pop Star
- The World's Worst Baby
- The World's Best Ghost
- The World's Best Cleaner
- The World's Best Radio Announcer
- The World's Best Pet
- The World's Best Tourist Guide
- The World's Best Fairy Godmother
- The World's Most Incredible Talking Dog

LANGUAGE

COMMUNICATION BREAKDOWN

Communication breakdown is sometimes the result of **ambiguity, tautology** or **circumlocution**. Let's look carefully at each of these causes of communication breakdown.

AMBIGUITY

If a sentence or expression can be interpreted in two ways, it is said to be ambiguous. Sometimes the cause of ambiguity is a misplaced phrase, incorrect punctuation, or the use of a word that has two meanings. The result is a communication breakdown that often contains unintended humour. The following advertisement is an example of ambiguity.

• Respectable lady seeks nice room where she can cook herself on an electric stove.

Here the obvious double meaning of the words 'cook herself' could be corrected by saying 'cook for herself'.

Avoiding Ambiguity

Identify the ambiguity in the following sentences and rewrite each sentence correctly.

1 Cats will be called for, fleas removed and returned to you for only one dollar. *the animals will be returned.*

2 Advertisement: Woman wants cleaning three days a week. *someone for cleaning job*

3 Securely pierced by a long brass toasting fork, Barry held a piece of bread to the *washed by Barry* glowing embers. *Barry securely* *the* *held → was held by the Barry*

4 Headline: Public health menace. Special committee to sit on "garbage." *speak subject of*

5 The umbrella was lost by a child, with silver ribs. *It had*

6 Shop sign: W. Williamsons—Dispensing chemists. We dispense with accuracy. *medicines*

7 The only thing to do with people who write insulting letters is to toss them straight into the rubbish bin. *when*

8 Eating quickly, the plate of bacon and eggs was soon emptied. *food* *by eating quickly*

9 Many of those homes were built roughly twenty years ago. *about*

10 If you take your dog in the car, don't let him hang out of the window while driving. *you*

TAUTOLOGY

Tautology means the needless repetition of an idea or a statement, often in different words. For example:

● It has been windy for eight consecutive days in a row.

The phrase 'in a row' repeats the meaning of 'consecutive' and so is an example of tautology.

Avoiding Tautology

Identify the tautologies in each of the following sentences and rewrite each sentence correctly.

1 Our forward progress was delayed when David reversed the Land Rover backwards.

2 Let's join together and give grateful thanks that this male bachelor is now being married and wedded to this lovely, feminine girl.

3 This theatre is fully filled to capacity because the show now on is known internationally, around the world.

4 Advertisement: Just circle once around the block on our new novelty skateboard and we are sure you will want to repeat the experience again.

5 Advertisement: Our new product kills flies and ants dead and yet it contains no toxic poison.

6 Advertisement: All our prices have been reduced down today so come in and receive a free gift at the door.

7 For those unemployed people who are out of work, the government is offering help.

8 Right now at this moment, a tediously boring TV show is being advertised as a wonderfully new innovation in the art of the mini-series.

CIRCUMLOCUTION

Circumlocution means speaking or writing in a roundabout or longwinded way. For example:

● The person on foot became the recipient of contusions occasioned by a car and himself impacting.

This sentence could be written simply and directly as:

● The pedestrian was bruised in a car accident.

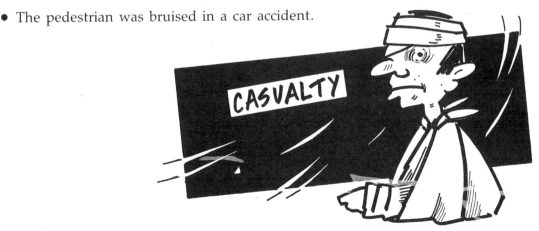

Avoiding Circumlocution

Each of the following sentences contains examples of circumlocution. Try rewriting the sentence in simple, direct English. Note that you are given the opening words for each answer.

1 The amount of solar emission in our urban areas has been below that normally experienced.
There has been less. *than normal sunlight*

2 The arrival time of the bus will be considerably delayed.
The bus will. *be late*

3 The failure of the boys to understand each other resulted in lack of agreement accompanied by the violent use of the feet.
When the boys misunderstood. *each other they disagreed and kicked each other*

4 The absence of speech is required of everyone who finds it necessary to work in the library.
No. *talking in the library.*

5 We will communicate with you in writing if we decide to acquire the car for a monetary settlement.
If we decide to buy. *the car we will write to you.*

6 They put their hands together to show their admiration for the way she inflicted a defeat on her opponent in the racquet-wielding tournament of Saturday last.
They clapped. *for the girl who won in the tennis tournament.*

7 When we enquired about her whereabouts we were told that she was at her dwelling in its rural location.
When we asked where. *she was she was at the countryside*

8 In the country of our birth the unemployment situation has suffered a deterioration.
In our country. *unemployment is getting worse.*

GETTING IT RIGHT

PROBLEM PAIRS

The following pairs of words are often used incorrectly.

Fewer/less
'Fewer' is used for a number of persons or things. For example:

• **Fewer** robots are being used in restaurants.

'Less' is used for quantity. For example:

• There has been **less** rubbish thrown on the tip lately.

Between/among

'Between' is used for two persons or things. For example:

- The pumpkin rolled **between** the two passengers.

'Among' is used for three or more persons or things. For example:

- The sunbather rose **among** the clouds.

Beside/besides

'Beside' means 'by the side of'. For example:

- An ostrich was racing **beside** him.

'Besides' means 'in addition to' or 'as well as'. For example:

- **Besides** his pumpkins, Sam had his bus pass to worry about.

Choosing the Correct Words

From the pairs of words in brackets, select the correct one to complete each sentence.

1 There are *fewer* storms in England this year. (less/fewer)

2 The huge old ostrich ran swiftly *beside* the boulder. (beside/besides)

3 Tension developed *between* the two boys. (among/between)

4 *Besides* carrying the schoolcase, the boy had to balance the huge vegetable. (besides/beside)

5 The group of robbers divided the money *among* themselves. (among/between)

6 *Besides* being too heavy, the pumpkin was cumbersome to handle. (beside/besides)

7 An ambulance ran off the road *between* two trees. (between/among)

8 The next day on the bus, the driver had *fewer* complaints about the students. (less/fewer)

DRAMA

Days of Joy and Heartbreak

By Bill Condon

CHARACTERS

Narrator
Tilly Tedium
Teddy Tedium
Bertie Tedium
José Tuesday
Sophia Sogood
Doctor Sunnyside/Horrible Helga
Jessica Bring'embackdeadoralive-Jones
Lottie Longarmofthelaw
an alien
a postie

It is a typical day at the home of Tilly and Teddy Tedium. They are seated on a lounge relaxing as the curtains open.

Narrator   Welcome to Chapter 3456 of 'Days of Joy and Heartbreak', a chronicle of life in the typical suburban home of the Tedium Family.

(The narrator exits.)

Tilly   Ah, Teddy, this is the life. No problems.
Teddy   Yes, Tilly, this is the life all right.
Tilly   We've worked hard all our days and now we can sit back and soak up life's rich twilight.
Teddy   Without a care in the world.

(Their son Bertie rushes in.)

Bertie Mother, Father!
Teddy and Tilly Yes, son?
Bertie I've made a terrible discovery!
Tilly Oh no!
Bertie Yes!
Teddy On a scale of one to ten, how terrible?
Bertie Fifteen!
Tilly Bertie, you haven't ...
Teddy It isn't possible!
Bertie But I have!
Teddy and Tilly Who told you?!
Bertie No one! I just looked in every cabbage patch in town—and there's no babies there!
Tilly We can explain, Bertie! Um, ask your father!
Bertie Well, Father?
Teddy We were only joking when we said babies came from cabbage patches.
Bertie Were you?
Tilly That's right—the stork brings them.
Bertie Oh, the stork. Right. Of course. Well thanks for straightening that out. I must dash now or I'll be late for medical school. Bye, bye.

(He exits.)

Teddy Quick thinking, Tilly.
Tilly What do you mean, dear? I just told him the truth.
Teddy You and I will have to have a long talk one day, Tilly.
Tilly Teddy, there's something I have to tell you—something awful.
Teddy Can it wait until I've taken a little nap, dear?
Tilly I don't know...

(Teddy falls fast asleep and begins to snore.)

Teddy Teddy...Teddy. Oh dear. I wanted to tell him there's a poisonous spider on his neck.

(José and Sophia enter.)

José Mrs Tilly Tedium?
Tilly That's me.
José I'm José Tuesday of Scotland Yard and I've got some devastating news for you.
Sophia And I'm Sophia Sogood, a positive thinking expert sent here to make you see the bright side of the bad news.
Tilly What is it?! What's happened?!
José It's your forgotten son, Rudy.
Tilly Who's Rudy?
Sophia She really has forgotten.

(Tilly wakes up Teddy.)

Tilly Hey, Teddy—have we got a son called Rudy?
José He's got a red nose—
Sophia And he looks like a reindeer.

Teddy 'Sure, I remember him. You must remember, Tilly—he was super intelligent—we called him Rudy the Red-nosed Brain, dear.

Tilly You don't mean our Rudolph—the nuclear dentist?

José That's him!

Tilly Why didn't you say so? What's happened to him?

José I'm afraid he's been taken by a shark.

Teddy Taken where?

Tilly Teddy, you imbecile! Our little boy's been ripped into shreds! He's been eaten! Devoured! Crunched up into bite-sized chunks and swallowed!

Sophia Yes. But there's a good side to this—we recovered his wallet. Empty of course, but we got it back!

Teddy Every cloud has a silver lining.

José Well, we've got a lot of calls to make so we'll be running along.

Tilly Thank you. You've both been very kind.

Sophia I know. We didn't even mention that your daughter Delores was the one who fed Rudy to the shark, or that she slipped into the water herself and was also unmercifully slaughtered.

Teddy That was very thoughtful, wasn't it, Tilly?

Tilly Delores!!!!

José and Sophia You have a nice day now, you hear?

(They exit.)

Tilly Oh, Teddy, I feel sick.

Teddy I don't feel too good myself.

Tilly Don't worry. It's probably only that poisonous spider biting into your jugular vein.

Teddy Tilly! That's no spider, that's...aarrghh!!!

(He collapses and remains in the same place for the rest of the play.)

Tilly Goodness me! It was a vampire bat!

(Doctor Sunnyside enters.)

Doc/Horrible Hello, I'm a door-to-door undertaker and I was wondering if you have any dead people you'd like carted off.

Tilly What's this! I know who you are! You're Doctor Horatio Sunnyside, the evil undertaker who trains vampire bats to kill people so he can get more business!

Doc/Horrible Curses! You've found me out!

Tilly I'm calling the police.

Doc/Horrible Please don't do that... Mum!

Tilly Mum?! You're not another one of my forgotten sons are you?

Doc/Horrible No! I'm your forgotten daughter—Horrible Helga!

(He takes off a wig to reveal flowing locks.)

Tilly Oh Horrible, how good to see you!

(They embrace.)

Doc/Horrible Sorry about Daddy.

Tilly Never mind, dear, no one's perfect.

Doc/Horrible It's great to see you again, Mum. Now we've been reunited nothing will ever take me away from you again.

Tilly That's wonderful!

(Jessica and Lottie enter.)

Jessica Stick'em up, Horrible Helga, alias Doctor Sunnyside!

Lottie We arrest you for the vampire murders of six hundred people.

Doc/Horrible It was an accident!

Tilly This is horrible, Horrible—what will I tell the neighbours?

Lottie Why don't you tell them the truth, Mrs Tedium?

Tilly The truth?!!!!...I have absolutely no idea what you mean.

Jessica I'm Jessica Bring'embackdeadoralive-Jones and this is my partner, Lottie Longarmofthelaw.

Lottie We've been staking out your house for the last fifteen years.

Jessica While cunningly disguised as garden gnomes.

Tilly Betrayed by gnomes!

Doc/Horrible Mum! Is there some dark and dastardly secret you've been hiding from your loved ones?!

Lottie Go ahead, Mrs Tedium, tell her the truth.

Tilly I'm just a little old pensioner.

Jessica A pensioner who has a flying saucer underneath her bed!

Tilly That's not mine!

Lottie It is!

Tilly It isn't! Mine's out in the shed!

Jessica Aha!

(A weirdly costumed alien enters.)

Alien Is anything wrong, Mother?

Tilly We've been nabbed by gnomes, son.

Lottie An alien being! Just as we thought. Horrible, I have some incredibly horrible news for you.

Doc/Horrible Are you trying to tell me I have an unidentified flying mother?!

Lottie I'm afraid so.

Tilly And that's not all. Horrible, my darling—I don't know how to tell you this, but I'm not your real mother—you were...

Doc/Horrible   Adopted?!

Tilly   No—I won you in a raffle.

Alien   You were the consolation prize.

Tilly   First prize was a chook.

Doc/Horrible   What foul news!

Lottie   You're all going to prison for a long, long time.

Jessica   It's the end of the Tedium dynasty!

Tilly   If only my great-great-granny were here—she'd know what to do.

Doc/Horrible   You mean great-great-granny's dead?

Tilly   Yes. She and her whole family were wiped out while attempting to ski Mount Everest.

Lottie   Did they get frostbite?

Tilly   No, their boat fell on top of them.

Lottie   What rotten luck.

Jessica   What was your poor old great-great-granny's name?

Tilly   Two Ton Tessy Tedium.

Jessica   Oh no!!!

Lottie   Don't go getting sentimental on me, Jessica.

Jessica   Good heavens! That's my long-lost Aunt Tessie!

Tilly   Now I recognise you! You're my long-forgotten stepdaughter's long-forgotten niece's fifth cousin's god-daughter!

Doc/Horrible   Yeah! The one who looks like a gnome!

(Jessica embraces Tilly, the alien and Doc/Horrible.)

Jessica   I've got a family! Hurray!

Lottie   Well I don't care! You're all still under arrestttttaaargghhhhhhh!!!

(Lottie screams and falls down in agony.)

Jessica   What's wrong, Lottie?!

Lottie   Oh no! My secret's out—I'm having a baby!

Alien   Stand back, everyone—I was a tree surgeon on Saturn.

Jessica   Is there anything we can do to help you?

Alien   Yes—get me a chainsaw.

Lottie   AARRGGHHH! My baby is going to be delivered by an alien!

(Bertie rushes on.)

Bertie   Mother, guess what?!

Tilly   What, Bertie?

Bertie   I've found out where babies come from!!

All   Where??!

Bertie   They're delivered by Australia Post! Gosh one learns a lot at medical school!

(A postie enters on a bike and blows a whistle. He is carrying a baby.)

Postie   Special delivery for Lottie Longarmofthelaw. Just sign here ma'am.

(She signs and takes her baby.)

Lottie It's a boy!
All Awwwwwwwww. *(A big sigh.)*

(The postie exits.)

Tilly Well, Lottie, you still want to turn us in—after all we've been through together?
Lottie No—we're like one big happy family now. In fact, I've decided to name my son in honour of the Tediums...I'm going to call him—Boring.
Tilly I'm moved.

(They all start swaying.)

Alien So am I!
Doc/Horrible We're all moving!
Jessica It's an earthquake!!!
All Argghh!!!!

(As everyone sways violently the narrator enters.)

Narrator Will a massive earthquake finally spell the end for the Tedium dynasty? Or will it be the cyclone and the tidal wave which, even as I speak, are hurtling towards them, followed closely by hordes of bloodthirsty looters hired by Tilly's power-hungry, brutal, ugly, no-good sister, Serenity. And most importantly of all, how will Lottie get the postmark off her son's forehead?
　　To discover the fate of the Tediums join us next week for Chapter 3457 of...'Days Of Joy and Heartbreak'.

Questions

1 What does the title 'Days of Joy and Heartbreak' suggest about the events of the play?

2 What is the play's setting?

3 The play's action begins with Bertie's 'terrible discovery'. What is this?

4 How do Tilly and Teddy reassure Bertie?

5 What is the terrible news about Rudy?

6 Why would the audience feel only amusement at the news?

7 What dreadful secret does Doctor Sunnyside reveal to Tilly?

8 But Tilly has a secret too. What is this?

9 Why does Bertie put in an appearance again towards the end of the play?

10 How is the humour in this play created?

4
FUTURE SHOCK

NOVELS

Survival in the Subways of New York

Slake is a poor boy who manages to exist in the New York streets until a race for survival forces him into the subway system where he finds a refuge.

So, the day of the sweater — the end of the beginning. Slake had found the sweater on the seat of a subway car only days before. Blue and grey diamond-patterned and nearly new. The day he had worn it to school, they had pulled it off his body, forcing his arms over his head, twirling him around until the sweater pulled free. They had grabbed it, waved it in the air, tossed it high above his head like a football while he ran this way and that trying to get it back.

'Over here, Alfie!'

'Big Joe! Hup, hip!'

'Zeke! Over here!'

'Here y'ar, Slake, man! Here y'ar.' A fake offer. Slake moved in for the promise to be kept.

'Hip, hup!' and over his head.

Then, as one, they moved towards him — a pack — the sweater held high now on a broom handle. And then the chase began, around the parking metres and fruit stands, through the alleys and junkyards, and had to end, as always, with more lumps and bruises or, if not, with escape into the subway.

Down in the subway it was, and Slake's dreams of being stronger than, bigger than, or even strong enough, big enough, slipped with his grasp on the handsome, eighty per cent reprocessed wool, nearly new sweater. Chased to the last ditch, he paid his token and leaped on to a train, just leaving.

The subway clattered and swayed its way downtown, and Slake with the instinct of other migratory creatures flew from the train at Seventy-seventh Street and Lexington Avenue. This was an unusual move in itself; Slake usually exited only at transfer points. Now he could not get home without the payment of another token, which he did not have.

He came up on to the street in a neighbourhood that he had never seen before, walked two blocks uptown to the splendid width of Seventy-ninth Street, and started to walk westward. Here were sparkling shops, large clean buildings, and neatly tended saplings along the edge of the relatively unlittered pavement. The absence of tin cans, garbage, and other refuse, the scarcity of steps and stoops, and the lack of people sitting or leaning about them interested Slake. As he crossed Park Avenue he waited on the kerb with respect as a young delivery boy drove a bicycle through heavy traffic as if it were a fine car. He continued along Seventy-ninth and finally crossed Fifth Avenue and walked into the autumn landscape of Central Park.

At the sight of the park, something came back to Slake. It was the recurrence of an old fantasy that *this year the leaves would stay on the trees*. Though there were few trees in Slake's life, this thought returned to him year after year. Now he broke into a run, winding and spinning through paths of the park, kicking up a kaleidoscope of fallen leaves, while above some leaves remained tenuously on the branches. Slake ran twenty blocks south, and well into the park. He was far from home . . . far from home, but his failing faith had given way once again to hope . . . a last hope. Slake, without sweater or subway token, put his faith in nature.

'This is the year . . .,' said Slake as he ran, '*this* is the year the leaves *will* stay on the trees.' And the enthusiasm of this hope in this new territory, and the momentary strength of this conviction made Slake heady. He looked about quickly and saw only an old lady dozing on a bench. Her mouth was open; her hair looked borrowed. Slake grabbed a bunch of tall dried grass from the foot of a poorly tended maple tree, leaped into its low branches and, squinting against the sun, tied several of the remaining leaves securely to the branches.

That was Slake at the tallest, strongest moment of his life till then. It lasted *just* a moment. Shouts broke into his ambitious dream as a park attendant appeared, running, shouting, and waving a rake.

'Get down out of there, you bum kid!'

Slake blinked.

'Get down, I said!' The attendant poked at the tree with his rake, but Slake had moved out of reach. 'The cops, then!' and the man was off and running to a nearby phone. The old lady awoke and started pointing.

Slake, now entirely ripped from his dream, abandoned it on the branch, leaped to the ground, spun around twice, ran several hundred yards through the park and out of it, down a flight of stairs and, committing still another crime, ran frantic and tokenless under the turnstile and into the subway at Columbus Circle.

He stayed one hundred and twenty-one days.

Slake rode the subway all that afternoon, crisscrossing the city, cutting it to pieces with the crashing cars, slicing through tunnels, burrowing through rock. He sat, a catapulted mummy, resurrecting himself from time to time, to exit at a transfer point, and enter another train headed to some other distant corner of the metropolitan subway system. It did not matter to Slake which corner. He touched base in the Bronx, Queens, Brooklyn, doubled back and clattered into the Upper West Side. Then, down again to the Battery and back again, finally to exit at the Forty-second Street station of the Lexington Avenue line — Grand Central Station.

What drew Slake from his getaway train at this particular place? Ask what put him on it. Something took him through the maze, the crush of people shoving each other through the turnstiles to a staircase. Slake started up. It was a crucial move.

But as he began to climb the stairs, a flying squadron of boys descended. A phalanx of leaping weight on the hoof, they appeared above him and seemed to fall thumping, jumping, yowling down the stairs faster than inertia and gravity should allow. Reality seized Slake by the throat and released his heels. He turned and ran, the sound of pounding feet mixed with the pounding blood in his ears. Back towards the platform ran Slake, committing the third crime of the day — under the turnstile and down the nearest flight of stairs.

'Stop him!' yelled the man in the change booth to no one who cared. But Slake ran as if pursued, through the station, past the dispatcher's windowed office to the very end of the platform; and realising that it was, indeed, the end, leaped off without a backward look and ran into the tunnel.

He had run only twenty paces when he awoke from his nightmare to the awareness of where he was and what he was doing — feet in a track bed, hands gripping gritty walls — terror behind, blackness ahead. Slake froze where he was, his spine pulling him back against the wall, away from the rails, away from any possible oncoming trains.

Oncoming trains!

Slake reached wildly for what he knew he should find — something he had seen many times from the station and the train itself — concrete alcoves in which the track workmen could stand while the trains were passing. Stepping carefully on the wood covering of the third rail, inching along, his hands groped for an alcove, but before they found one, they found something else — a hole — a jagged opening in the subway wall.

Slake bent forward, and in the dim light that came from the nearby tunnel lights, Slake could make out what looked like walls on the other side of the hole. With shaking and numbed limbs, Slake moved through this opening, slipping a leg through first, feeling for solid ground and finding it, and then snaking the rest of his body through. He stood up carefully, not sure of the height of his rabbit hole. He hit nothing, and his feet were not on track bed but on flat rock and a few loose stones and timbers.

Slake moved slowly—a blind man who was beginning to see—and found that he was in a small enclosure whose only opening was the jagged entrance, left by fallen concrete, through which he had just come. Unoccupied and unused, it appeared to be, for want of a better term, a 'room' in the subway. Slake sat down with his back against the farthest wall. Indeed, as it ultimately turned out, *Slake moved in*.

from *Slake's Limbo* by Felice Holman

Reading for Meaning

1 What happens to the sweater Jake found on the train?

2 What choice faces Jake as he flees from the pack?

3 How does Jake finally end the chase?

4 'He came up on to the street in a neighbourhood that he had never seen before...' How does this neighbourhood contrast with the one he knows?

5 What old fantasy comes back to Slake when he arrives in Central Park?

6 How does Slake proceed through Central Park?

7 Why does Slake leap into the lower branches of a maple tree?

8 Why is Slake's 'moment' in the maple tree important for him?

9 How is Slake 'ripped from his dream'?

10 What crime does Slake commit soon after he leaves the park?

11 'Slake rode the subway all that afternoon...' How does the writer go on to suggest that Slake becomes almost a part of the subway?

12 What prevents Slake from returning to the outside world at Grand Central Station?

13 'He turned and ran...' What two sounds does Slake hear as he does this?

14 What happens immediately after he commits his third crime of the day?

15 In the subway tunnel, what is behind and ahead of Slake?

16 While searching for a safety alcove in the tunnel wall, what does Slake find instead?

17 How does Slake feel as he moves through the subway wall?

18 How do we know that Slake will eventually think of this enclosure as home?

19 What makes us always feel sympathetic towards Slake, even though he commits three crimes?

20 Thinking back over the passage, what would you say were its four most exciting incidents?

The War Begins

The thermo-nuclear war had started and thousands of missiles fell on the cities and towns of Earth. There were few survivors. One boy tells why he was unfortunate enough to be one of those survivors. In the first section, he describes how the war started and the extent of the destruction it brought. In the second section, he describes what he was doing on that day, and how, by chance, he managed to survive.

1

East is East and West is West, and maybe it was a difference of opinion or just a computer malfunction. Either way, it set off a chain of events that nobody but a madman could have wanted and which nobody, not even the madmen, could stop.

There were missiles.
Under the earth.
In the sky.
Beneath the waves.
Missiles with thermo-nuclear warheads, enough to kill everybody on earth.
Three times over.

And something set them off; sent them flying, West to East and East to West, crossing in the middle like cars on a cable-railway.

East and West, the sirens wailed. Emergency procedures began, hampered here and there by understandable panic. Helpful leaflets were distributed and roads sealed off. VIPs went to their bunkers and volunteers stood at their posts. Suddenly, nobody wanted to be an engine-driver anymore, or a model or a rock-star. Everybody wanted to be one thing: a survivor. But it was an overcrowded profession.

The missiles climbed their trajectory arcs, rolled over the top and came down, accelerating. Below, everyone was ready. The Frimleys had their shelter in the lounge. The Bukovskys favoured the cellar. A quick survey would have revealed no overwhelming preference, worldwide, for one part of the house over the others.

Down came the missiles. Some had just the one warhead, others had several, ranging from the compact, almost tactical warhead to the large, family size. Every town was to receive its own, individually programmed warhead. Not one had been left out.

They struck, screaming in with pinpoint accuracy, bursting with blinding flashes, brighter than a thousand suns. Whole towns and city-centres vaporised instantly; while tarmac, trees and houses thirty miles from the explosions burst into flames. Fireballs, expanding in a second to several miles across, melted and devoured all matter that fell within their diameters. Blast-waves, travelling faster than sound, ripped through the suburbs. Houses disintegrated and vanished. So fierce were the flames that they devoured all the oxygen around them, suffocating those people who had sought refuge in deep shelters. Winds of a hundred-and-fifty miles an hour, rushing in to fill the vacuum, created fire-storms that howled through the streets, where temperatures in the thousands cooked the subterranean dead. The very earth heaved and shook as the warheads rained down, burst upon burst upon burst, and a terrible thunder rent the skies.

For an hour the warheads fell, then ceased. A great silence descended over the land. The Bukovskys had gone, and the Frimleys were no more. Through the silence, through the pall of smoke and dust that blackened the sky, trillions of deadly radioactive particles began to fall. They fell soundlessly, settling like an invisible snow on the devastated earth.

Incredibly, here and there, people had survived the bombardment. They lay stunned in the ruins, incapable of thought. Drifting on the wind, the particles sifted in upon them, landing unseen on clothing, skin and hair, so that most of these too would die, but slowly.

Most, but not all. There were those whose fate it was to wander this landscape of poisonous desolation. One of them was me.

2

It was a hot day in the summer holidays. People kept coming in the shop for ice-cream and lollies and coke. We lived in Skipley, behind the shop, open seven days a week and the bell drove you daft. I'd have gone off on the bike but Mum said I had to play with Ben.

You know what it's like playing with a kid of seven. They always want to play at being in the army or something. They get so wrapped up being a soldier that they yell stupid stuff at the tops of their voices so the grownups can hear. It's embarrassing.

Anyway, I played with him a bit in the back where Dad stacked the crates. It was all right at first but then he started wittering; so when Dad went off in the van, I gave him ten pence for a lolly. He ran inside and I got on the bike and left.

It didn't matter where I went, so long as I got away by myself. I had thought of going into Branford but there were too many people there, so I took the road that goes up over the moor. It's a hard pull and I was sweating like a pig when it flattened out. There's nothing to stop the sun up there and it beat down so you could hear it. The heat made the horizon shimmer and the road look wet. I kept pedalling till I was well away from Skipley, then got off and lay on my back in the needle-grass and looked for UFOs.

It was so quiet you could hear bees in the heather sounding like a sawmill a long way off. The air smelt of peat and hot tar. The sweat on my shirt made my back cold while the sun burnt my knees through my jeans. Now and then a car went by. It sounds kind of sad now, bees and cars and heather, but that's how it was then.

I must have dozed off, because the next thing I knew the sun was gone and half the sky had vanished behind these great black clouds. It was still hot, but with a different sort of heat; that close, threatening heat you get before a storm.

I didn't fancy being caught out here in a storm. They say lightning strikes the highest point, and there were no trees on the moor. As soon as I stood up, I'd be the highest point. I got up, grabbed the bike and began pedalling like mad towards home.

I nearly made it. The top of the last upward bit was in sight when there came a rumbling in the distance and the first big raindrops fell. Pennies from Heaven, my mum called them.

I might easily have gone on. I had only to top that little slope and I'd have free-wheeled all the way down into Skipley, and I'd have been dead, like everybody else. The reason I didn't was because I spotted the pillbox.

It was one of those concrete bunkers left over from the war, World War Two, not the last one. It was just beyond the ditch, on the edge of farmland, partly sunk into the ground and half-hidden in a clump of elder bushes. I'd been in it before, years back when Dad brought Mum and me and Ben up for a picnic one day when Ben was a baby. I'd gone crouching into the musty dimness, half expecting to find a machine-gun or a skeleton or something. There'd been an empty bottle and the remains of a fire, and I'd played at shooting up passing cars through the narrow slot.

I couldn't crouch into it now. It had sunk a bit deeper and I was a lot taller and I had to get down on my hands and knees. I lugged the bike across the ditch, propped it against the pillbox and crawled in. The remains of the fire were still there, or perhaps it was another one. I didn't go right in, just far enough so I could watch the storm without getting wet. I used to like thunderstorms as long as I was somewhere safe.

As I crawled in there was this sudden gust of wind and a clap of thunder, and the rain really started coming down. It fell so hard you could feel the ground trembling under you. It poured off the top of the pillbox in a solid curtain. I sat looking out through it, hugging my knees and thinking how smart I'd been to get myself under cover.

Then I saw the flash. It was terrifically bright. I screwed up my eyes and jerked my head away. I thought the bunker had been struck: I expected the whole thing to split apart and fall on top of me.

Then the ground started shaking. It quivered so strongly and so fast that it was like sitting with your eyes closed in an express train. Bits started falling on my head; dust and that. I was choking. I rolled over and lay on my side with my arms wrapped round my head.

There was this sudden hot blast. It drove rain in through the doorway and spattered it on my arms and neck; warm rain. I opened my eyes. The pillbox was flooded with bright, dusty light which flickered and began to fade as I watched. My ear was pressed to the ground and I could hear rumbling way down, like dragons in a cave; receding, growing more faint as the dragons went deeper, till you couldn't hear them at all. The light dimmed and there was only silence, and a pinkish glow with dust in it.

Sometimes, I wish I'd stayed there. The dust would have covered me and I would have slipped away, to follow the dragons down into silence. There are worse things than dragons. I've seen them.

from *Brother in the Land* by Robert Swindells

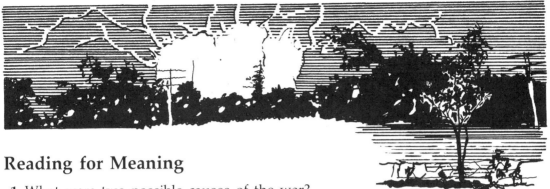

Reading for Meaning

1 What were two possible causes of the war?

2 Why were the missiles especially to be feared?

3 'Everybody wanted to be one thing: a survivor.' Why was this going to be difficult?

4 'Every town...' In the two sentences following these words, what grim facts emerge?

5 What comparison is used to describe the brightness of the missile explosions?

6 What happened to the towns and cities at the centres of the explosions?

7 What happened to the people who sought refuge in deep shelters?

8 What were created by the terrible winds?

9 What happened in the silence after the explosions?

10 What was the fate of many of the survivors?

11 During the summer holidays, why was Skipley a busy place for the boy?

12 'It didn't matter where I went, so long as I got away by myself.' Why did the boy want to do this?

13 What sounds, smells and feelings did the boy sense as he lay in the needle-grass?

14 The boy didn't quite make it to the top of the slope and, although he didn't know it at the time, this failure was critical to his survival. Why was this?

15 What two natural happenings preceded the rain?

16 'Then I saw the flash.' How did he react to it?

17 After the flash, what was the next sign of the falling missiles?

18 What accompanied the 'sudden hot blast'?

19 What did the rumbling noise seem like to the boy as he pressed his ear to the ground?

20 The writer succeeds in making the idea of nuclear war realistic to the reader. What are some of the ways in which he does this?

Besieged!

Triffids are large, intelligent plants. Their poisonous stings are deadly for humans. They are rapidly moving to invade the territory of their enemy, the human race. In this scene, the human beings, Susan, Bill and Josella, who have made a fortress of their farm, find that the fences have been broken and the 'things' have besieged the house itself. Bill is telling the story.

Susan came running into our room early one morning to tell us that the *things* had broken in, and were all round the house. She had got up early to do the milking, as usual. The sky outside her bedroom window was grey, but when she went downstairs she found everything there in complete darkness. She realised that should not be so, and turned on the light. The moment she saw leathery green leaves pressed against the windows, she guessed what had happened.

I crossed the bedroom on tiptoe, and pulled the window shut sharply. Even as it closed a sting whipped up from below and smacked against the glass. We looked down on a thicket of triffids standing ten or twelve deep against the wall of the house. The flame-throwers were in one of the outhouses. I took no risks when I went to fetch them. In thick clothing and gloves, with a leather helmet and goggles beneath the mesh mask I hacked a way through the throng of triffids with the largest carving knife I could find. The stings whipped and slapped at the wire mesh so frequently that they wet it, and the poison began to come through in a fine spray. It misted the goggles, and the first thing I did in the outhouse was to wash it off my face. I dared not use more than a brief, low-aimed jet from one of the throwers to clear my way back for fear of setting the door and window frames alight, but it moved and agitated them enough for me to get back unmolested.

Josella and Susan stood by with fire-extinguishers while I, still looking like a cross between a deep-sea diver and a man from Mars, leant from the upper windows on each side of the house in turn and played the thrower over the besieging mob of the brutes. It did not take very long to incinerate a number of them and get the rest on the move. Susan, now dressed for the job, took the second thrower and started on the, to her, highly congenial task of hunting them down while I set off across the fields to find the source of the trouble. That was not difficult. From the first rise I was able to see the spot where triffids were still lurching into our enclosure in a stream of tossing stems and waving leaves. They fanned out a little on the nearer side, but all of them were bound in the direction of the house. It was simple to head them off. A jet in front stopped them; one to either side started them back on the way they had come. An occasional spurt over them and dripping among them hurried them up, and turned back later-comers. Twenty yards or so away a part of the fence was lying flat, with the posts snapped off. I rigged it up temporarily there and then, and played the thrower back and forth, giving the things enough of a scorching to prevent more trouble for a few hours at least.

from *The Day of the Triffids* by John Wyndham

Reading for Meaning

1 How did Susan first become aware that the 'things' had broken in?

2 What was Susan's first sight of the triffids?

3 'I crossed the bedroom on tiptoe, and pulled the window shut sharply.' Why was Bill's precaution justified?

4 What word is used by the writer to describe the mass of triffids?

5 'I took no risks...' How did Bill protect himself from the triffids?

6 How did Bill attack the triffids as he went to one of the outhouses?

7 How did the poison spray come into contact with Bill's skin?

8 How did Bill manage to get back to the house unmolested?

9 What did Bill think he looked like in his protective gear?

10 How was Bill's use of the thrower from the upper windows successful?

11 What did Susan think of the task of incinerating the triffids?

12 Why did Bill set off across the fields?

13 As the triffids lurched into the enclosure, how is their movement described?

14 How did Bill head off the triffids from the house?

15 How did Bill prevent more trouble for a few hours at least?

16 In this passage, how do you think the writer manages to convey the threat of the triffids to human beings?

17 What have you learned about the character of Bill from this incident?

18 If you were asked to describe a triffid for someone who has not read the novel, what would you say?

POETRY

POEMS TO MAKE US THINK

Adman

I'm the new man
in the ivory tower
the new man
the man with the power
the old village chief
used to lay down the law
but the medicine man
had his foot in the door
he taught me the secret
of how you tick
to use psychology
like a conjuring trick
so I've found the doorway
into your brain
when you get a bargain
you lose—I gain
I can get in your bath
I can get in your bed
I can get in your pants
I can get in your head
you're like a man on the cross
you're like a priest at the stake
you're like a fish on a hook
make no mistake
I can tie you up
I can take you down
I can sit and watch
you wriggle around
'cos I'm the medicine man
with the media touch
the man with the power that's
too much

Nigel Gray

Questions

1 What does the adman claim to possess?

2 What is the secret from the past that is acquired by the adman?

3 'When you get a bargain/you lose — I gain'. What do you think this means?

4 How can the adman destroy the privacy of the individual?

5 What three similes does the adman use to show that he has you under control?

6 What is the meaning of '...I'm the medicine man/with the media touch'?

7 What point is made in the last two lines of the poem?

8 Do you think this poem presents a true picture of modern advertising? Explain your viewpoint.

Mad Ad

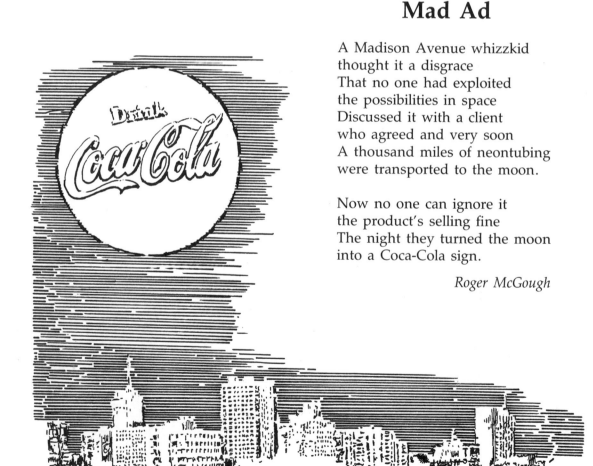

A Madison Avenue whizzkid
thought it a disgrace
That no one had exploited
the possibilities in space
Discussed it with a client
who agreed and very soon
A thousand miles of neontubing
were transported to the moon.

Now no one can ignore it
the product's selling fine
The night they turned the moon
into a Coca-Cola sign.

Roger McGough

The Way is Open

I heard that the man
who played Superman
really died...

No make-believe death
this time.
No edge-of-the-seat,
come-back-next-week
death.

It came out of the radio
like a message from his enemies,
lacking only their laughter
to make me believe
I'd heard wrongly.

It hung on the air
like a warning of doom,
filled the rooms with silence
as each one present
considered the news.

No safety net now
with which to catch
America
when she lapses.

No tough guy waiting
to bring some mad man
to his knees.

The way is open
for crooks and politicians
to do as they please.

Brian Moses

Tracey's Tree

Last year it was not there,
the sapling with purplish leaves
planted in our school grounds with care.
It's Tracey's tree, my friend who died,
and last year it was not there.

Tracey, the girl with long black hair
who, out playing one day, ran
across a main road for a dare.
The lorry struck her. Now a tree grows
and last year it was not there.

Through the classroom window I stare
and watch the sapling sway.
Soon its branches will stand bare.
It wears a forlorn and lonely look
and last year it was not there.

October's chill is in the air
and cold rain distorts my view.
I feel a sadness that's hard to bear.
The tree blurs, as if I've been crying,
and last year it was not there.

Wes Magee

Questions

1 What mystery is present in the first three lines of the poem?

2 Who was Tracey?

3 What happened to Tracey?

4 What change will soon come over the tree?

5 In the third verse, how is the tree given human qualities?

6 'The tree blurs, as if I've been crying? What has really caused the tree to blur?

7 The last line of each verse is the same. What do you think is the poet's reason for doing this?

8 What is the main feeling that runs through the poem?

The Face at the Window

I used to catch the bus to school alone.
On a corner where the wind blew from the shore
There was a church, and where I had to stand
A garage where they brought crashed cars to mend.
And one day, early morning as I stood
And watched the traffic on the quiet road
I saw a face in one of the crashed cars
Whose door and wing and seats were torn apart
I knew that there was no-one in the place
And yet in that crashed car I saw a face.
I didn't want to look and yet I must
And each glance brought the moment of that crash.
I knew exactly what the girl was like
Twenty or so, and pretty, and her look
Told me how suddenly the crash had come
Her mouth was barely opening to scream
She couldn't close her eyes or turn her head
Or stop that moment. And was she dead?
I couldn't turn away or look at her
The car was empty yet the face was there.
It stayed in front of me all day at school
Next day I said I mustn't look, but still
The woman's face was there in that crashed car
And she and I touched hands with that same fear
And every day that week we shared a glance
That stopped our breath and chilled our blood to ice.
Asleep or waking I would know that face.
That smashed against the windscreen with such force
That her make-up had been pressed into the glass
And into my memory, never to be erased.

Berlie Doherty

Questions

1 How does the poet introduce an eerie feeling in the opening lines of the poem?

2 What words tell us that the poet felt reluctant yet at the same time compelled to look at the face in the car?

3 What did each glance bring?

4 The girl was 'twenty or so, and pretty' but what did her 'look' seem to tell the poet?

the face causes the poet to wonder if the girl was dead

5 What question does the face cause the poet to ask? *whether she was dead*

He almost feels the girl

6 To what extent did the poet come to identify with the girl? *he knew the girl 20 or so.*

7 How do the last lines of the poem explain the face in the car? *The face is pressed against the lines*

8 What are the main feelings expressed in this poem?

The poem expresses fear and insecurity/curiosity of the boy and sadness of the sight of accident to look at the smashed car again & again → for the death

The Boys of Winter

Snow around their boots, they gather
Like an embodiment of the weather:
Huddled there, herded like cattle,
They are animals dressed for battle.
One smokes, another sprawls,
Three of them sloganise the walls.
They look askance at Princes Street
Defiantly in their defeat:
Their breath clouds in the cold.
These young boys, horribly old,
Having nothing (heads shorn of hair).
They do nothing, pollute the air
With verbal debris, have nothing to declare.
They look ahead and blankly stare:
Their eyes are onions of despair.

Alan Bold

WRITING

LETTER WRITING

Letters are written to communicate information, ideas, suggestions, complaints, requests and for many other reasons. The layout of most letters follows a simple pattern that makes for clear and direct communication.

On the following page you will find an imaginary, entertaining letter that is supposed to have been written early last century by a tailor in Paris. The addressee (the person to whom the letter is sent) is the Emperor Napoleon. As you read the letter, note the way it is set out.

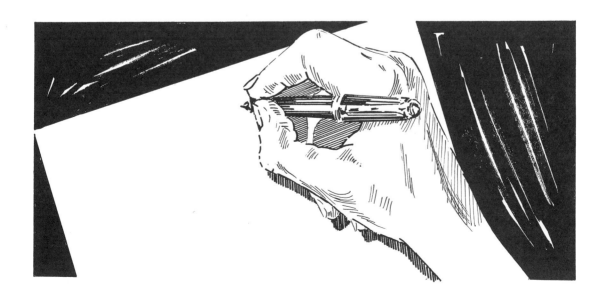

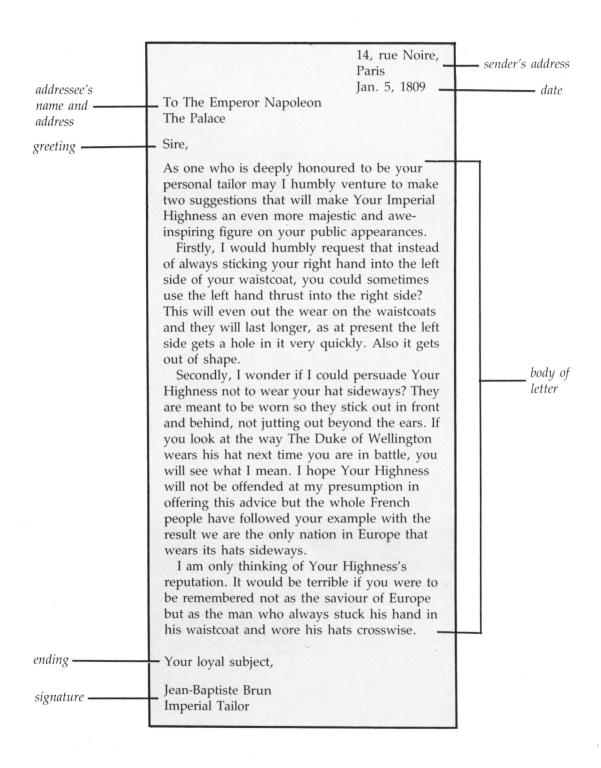

sender's address

date

addressee's name and address

greeting

14, rue Noire,
Paris.
Jan. 5, 1809

To The Emperor Napoleon
The Palace

Sire,

As one who is deeply honoured to be your personal tailor may I humbly venture to make two suggestions that will make Your Imperial Highness an even more majestic and awe-inspiring figure on your public appearances.

Firstly, I would humbly request that instead of always sticking your right hand into the left side of your waistcoat, you could sometimes use the left hand thrust into the right side? This will even out the wear on the waistcoats and they will last longer, as at present the left side gets a hole in it very quickly. Also it gets out of shape.

Secondly, I wonder if I could persuade Your Highness not to wear your hat sideways? They are meant to be worn so they stick out in front and behind, not jutting out beyond the ears. If you look at the way The Duke of Wellington wears his hat next time you are in battle, you will see what I mean. I hope Your Highness will not be offended at my presumption in offering this advice but the whole French people have followed your example with the result we are the only nation in Europe that wears its hats sideways.

I am only thinking of Your Highness's reputation. It would be terrible if you were to be remembered not as the saviour of Europe but as the man who always stuck his hand in his waistcoat and wore his hats crosswise.

body of letter

ending

Your loyal subject,

signature

Jean-Baptiste Brun
Imperial Tailor

from *Tonight Josephine* by Michael Green

LETTERS OF COMPLAINT

The following letters of complaint show Spike Milligan's efforts against some packaging that he considered was environmentally unsound.

To: Ms Daphne Charters,
Beauty Without Cruelty

<—   19th June, 1976

Dear Ms Charters,   ✓

Sub (a short phrase) - complaint about packaging

Para I.
reason for writing with reference

May I make a kindly suggestion to you. I notice when I receive parcels of goods from Beauty Without Cruelty, what is well-intentioned packing, but in essence is overpackaging on a large scale. For instance, I ordered some Beau aftershave — four bottles, which are all in plastic unbreakable bottles, then they are wrapped in a plastic resilience pack, then they are placed in a cardboard box (a) with tissue paper on top, and then (b) a lot of plastic shock absorbers.

Para II.
details of complaint with reason

I find this all excessive in terms of the run down of our planet, forests are being depleted at an alarming rate for paper, and the tissue paper looks very nice in the box, but it is not necessary, likewise all the other things I have mentioned. So, in future, might I suggest in the interests of us all that the packaging is less extravagant. It would be an economic saving for a start, and also help towards easing the use of the earth's products.

Para III
suggest suitable solution

I do hope you take this in the spirit it is meant.

Para IV - Conclusion

Again thank you for your service, and I shall give you my continued support.

<—   Love, light and peace,

<—   *SPIKE MILLIGAN*

Spike had a reply from Ms Charters explaining that the amount of packaging used is based on past experiences, liquid substances having to receive special care as other items are usually spoilt if the containers break, etc...

29th June, 1976

Dear Ms Charters,

Thank you for your letter, I take your points, now here are mine:

I have taken one of the bottles of aftershave, and thrown it at the wall, I even jumped on it, and it didn't break. So, whereas you might like to pack other people's goods, as you suggest, I most certainly will take the responsibility for my aftershave being packed in a cardboard box and nothing else, and that way I will feel better, O.K.?

Love, to all,

Love, light and peace,

SPIKE MILLIGAN

from *The Spike Milligan Letters*

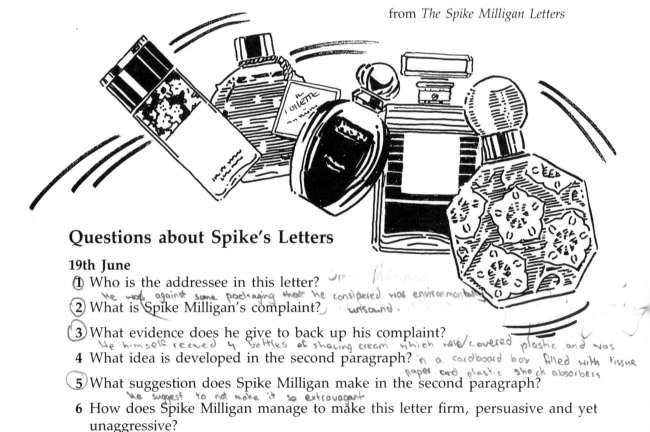

Questions about Spike's Letters

19th June

1 Who is the addressee in this letter? *Spike Milligan*
   He was against some packaging that he considered was environmentally
2 What is Spike Milligan's complaint? *unsound.*

3 What evidence does he give to back up his complaint?
   He himself received 4 bottles of shaving cream which were covered plastic and was
4 What idea is developed in the second paragraph? *in a cardboard box filled with tissue*
   paper and plastic shock absorbers
5 What suggestion does Spike Milligan make in the second paragraph?
   He suggest to not make it so extravagant
6 How does Spike Milligan manage to make this letter firm, persuasive and yet unaggressive?

7 What is unusual about the letter's ending?

29th June

8 In what two ways did Spike Milligan go about proving that Ms Charters' points were wrong? *to take responsibility of the aftershave being packed in cardboard.*

9 In the future, what conditions does Spike require to make him 'feel better'?

10 In what way does this letter differ slightly from the usual layout of a letter?

11 Why is the letter likely to produce positive results?

12 How does Spike add a touch of humour to his complaint to make it more effective?

JOB APPLICATION LETTERS

Here is an example of the kind of letter you might write in applying for a job. However, before you look at the letter, keep these points in mind.

- Be sure to work on a rough draft of your letter so that the points you want to make can be arranged in a logical and well-organised way. Check the spelling of any words you are unsure of.
- Be brief and concise in your letter. It is best to provide detailed information on a separate sheet of paper under headings such as:
  —**Personal** (your name, age, etc.)
  —**Educational** (schools attended, exams passed, etc.)
  —**Work Experience** (where and when you have worked)
  —**Other Information** (your interests, community activities, etc.)
- The setting out of a job application letter is similar to other letters. Either 'Yours sincerely' or 'Yours faithfully' is a good ending for any business letter.
- Each point you wish to make should be given a separate paragraph. The tone should be polite.
- Write neatly or type the final letter you will send. Make sure it is free of errors and corrections.

15 Compass Street
Toomley 5270
1 February, 199_

The Manager
Universal Computers
1 Software Crescent
Mainframe 5285

Dear Manager

I would like to apply for the position of computer salesperson, which was advertised in the 'Advertiser' on 27 January, 199_.

I am eighteen years old and have successfully completed Year 12. My school work experience consisted of three weeks at the Computerland sales offices.

I consider myself to be a suitable applicant for the job as I am enthusiastic about the use and potential of computers, and I have owned and used several kinds.

I would be pleased to attend an interview at any time convenient to you.

Yours sincerely

Robert Mann

(Mr) Robert Mann

WRITING YOUR OWN LETTERS

Choose one of the following situations and write the type of letter that is suggested.

1 Your friend has moved to a country school. Write him or her a letter giving the news of a crisis that you have just been through.

2 You want to meet your next-door neighbour socially. Write a letter introducing yourself.

3 You have found a worm in the can of tomatoes you opened. Complain by letter to the manufacturer.

4 Your local council plans to cut down a cluster of trees to make way for a supermarket car park. Write a letter of protest.

5 From the employment section of your newspaper, choose a job you would be keen to do and write a letter applying for it.

6 Your uncle or aunt has just won first prize in the lottery. Write a letter of congratulation.

7 Write a humorous letter about some aspect of your school to the Letters to the Editor column of your local newspaper.

8 A cousin has just written to you asking for a substantial loan. Write a letter giving the reasons why you must refuse the request.

LANGUAGE

WORDS AND MEANINGS

Words are the basis of our language as they represent the ideas we use in speaking and writing.

The Right Word

Replace each of the following meanings with a single word. The first one has been done for you.

1 The desire for food   appetite

2 To donate   g i v e

3 To tell the future   pr edic t

4 The period after childhood   ad olescen c e

5 The place where earth and sky meet   ho rizon n

6 A person owing money   d ebto r

7 A person who goes on foot   p edestria n

8 The hundredth anniversary of an event   c entror y

9 A time without rain   d rough t

10 A gathering of people who listen or watch   a udienc e

11 To look like someone or something   re sembl e

12 To leave uncared for   n eglec t

13 In the shape of a circle   c.ircula.r
14 To go forward   a dvanc...e
15 A personal record of daily events d.iar....y
16 The wide mouth of a river   es.tuar..y
17 No longer in existence   e xtinct..t
18 The outer section of a city   su b.ur..b
19 Done on purpose   de liberat.e
20 Able to be seen   v .isible..e

Employment Words

Each of the employees listed below can be linked to one of the employment categories in the box. Match them correctly. The first one has been done for you.

medicine	water and sewage	transport	police
entertainment	beauty care	law	tourism
pharmacy	agriculture	broadcasting	computer science
journalism	corrective services	banking	government
retail trade	horticulture	building	education
real estate	army	aviation	fashion industry

1 doctor   medicine
2 farmer   agriculture
3 carpenter   building
4 politician   government
5 comedian   entertainment
6 teacher   edcuation
7 driver   transport
8 reporter   journalism
9 soldier   army
10 constable   lahv..
11 announcer   broadcasting
12 programmer   computer science

13 chemist   pharmacy
14 model   fashion industry
15 teller   banking
16 gardener   horticulture
17 travel agent   tourism
18 warder   police
19 manicurist   beauty care
20 solicitor   corrective service
21 shop assistant retail trade
22 pilot   aviation
23 estate agent   real estate
24 plumber   water and sewage

Similar and Opposite Meanings

1 Find the words in the box that have **similar** meanings to:

a expect *anticipate*
b cause *reason*
c begin *commence*
d choose *select*
e yearly *annually*
f quantity *amount*
g frequent *often*
h depend *rely*
i delay *postpone*
j separate *divide*

2 Find the words in the box that have **opposite** meanings to:

a love *hate*
b fail *succeed*
c question *answer*
d victory *defeat*
e creditor ~~lose~~ *debtor*
f profit *loss*
g public *private*
h ignorance *knowledge*
i inferior *superior*
j deny *admit*

> **Words**
> admit
> annually
> debtor
> private
> rely
> anticipate
> hate
> postpone
> knowledge
> answer
> commence
> reason
> superior
> amount
> select
> loss
> often
> divide
> succeed
> defeat

Same Sounds, Different Meanings

Words that have the same sounds but different meanings are called **homonyms**. Complete each of the following sentences by inserting in each space the correct homonym from the pair in the brackets.

1 A fruit .*dessert*. was enjoyed by the sheik in his oasis in the .*desert*. (desert/dessert)

2 She ate her .*cereal*. as she listened to the .*serial* on the radio. (serial/cereal)

3 At .*night*. the .*knight*. removes his armour. (night/knight)

4 .*Eight*.. greedy students .*ate*... their hamburgers. (eight/ate)

5 The van carrying .*stationery* stood .*stationary* at the kerb. (stationery/stationary)

6 As the doctor was very busy, the .patient. waiting to see her had to have .patience. (patience/patients)

7 A .miner... suffered a .minor.. injury to the hand.   (miner/minor)

8 All the school .principals. attended a meeting at which some .principles. of good behaviour were discussed.   (principles/principals)

9 The children listened to the .story... in the library, which was situated in the school's second .storey. .   (story/storey)

10 The plasterer spent some time .sealing. the holes in the .ceiling. . (ceiling/ sealing)

Dictionary Words

Here is a definition of the word 'dictionary' from *The Pan English Dictionary*:

> **dictionary** (*say* **dik**-sh'n-ree) *noun* a book listing words of a language in alphabetical order with their meanings, pronunciation, use and derivation.

Let's look at a 'C' page from the same dictionary. Note that in each dictionary entry you are given the meaning or meanings and the part of speech of the word (for example, *noun*). Sometimes you will also find the word's pronunciation in brackets just after the word. At the end of the entry, the word's origin is sometimes given in square brackets.

Your task is to answer each of the questions by referring to the appropriate word on the dictionary page.

Cc

cab *noun*
1. a taxi.
2. any of various horse-drawn carriages formerly for public hire.
3. see CABIN.
[short form of CABRIOLET]

cabal (*say* ka-bahl) *noun*
a faction or group of people working towards a common aim, especially by secret methods.

caballero (*say* kabbal-yairo) *noun*
a Spanish gentleman.
[Spanish, horseman]

cabaret (*say* kabba-ray) *noun*
a form of entertainment consisting of songs and dances, usually performed in a restaurant or nightclub.
[French, a tavern]

cabbage *noun*
a large, broad-leafed vegetable, with the leaves arranged in a tight head.

cabby *noun*
(*informal*) a taxi driver.

caber (*say* kay-ber) *noun*
a long, heavy pole which is lifted at one end and tossed in Scottish Highland games.

cabin *noun*
1. a small, simple house, often in the country.
2. a) a room for the accommodation of passengers on a ship. b) the space available for passengers or crew on an aircraft.
3. the covered part of a vehicle where the driver sits. Short form is **cab**.

cabinet *noun*
1. a piece of furniture with shelves and drawers for storage or display.

2. *Parliament:* (*capital*) a group of ministers from the ruling political party, which advises the Prime Minister on policy and each of whom leads a government department.

cabinet-maker *noun*
a person who builds household equipment such as cupboards, shelves, etc.

cable *noun*
1. a thick, strong rope or chain.
2. a bundle of insulated wires for carrying electricity.
3. an overseas telegram. Short form of **cablegram**.
cable *verb*
1. to send a telegram overseas.
2. to secure with a cable.

cable car
a vehicle suspended from an overhead cable and forming part of a transport system.

caboodle *noun*
(*informal*) the whole lot.

cabriole *noun*
a curved and tapering furniture leg, often ending in the form of an animal's paw.

cabriolet (*say* kabrio-lay) *noun*
an open, horse-drawn, two-wheeled carriage with a hood.

cacao (*say* ka-kayo) *noun*
the seeds from a small, evergreen, tropical tree, from which cocoa, chocolate, etc. are made.

cache (*say* kash) *noun*
a) a hiding-place. b) a supply of things hidden or stored.
[French *cacher* to hide]

cachet (*say* kashay) *noun*
an indication, usually of distinction.
Usage: 'his music has the *cachet* of genius' (= all the signs of).
[French, a seal]

cachou (*say* kashoo *or* ka-shoo) *noun*
a tablet for sweetening the breath.

cackle *verb*
1. to make a shrill, broken sound similar to that of a hen after it lays an egg.
2. to laugh or chatter noisily.
Word Family: cackle, *noun.*

cacophonous (*say* ka-koffa-nus) *adjective*
having a harsh, discordant sound.
Word Family: **cacophony** (*say* ka-koffa-nee), *noun.*
[Greek *kakos* bad + *phoné* sound]

from *The Pan English Dictionary*

Dictionary Questions

1 What kind of public transport does a **cabby** drive?

2 If you had a **cache** of money what would you have?

3 Where would you go to be entertained by a **cabaret**?

4 What two drinks might you obtain from the seeds of the **cacao** plant?

5 At what games would you see people tossing the **caber**?

6 With what animal is the word **caballero** linked?

7 If a **cacophony** was keeping you awake at night what would you be hearing?

8 What is the interesting origin of the word **cacophonous**?

9 What two very different meanings are possessed by the word **cabinet**?

10 What comparison is linked with the word **cackle**?

11 How much is suggested by the word **caboodle**?

12 What are the two things that are characteristic of a **cabal** of people?

13 What is the difference between a **cabin** on land and one at sea?

14 If you were a **cabinet-maker** what would you usually build?

15 If you were asked to use the word **cachet** in a sentence, what could you say?

16 Why would you chew a **cachou**?

17 What would you often find resting on the floor at the end of a **cabriole**?

18 What would you be sitting in if you were being transported in a **cabriolet**?

19 What kind of rope or chain is a **cable**?

20 If you sent a **cable** how would you have been communicating?

21 How are the leaves of the **cabbage** arranged?

22 If you were in a **cable car** why would you be up in the air?

GETTING IT RIGHT

THE SUBJECT AND THE VERB IN A SENTENCE

The subject of a sentence is linked to the verb (or action word) in that sentence by **agreement**. Here are some important rules to follow. In each sentence the subject is shown in heavy type and the verb is shown in italic type.

1 A singular subject is followed by a singular verb. For example:

- A **triffid** *has broken* through the fence.

2 A plural subject is followed by a plural verb. For example:

- Many **triffids** *have broken* through the fence.

3 Two words forming a subject but joined by the word 'and' are followed by a plural verb. For example:

- **Bill and Josella** *were fighting* them with flamethrowers.

Selecting the Correct Verb

From the pairs of verbs in brackets, select the singular or plural verb to complete the sentence.

1 Slake .... chased into the subway by the gang.   (were/was)

2 A building and a car .... vanished in the explosion.   (have/has)

3 The boy and his brother .... running through the smoke.   (are/is)

4 The deadly plants .... towards the houses.   (move/moves)

5 Slake and the park attendant .... not to blame.   (is/are)

6 She and I .... leaving the city.   (am/are)

7 The thunder .... us to tremble.   (causes/cause)

8 The nurses .... what they can for the wounded.   (do/does)

9 All trees and bushes .... destroyed immediately.   (were/was)

10 Both the triffid and the human being .... intelligence.   (possess/possesses)

DRAMA

WRITE YOUR OWN SCRIPT

Form small groups to write your own scripts on the subject of 'Future Shock'. Here's a good approach to use. Each group should appoint one or two script-writers. This leaves the other group members free to discuss ideas for the script, based on the following characters, settings and plots. Start by choosing the characters for your script, then select one setting and one plot from those offered. So, all aboard for Future Shock!

CHARACTERS

Captain Krag Hest

Engineer Trank Flok

Lieutenant Ixon Klor

Navigator Rollo Burr

SETTINGS

1 The Control Deck with observation ports of the spaceship 'Quantum Leap'.

2 In an Astrodome on the savage, swirling surface of Neptune.

3 In the submarine 'Proton' deep down in an alien sea. Vision screens are in operation.

4 On a far-distant planet in the jungle-crawling vehicle 'Thunderer'. A jungle clearing surrounded by weird plant growths has been reached.

Dr Frome Pheryl

Computer Director Smol Trink

Biologist Proon Rux

Robot Tylo Nolo

PLOTS

1 During an expedition into unknown territory, an alien creature appears and carries off one of the crew. A rescue has to be attempted. Is it successful?

2 In conditions of terrible stress, the robot member of the crew runs wild with terrible results.

3 When an accident occurs and oxygen leaks away, some crew members become heroes and save the expedition.

4 A 'mission impossible' situation causes a crisis in crew relations and an awesome discovery.

5

RADIO AND TELEVISION

RADIO

When television arrived in Australia in 1956, many people predicted that this would signal the death of radio. It is obvious that all such predictions were wrong. Radio is very much alive and well. It was able to survive the challenge of television mainly because radios could be carried to the beach or could be listened to while someone worked, whereas television was less portable and required fuller attention.

However, radio programmers were also successful in creating new formats with high listener appeal. One of the most important changes was the introduction of programs that played big 'blocks' of time. The best-known of these are the programs that play Top 40 hits continuously. Some stations exist by doing virtually nothing else. Other stations provide music for particular tastes such as easy-listening, classical and rock.

One other popular radio program that has proved to have wide listener appeal is the talk-back program. In these programs radio personalities encourage listeners to phone in and give their opinions on controversial subjects. Usually the radio commentator provides considerable personal input, and sometimes uses humour, often at the expense of the person phoning in.

The best radio programming tends to include interviews with well-known personalities from many different areas of life. It also offers news and news commentaries, documentaries, discussions and, for some stations, descriptions of sports events. Along with the variety of musical programs, this makes radio still a very important medium for informing, entertaining and educating.

Let's look at some of the kinds of programs that radio has to offer.

RADIO INTERVIEWS

One of the outstanding interviewers on national radio is Margaret Throsby, noted for her warm, informed interviewing style. In this excerpt she is talking with Densey Clyne, one of Australia's best-known naturalists. Ms Clyne, as the interview demonstrates, loves to present the wonders of nature to the public.

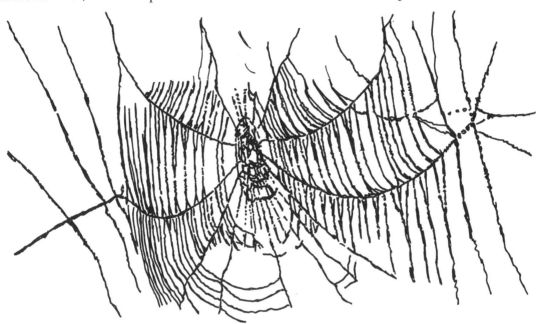

An Interview with Densey Clyne

Throsby Do you like spiders?

Clyne I love spiders. I think they have the most fascinating lives...secret lives people don't know about. They're really, in their own way, much more interesting than insects are. We don't realise what fascinating spiders we have around the garden.

Throsby Are spiders different from insects only structurally, or are they different in other ways?

Clyne They're very different. Very different in their behaviour—certainly structurally. To start with, they've got eight legs and insects have only six legs. But, they're quite different. They probably had different origins. The insects' life and the courtship and mating procedures are totally different from spiders.

Throsby What about that incredible phenomenon of spiders spinning the web, which I watched over the summer holidays. I couldn't work out how the spider got that first strand to go between two points. Has that ever been explained?

Clyne That puzzles most people. Actually they do it in a quite simple way. They let out a thread of silk from the tip of their body—and they just sit there. There are always currents of air around that we're not aware of. The thread gets pulled out and lifted and it drifts across in the direction of the air current until it comes to a solid object—like a leaf or a branch—and it sticks there.

Throsby   Why doesn't the spider stick in its own web?

Clyne   Ah! Well, that's a thing that not many people know about. Because only part of the web is sticky. That's the spiral. Let's go into the structure of the web a little bit — it's quite fascinating. When the spider puts down that spiral part that we all see in the middle of the web — the part that actually catches insects — it starts from the inside, from the hub, and it puts down a very broad spiral of non-sticky silk. Now that's a sort of scaffolding the spider works on. When it reaches the outside of the structure, it starts coming in again, making a spiral inwards, and that spiral is a sticky spiral — braided with tiny sticky droplets. Presumably the spider, when it walks on the web, knows where to put its feet. I think this is awfully clever, because spiders have eight feet, but they have claws on the end of their feet which are quite minute and delicate and they probably know where to put them.

Throsby   It's an incredible story. It's one that is fascinating not only for its beauty and intricacy, but for the smallness of it, too.

from *The Throsby Tapes* by Margaret Throsby

Questions

1 What words in Densey Clyne's opening speech tell us how she feels about spiders?

2 How many legs does a spider have? How is this different from insects?

3 What other differences are there?

4 What aspect of nature does the spider make use of in getting its first thread of silk attached to a solid object?

5 Why is it important for the spider to be able to spin some non-sticky threads?

6 What purpose is served by the sticky spiral?

7 Why does Densey Clyne think that spiders are 'awfully clever'?

8 How would you describe Densey Clyne's personality, judging from this interview?

9 How does Margaret Throsby feel about Densey Clyne's description of the making of a spider web?

10 From your reading of this transcript, do you think Margaret Throsby is a good interviewer? Why?

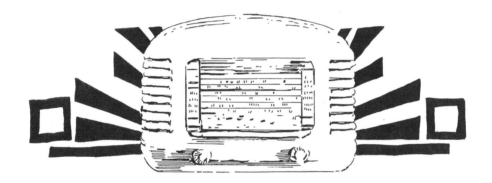

RADIO PLAYS

Radio plays rely completely upon the script-writer's ability to capture our imagination through sounds and words. When we attend a play at a theatre, or watch a film or a television drama, we take in a lot of information through our sight. The setting, the age of characters, facial expressions, any physical peculiarities — all of these we can see. However, in radio plays this information all has to be conveyed by sounds and words. This makes the radio play different but, if it is well written, our imaginations can easily fill in the gaps.

In the following extract from the humorous radio play *Yes What*, the teacher is easily 'confused' by some of the students. They don't seem to be making much progress in the world of learning!

Yes What

The school bell rings.

Teacher That was disgraceful behaviour last lesson.

Bottomley Er, you mean when you fainted because Greenbottle was early.

Teacher Er...yes...and I mean your insolent remarks and impertinent behaviour as well.

Bottomley Ah well, strike, I didn't think it was impertinent, sir.

Teacher No, but...if...if...if...I...you didn't think who was impertinent?

Bottomley Oh, er Greenbottle, sir.

Teacher Greenbottle? Alright. I don't think he was either.

Bottomley You don't, sir?

Teacher No, I don't.

Bottomley Oh, well, that's alright then.

Teacher Is it?

Bottomley Yes, we'll say no more about it.

Teacher No.

Bottomley We'll make a start with the lesson.

Teacher Yes, exactly. Er...no, wait a minute. We won't do anything of the kind.

Bottomley Why not, sir?

Teacher Why not? Because I don't want to start the lesson, that's why not.

Bottomley Aren't you going to have a lesson today, sir?

Teacher No, we are not...er, er,...er. Yes, we most certainly are.

Bottomley Well, when do we start? Tomorrow?

Teacher No, yesterday.

Bottomley Oh.

Class Er, eh?

Teacher Er...er, listen. Bottomley, are you just trying to get me muddled up with the idea of...er...er...with the idea of er...er wasting time.

Bottomley No, sir, of course I'm not.

Teacher Well, it sounds very much like it to me.

Bottomley No, sir. I don't wanna waste time. I want to start the lesson.

Teacher Well for heaven's sake, keep quiet and allow me to start the lesson.

Bottomley Yes, sir.

Teacher You just sit there and talk your head off and before we know where we are, half the lesson is gone.

Bottomley   Ah, yeah.

Teacher   I can't ever seem to er...er...er...get straight on to a subject. Every day I seem to have to spend the...er...er...first five minutes...in...in futile argument.

Class   Ah, ah...yes, sir!

Teacher   Alright then. As you know I have been trying to make some headway lately with the...er...geography, but as usual the progress has been non-existent.

Class   Er...er...yes, sir!

Teacher   Today, however, things are going to be much improved.

(Greenbottle enters.)

Greenbottle   Yessss.

Teacher   O...er...Greenbottle!

Greenbottle   Yes, hullo.

Teacher   Listen. This is one lesson that you are not going to disturb, Greenbottle. So if you have any idea of making a nuisance of yourself, you'd better forget it straight away.

Greenbottle   Making a nuisance of meself?

Teacher   Yes and there's no need to be horrified at that remark. You've been making a nuisance of yourself for years.

Greenbottle   Yes, er, eh?

Teacher   If you're not outlining some ridiculous proposition and disturbing us that way, you arrive late and disturb us that way.

Greenbottle   Yes, but it wasn't my fault I was late today.

Teacher   No, I know very well it wasn't. It never is.

Greenbottle   I've been rejoicing.

Teacher   Yes alright well, there's no need to tell us about it. We all know that...that...that...er...all of us...er...er. I...I beg your pardon?

Greenbottle   But, I was just telling you why I was late.

Teacher   Why?

Greenbottle   Because I thought you'd like to know.

Teacher   Er...I don't mean why were you telling me, I want to know why were you late.

Greenbottle   Why?

Teacher   Because I want to know.

Greenbottle   Ah.

Teacher   Er...I mean...yes, why? Why were you late?

Greenbottle   I told ya. We've been rejoicing.

Teacher   Oh, well that explains it. I...I thought you'd been...er...er...er...You've been what? Rejoicing?

Greenbottle   Yes. My aunty's lost.

Bottomley   So's your head.

Teacher   Yes, so's your head. But what do you mean rejoicing?

Greenbottle   Ah, you pipe down, Bottomley.

Teacher   Yes you pipe down, Bottomley.

Greenbottle   Or I'll dong you.

Teacher   Or I'll dong you.

Bottomley   Ah?

Greenbottle Yer see if I don't.

Teacher Now, wait a minute, wait a minute. Look I didn't give anybody permission to start an argument.

Greenbottle No and I don't want to argue neither.

Teacher Oh, don't you?

Greenbottle No, 'cause I'm rejoicing.

Teacher Yes, well that's exactly what I...er...listen, Greenbottle, what is this business. What are you talking about?

Greenbottle Ah, about me old man being better.

Teacher About your father being better?

Greenbottle Yes. He's as right as a bank now.

Teacher Well, that's a change. But, I'm pleased to know that he's been ill.

Greenbottle Yes, well, he's...er.

Teacher Yes?

Greenbottle He hasn't been ill.

Teacher He...he hasn't been ill?

Greenbottle No, he's just had a sore foot.

Teacher Oh! I see.

Greenbottle For three weeks he's had it now.

Teacher Three weeks?

Greenbottle Yes, but now he's better.

Teacher That's a pity.

Greenbottle Yes, now, we've been rejoicing.

Teacher Er, Greenbottle.

Greenbottle Yes.

Teacher While the fact that your father has had a sore foot for the last three weeks might be of great interest to you and your father, I fail to see that it interests this class in any way whatsoever, so I'd be pleased if you stopped talking about it.

Greenbottle Yes, well you asked me.

Teacher I didn't ask you at all. I merely asked you why you were late.

Greenbottle Yes.

Teacher Yes, what?

Greenbottle Yes, well I been rejoicing.

Teacher Ah, well, you had no right to be rejoicing what...whatever that might mean. You should've come along to school at the proper time and d...done your lessons.

Greenbottle Oh!

Teacher The mere fact that your father has got a sore foot d...doesn't allow...er...er...er can't be allowed to hold up our school work.

Greenbottle My old man hasn't got a sore foot.

Teacher No! Well, if he ever gets a...I...er...er. What?

Greenbottle I told you his foot's better.

Teacher Ah!

Greenbottle It's been sore for three weeks, then this morning he went to the doctor and the doctor fixed it up in two minutes.

Teacher He fixed it up in two minutes?

Greenbottle Yes, of course he did.

Teacher Well, what was the matter with his foot?

Greenbottle What?

Teacher   What was it that made his foot sore for three weeks?
Greenbottle   There was a stud in his sock.
Teacher   Oh, I see a stud in the sock. I...well...I...what?

(Class goes into an uproar, everyone talking and calling out at once.)

For goodness sake, stop this terrible noise.
Greenbottle   We were rejoicing that he didn't have to have his foot off.
Teacher   Greenbottle!
Greenbottle   Yes?
Teacher   If you dare utter another word this lesson, you'll have more than your foot off...you'll have your head off.

Questions

1 What sound occurs at the beginning of this radio play? What setting does it bring to our imagination?

2 When Bottomley says 'We'll make a start with the lesson', what confusing change seems to have taken place?

3 Why does the teacher get so frustrated?

4 Why isn't the teacher surprised when Greenbottle explains that it wasn't his fault for being late?

5 Why do you think the teacher echoes Greenbottle's remarks when he tells Bottomley to pipe down or he'll dong him?

6 Greenbottle explains that he is late because he has been 'rejoicing'. What effect does this word seem to have on the teacher?

7 Why did Greenbottle's father have a sore foot? What does this tell us about his father?

8 What part would you prefer to play in this radio play? Why?

9 Why do you think this radio play has been so popular over the years?

10 Give two ways in which the writer of radio plays has a more difficult task than the writer of television plays?

RADIO DOCUMENTARIES

A radio documentary takes a subject and explores it by description, interview, narration, summaries and, where possible, music. It seeks to present an in-depth picture of the subject so that the public has a more informed understanding.

In *Ashes of Vietnam*, an ABC radio series focusing on the Vietnam War, the attempt was made to help ordinary Australians understand the war. As part of this effort, interviews with Australian soldiers were presented. Here is one of them.

Bob Stephens

It was late in the afternoon and we were called up into the Long Hais, a treacherous part of the province. We had to pick up some wounded, some South Vietnamese troops with some Australian advisers.

We came into the position. They threw us smoke so we knew where they were but couldn't land because of the rough terrain.

We went in, hovering about twenty feet above the ground, everything was going all right, and I sent a winch down. I could see wounded and bodies lying there. The first bloke they put into the litter was a fellow that had both legs blown off at the knees, a South Vietnamese, and I remember he had a piece of bone about three or four inches protruding from one knee.

I'd just started to winch this guy up when we were shot down by automatic weapons fire. You could hear the rounds hitting the aircraft and they must have hit the engine because the next thing there was no noise.

We hit the rocks, the aircraft rolled over onto its right side. As it was rolling I was looking out the door and I could see the fellow in the litter, who thought that the aircraft was rolling onto him. He didn't scream, but just the look of despair on his face . . .

I dived in behind the back of the pilot's seat for safety and the aircraft shook itself to pieces until the rotor broke itself off and the aircraft stopped. Straight away there was a lot of smoke, there was screaming. The air-craft was on its side and I was standing in the opening on the ground realising that I was still alive. The gunner and then the co-pilot brushed past me and went up through the opening. I watched the co-pilot slide to the ground alongside the aircraft and I watched him rolling down the hill. Then the Army medic, who had taken my machine-gun while I was on the winch, yelled out 'Help me, I'm stuck, I'm stuck.' Something had rolled forward onto the back of his legs and he was sort of kneeling. I put my arms under his armpits to lift him out but I couldn't move him.

I could hear screams coming from the front somewhere and I didn't know whether it was the pilot or some of the men who had been underneath the aircraft when we crashed. I thought I would get out and smash the windscreen in but I couldn't climb out and I thought, 'I'm caught, I'm going to be the next one.' Then I realised that I still had on my safety harness, which stops you from falling out of the aircraft. I got outside and I was about to knock the windscreen in when the aircraft captain, who had already got out, yelled to me to get away before it blew up. He was down behind a large boulder.

I started to run to where he was and I saw the body of one of the Australian advisers who had been assisting in putting that wounded fellow in the litter. He was killed.

It wasn't long after that you could hear the aircraft burning and the ammunition was going off. Once I heard that I knew that I couldn't have gone back even if I had wanted to.

A helicopter came in to get us out just on dusk. There was a wounded South Vietnamese fellow who had taken shrapnel wounds to the head. He was bandaged up, but he was standing underneath the aircraft to be winched up and the downwash from the rotor blades was just swirling his blood everywhere. You could see it going against all the rocks and everything.

When I got on, there was wounded and dead everywhere. Normally they probably would have had a couple of aircraft to remove that many people, but it was right on dark and I suppose if they didn't get us out then, they wouldn't have been able to get us out.

I went around and I sat next to the gunner and I just broke down and cried. I was relieved to be getting out of that place and I thought of what had happened and I just broke down and cried. The gunner put his arm around my shoulders and tried to comfort me. I just felt exhausted, as though all my strength and energy had been drained right out of me.

We landed on the pad at the hospital at Vung Tau and the place was all packed with people ready to tend the wounded and the dead and I just stepped straight off and sort of ambled over. I still had my pistol at that stage and I was trying to get the magazine out and an Army fellow quickly snatched that off me in case something happened there. I was just sort of lost. I felt I was nowhere.

from *Ashes of Vietnam* edited by Stuart Rintou

Questions

1 What was the purpose of the mission described by Bob Stephens?

2 The landing area was marked by smoke bombs. Why couldn't the aircraft land?

3 What horrifying detail about the first casualty does Stephens note as the rescue begins?

4 When the helicopter crashes, what causes the man in the litter to look on in despair?

5 Why couldn't Stephens lift the Army medic up?

6 Why did Stephens want to smash the aircraft windscreen in?

7 Why did the aircraft captain tell Stephens to get away from the plane?

8 Normally more than one aircraft would have come to rescue them. Why did only one come this time?

9 What caused Stephens to break down and cry on the plane?

10 How did Stephens feel while on the rescue aircraft?

11 Why did the Army person quickly grab Stephens' pistol?

12 What effect did the mission have on Stephens?

13 What aspects of the Vietnam War does this extract portray for radio listeners?

14 Why do you think this radio documentary would interest radio listeners?

15 What do you think is the purpose of this radio documentary? Judging from this extract, do you think it achieves its purpose?

16 Give two pieces of advice that you think would be essential to anyone thinking of preparing a radio documentary.

RADIO ADVERTISING

Commercial radio stations rely almost totally on the advertisements they play and the money paid for this privilege by advertisers.

Radio advertisements depend on sound to convey their message. Sometimes they simply have a person present a product or service, using some persuasive language such as 'It's the *real* thing' or 'Don't leave home without it'. Often the advertisement uses an attractive musical jingle. Sometimes the advertisement is a dramatisation in which the product or service is presented to us in an interesting way. Sound effects are usually quite important in setting the scene in these dramatisations.

Look carefully at the following radio advertisement script. MVO means 'male voice-over' and SFX stands for 'sound effects'.

CLIENT: JAPAN AIRLINES
PRODUCT: EUROPE VIA JAPAN
MEDIA: 30" RADIO
DATE: 4.10.89
TITLE: SKIPPY
DRAFT: 3

MVO: Most people who fly to Europe go via the old tried and trusted Kangaroo route.

SFX: Boing, Boing, Boing, Boing ...

MVO: Problem is, if you fly often enough it gets a trifle boring.

SFX: Boing, Boinggg ...

MVO: For a change you should fly with Japan Airlines via......

SFX: SOUND OF A GONG.

MVO: ...Japan. Japan Airlines has daily flights from Sydney to Tokyo and on to Europe. So fly Japan Airlines and give the old Kangaroo route the ...

SFX: Boing, Boing, Boing. (GONG)

Questions

1 What sound is used to suggest a kangaroo hopping?

2 What sound is intended to give an oriental impression?

3 How is a sense of things being 'a trifle boring' created?

4 How might the tone of the MVO's voice vary at the beginning of the line 'For a change...'?

5 What factual information about Japan Airlines is conveyed in the ad?

6 What message is the sound of the gong at the end aiming to convey?

7 How is humour created in this ad?

8 Whom do you see as the target audience for this ad?

9 Identify one aspect of radio advertising that is evident in this ad?

10 What do you see as the strength of this ad? Why?

TELEVISION

As noted earlier in this chapter, television made its entrance into Australia in 1956. In the earliest years most material was simply imported from the United States. These early programs tended to follow radio-program format. Quiz shows, westerns, suspense shows, 'soapies' and comedy programs were all direct descendants of radio-program formats. The earliest television 'stars' usually came from backgrounds of working in radio. The Australian public was used to radio advertising and recognised that it provided the funds to produce radio programs, so the presence of television commercials was readily accepted by most people.

Australian content gradually began to increase in response to demand and also to fit in with laws passed by the government which required that certain percentages of 'air time' be given to Australian-content programs. The earliest Australian shows were mainly news and current affairs programs, sports telecasts, quiz shows and talent quests. Most drama shows continued to be imported from the United States and later Great Britain. The reason for this lay in the fact that producing a drama cost up to seven times as much as producing a sports program, or twice as much as producing a quiz program. Since these early times Australian drama—'soaps', mini-series and full-length television movies—have greatly increased in number as the experience and quality of the Australian television industry has grown, and as advertisers willing to pay large amounts have emerged.

Television today is a huge industry. It is incredibly costly (compared to radio or newspapers) but it fulfills a special role as a mass entertainer, educator and persuader. Most Australian homes have a television set and viewing television is the main leisure-time activity of Australians.

TELEVISION NEWS

The evening news is the central feature of the menu offered by television stations. It has been established by research that viewers tend to stay mainly on the channel that they watch the news on. For this reason, channels work hard to develop news teams that are popular and appealing, from the news writers and main presenters to the sports and weather people.

The anchorperson, or news presenter, has a crucial role. These people have been promoted as personalities, in order to win viewers to their channel. In Australia we seem to prefer a news presenter who is competent and reassuring, someone who can make the most tragic news somehow seem under control.

Read the news report that follows.

Adelaide Shoot-Out

V/Tape: *3 mins. 44 secs.*
[*Take* VT *first word*]
A man armed with a shotgun held police at bay in Adelaide's Rundle Street today for about one-and-a-half hours before he was shot by a police marksman. The man later died from the wound in his stomach. The incident began about eleven o'clock in Hambly Clark's gun shop when the man is said to have grabbed a double-barrelled twelve-gauge shotgun from a shelf and loaded it with cartridges.
[CUE: *30 secs.*]
Police were quickly on the scene. They cordoned off the area, and began firing tear gas into the shop after appealing to the man to come out.
[CUE: *43 secs.*]
The man fired about six shots at police during the siege. Four people in the shop, including the owner, Mr W. Hambly Clark, managed to escape through a back entrance.
[CUE: *Pan and Z/O men in building site*]
Hundreds of people, many crouched in doorways and any other areas that afforded cover, watched the drama play its course. During the siege, members of the Police Armed Offenders Squad covered the man with armalite rifles. Finally the man climbed out over the smashed plate glass into the street. He was armed with two shotguns.
[*Bring up* FX]
[CUE: *1 min. 52. W/S police and ambulance after the kill.*]
The final stages of the siege were over in a matter of seconds. The man fell to the ground after a single shot, and was rushed to hospital where he died a short time later.
[CUE: *2 mins. 06*]
The shot which mortally wounded the man was fired by a police marksman from the first floor of a building across the road. Police say they have no idea of his motive. Reporter Michael Duggan spoke to the owner of the shop, Mr W. Hambly Clark.
[*Up sound*
First words: 'Well I was out . . .'
Super: Hambly Clark
Last words: '. . .we did not get shot.'
VT: Duration: 140-ft. 3 mins. 44 secs.]

Looking at the News

1 How long did this news segment run?

2 This is a reasonably long news item. Why do you think it was given so much time?

3 What are some of the visual shots that would have accompanied this item?

4 Why is 'grabbed' a better word than 'taken' in the sentence '...the man is said to have grabbed a double-barrelled twelve-gauge shotgun...'?

5 The last speech by the newsreader contains an ambiguous sentence: 'Police say they have no idea of his motive.' How would you correct this sentence so that we know exactly who is meant by 'his'?

6 Who do you think is the best news presenter in Australia? What are the qualities that make him or her outstanding from your point of view?

7 By thinking about some of the news presenters you have seen (including sports and weather presenters) identify three qualities that seem to be important in these people.

8 Sometimes the news finishes with a report on a light-hearted or humourous event. Why do you think this is done?

TELEVISION DRAMA

Television is ideally suited for the presentation of drama. Television dramas may take the form of:

- **Series.** These include long-running 'soaps', comedy shows and serious dramatisations that are scheduled regularly week after week.
- **Mini-series.** Usually these run for a few consecutive nights, or a few consecutive weeks.
- **Movies.** Often these are re-runs of movies made for the picture theatres but occasionally special television movies are made.

Here is an extract from the celebrated series *Fawlty Towers*. Fawlty Towers is a run-down English hotel, owned and managed by the snobbish, manic Basil Fawlty and his domineering wife, Sybil. In this extract some late-arriving American guests try to order a meal.

The cast of the television series *Fawlty Towers*. From left: Polly, Basil, Sybil and Manuel.

Ordering Dinner

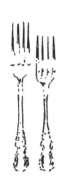

```
CAST
Basil
Sybil
Mr Hamilton
Mrs Hamilton
```

The dining room. Sybil is sitting at a table near the door, reading a Harold Robbins novel. The door opens and Basil ushers in the Hamiltons.

Basil   Thank you. If you'd care to sit over there...
Sybil   Good evening.
Mr & Mrs Hamilton   Good evening.
Sybil   Is your room to your liking?
Mr Hamilton   Yes, it's very nice.
Mrs Hamilton   Very nice, thank you.
Sybil   Oh good. *(she rises and goes into the kitchen)*
Basil   I'll just get you tonight's menu...Oh, would you care for a drink before
      your meal?
Mr Hamilton   A scotch and water and screwdriver, please.
Basil   Um...and for you, madam?
Mrs Hamilton   The screwdriver's for me.
Basil   I see...um...would you like it now or after your meal?
Mrs Hamilton   Well, now, please.
Basil   There's nothing I can put right?
Mrs Hamilton   What?
Basil   Absolutely. So it's one scotch and one screwdriver.
Mr Hamilton   I think I'll join you. *(to Basil)* Make that two screwdrivers, will you?
Basil   You'd like a screwdriver as well?
Mr Hamilton   You got it.
Basil   Fine. So it's one scotch and you each need a screwdriver.
Mr Hamilton   No, no, no. Forget the scotch. Two screwdrivers.
Basil   I understand. And you'll leave the drinks.
Mr Hamilton   What?
Basil   Nothing to drink.
Mr Hamilton   What do you mean, 'Nothing to drink'?
Basil   Well you can't drink your screwdrivers, can you. Ha ha.
Mr Hamilton   What else would you suggest that we do with them?
Mrs Hamilton   Vodka and orange juice.
Basil   Ah, certainly madam.
Mr Hamilton   Make that two. And forget about the screwdrivers.
Basil   You're sure?
Mr Hamilton   We can manage without them.

Basil   As you wish, sir. *(he goes into the kitchen)*

Mr Hamilton   *(reading from a tourist magazine)* 'Relax in the carefree atmosphere of old English charm...' *(he sees Sybil who has just come back in)* I hope we're not intruding on your dinner hour.

Sybil   *(sitting at her table)* Not at all, no. You're American?

Mr Hamilton   That's right.

Sybil   Where are you from?

Mrs Hamilton   California.

Sybil   How lovely. *You're* English, though?

Mrs Hamilton   Yes, but I've been over there ten years now.

Sybil   *Ten* years. Do you ever get home-sick?

Mrs Hamilton   Oh, yes. But I love it there—the climate's so wonderful. You can swim and sunbathe and then after lunch drive up into the mountains and ski.

Sybil   How wonderful. *(Basil enters)*

Mr Hamilton   I like England and the English people, but I sure couldn't take this climate.

Mrs Hamilton   Harry finds it too gloomy.

Basil   *(putting the drinks on the Hamiltons' table)* Oh, I don't find it too gloomy. Do you, Sybil?

Sybil   Yes I do, Basil.

Basil   Well, yes, my wife finds it too gloomy. I find it rather bracing.

Sybil   What do you find bracing, Basil?...the damp, the drizzle, the fog...

Basil   Well, it's not always like this, dear. It changes.

Sybil   My husband's like the climate. *He* changes. This morning he went on for two hours about the 'bloody weather', ha ha ha.

Basil   Yes, well, it has been unusually damp this week, in fact, but normally we're rather spoiled down here on the English Riviera.

Sybil   Mr and Mrs Hamilton were telling me about California. You can swim in the morning and then in the afternoon you can drive up into the mountains and ski.

Basil   It must be rather tiring.

Mr Hamilton   Well, one has the choice.

Basil   Yes, but I don't think that would suit me. I like it down here. It's very mild all the year round. We have palm trees here in Torquay, you know. Do you have palm trees in California?

Mr Hamilton   Burt Lancaster had one, they say. But I don't believe them. *(he tastes his screwdriver)* What the hell is that?

Basil   Er...Vodka and orange juice...

Mr Hamilton   Orange juice?

Mrs Hamilton   I'm afraid it's not fresh.

Basil   Isn't it? *(he takes it and sniffs it)*

Mrs Hamilton   No.

Basil   We've just opened the bottle.

Mr Hamilton   Look, fresh means it comes out of an orange, not out of a bottle.

Basil   Ah! You'd like freshly *squeezed* orange juice.

Mr Hamilton   As against freshly unscrewed orange juice, yes.

Basil   ...Leave it to me, I mean, I'll get chef on to it straight away. *(he bustles off into the kitchen)*

Sybil   Sorry about that. A lot of English people are used to the flavour of the bottled...

Mrs Hamilton   Oh, that's all right. It's just that back home fresh orange juice comes like running water.

Sybil   Does it really? 'Course, it's so good for your skin, isn't it. I'd love to go to California some day. It looks so exciting. *(she indicates her book)*

Mrs Hamilton   Oh! *Never Love A Stranger*. Do you like it?

Sybil   Oh, I love Harold Robbins. I've read this one three times.

Mrs Hamilton   *The Pirate* is his best, I think. I read them when Harry's away. I just don't seem to have the time when he's home.

Sybil   Who needs Harold Robbins when you've got the real thing. *(she laughs; Basil enters)*

Mrs Hamilton   How long have you been married, Mrs Fawlty?

Sybil   Oh, since 1485.

Basil   *(putting the screwdrivers down)* There we are, fresh orange juice.

Sybil   But seriously though, his men are all so interesting. Ruthless and sexy and...powerful.

Basil   *(handing out the menus)* Who's this, then, dear? Proust? E.M. Forster?

Sybil   Harold Robbins.

Basil   Oh, of course, yes. My wife likes Harold Robbins. After a hard day's slaving under the hair-dryer she needs to unwind with a few aimless thrills.

Sybil   Basil! *(she exits to the kitchen)*

Basil   Have you ever read any? It really is the most awful American...well, not America, but trans-Atlantic tripe. A sort of pornographic muzak. Still, it keeps my wife off the streets.

Mr Hamilton   We both like him.

Basil   *(looks disturbed for a moment)* Oh! *Robbins*!

Mr Hamilton   What?

Basil   Harold *Robbins*. I thought you meant that awful man, what's his name, oh, Harold...Robinson. Have you read any Harold Robinson? Ah! Painful!

Mr Hamilton   How about Waldorf salad.

Basil   Was that one? Yes, you're absolutely right. Oh, that was a shocker, wasn't it.

Mr Hamilton   ...Could you make me a Waldorf salad.

Basil   Oh...a...Wa...?

Mr Hamilton   Waldorf salad.

Basil   ...I think we're just out of Waldorfs.

Mr Hamilton   *(to Mrs Hamilton)* I don't believe this.

Mrs Hamilton   It's not very well known here, Harry.

Basil   Yes, may I recommend tonight the...

Mr Hamilton   Look, I'm sure your chef knows how to fix me a Waldorf salad, huh?

Basil   I wouldn't be too sure.

Mr Hamilton   Well, he's a chef, isn't he?

Basil   Yes, you wouldn't prefer...

Mr Hamilton   *(shouting)* Well, find out, will you? Just go out there and see if he knows how to fix me a Waldorf salad!

Basil   ...Of course. *(he goes into the kitchen, but re-appears almost immediately)* He's not *absolutely* positive...he's almost got it. It's lettuce and tomatoes, walled in with...?

Mr Hamilton   No, no, no, it's celery, apples, walnuts, grapes.

Mrs Hamilton   In a mayonnaise sauce.

Basil   Right. Incidentally, he did ask me to say that he does specially recommend the pâté tonight.

Mr Hamilton   I don't want pâté.

Basil   Or the...the grapefruit.

Mr Hamilton   Grapefruit?

Basil   The grapefruit.

Mr Hamilton   How's it done?

Basil   Well, it's halved, with a cherry in the centre. *(Sybil re-enters)*

Mr Hamilton   Look! I haven't paid you twenty pounds to have some guy cut a grapefruit in half and stick a cherry in the centre. *(Sybil reacts to the 'twenty pounds')*

Basil   Exactly.

Mr Hamilton   I want a Waldorf salad.

Basil   Absolutely. One Waldorf salad.

Mrs Hamilton   And a green salad for me.

Basil   And one green salad. Yes. And if we can't manage the Waldorf salad...?
Mr Hamilton   *(loudly)* I want a Waldorf salad! And a couple of *filets mignons. (Basil is flummoxed)*
Mrs Hamilton   Steaks.
Mr Hamilton   Steaks!!
Basil   Steaks!
Mr Hamilton   Done rare.
Basil   Done rare!
Mr Hamilton   Not out of a bottle
Basil   Not out of a bottle. Right. *(he disappears into the kitchen)*
Sybil   Would you like to see the wine list? *(she gives it to them)*
Mr Hamilton   Thank you.
Sybil   May I ask, did you say you'd paid twenty pounds...?
Mr Hamilton   Yes, but it's not the money, my wife and I, we wanted dinner and your husband said your chef usually leaves at nine o'clock...
Sybil   Well, this can't be right. There's no reason chef couldn't stay...
Basil   *(re-appearing from the kitchen)* I'm awfully sorry, he's forgotten already...walnuts, cheese...
Mr Hamilton   No! No cheese! It's celery, apples, walnuts, grapes!
Basil   Right!
Mr Hamilton   In mayonnaise.
Basil   Right! *(shouting into the kitchen)* Now come on! *(goes into the kitchen)*
Sybil   Um...would you excuse me one moment?
Mr Hamilton   Excuse me...a bottle of the Volnay, please.
Sybil   Of course. Thank you. *(she goes into the kitchen)*

In the kitchen, Basil is rummaging frantically in a large cardboard box.

Sybil   What's this about twenty pounds, Basil?
Basil   There's no celery. Would you believe it?
Sybil   I'll find the celery. What about this twenty pounds?
Basil   He gave me twenty pounds to keep the kitchens open, but chef wouldn't...I mean, where does he put things?
Sybil   If you'd just look...
Basil   I *have* looked. There's no celery, there's no grapes...walnuts! That's a laugh, easier to find a packet of sliced hippopotamus in suitcase sauce than a walnut in this kitchen. *(he looks in the fridge)*
Sybil   Now, we've got apples. *(holding up some)*
Basil   Oh, terrific! Let's celebrate. We'll have an apple party. Everybody brings his own apple and stuffs it down somebody's throat.
Sybil   Basil, I'll find everything. Just go and get a bottle of Volnay.
Basil   What's a waldorf, anyway—a walnut that's gone off?
Sybil   It's the hotel, Basil. The Waldorf Hotel. In New York.
Basil   *(struck with an idea)* Wait, wait.
Sybil   *(warningly)* Basil.
Basil   *(going into the dining room)* Everything all right?
Mrs Hamilton   Yes thank you.
Mr Hamilton   Never been better.
Basil   Oh good. Um...by the way. I wonder...have you by any chance ever tried a Ritz salad?

Mr Hamilton   A Ritz salad?

Basil   Yes—it's a traditional old English...thing. It's apples, grapefruit and potatoes in a mayonnaise sauce.

Mr Hamilton   No, don't think I ever tried that.

Basil   Ah!

Mr Hamilton   Don't think I ever will, either.

Basil   No, well, that's probably pretty sound. Well, look, um...about this Waldorf salad of yours...

Mr Hamilton   Yes?

Basil   Um...I've had a bit of a tête-a-tête with chef, and the point is, we're all right on the apples. Absolutely no problem with them at all. Now...on the celery front, well, er...perhaps I should explain, we normally get our celery delivered on a Wednesday, along with our cabbages, onions, walnuts, grapes...that sort of thing, but this week the driver...

Mr Hamilton   Mr Fawlty.

Basil   Yes, he was putting the crate into the van...

Mr Hamilton   I'm not interested.

Basil   ...and he sort of slipped forward and the van door caught his arm, like that, and he may have fractured it...

Mr Hamilton   You don't have any.

Basil   They did the X-rays and we'll know tomorrow whether they're going to have to operate, and to cut a long story short...we don't have any, no. But...um...still...it makes you think how lucky you are, doesn't it. Here we are, with all our limbs functioning. I mean, quite frankly, if you've got your health, what else matters?

Mr Hamilton   What a bunch of crap!

Basil   *(interested)* Oh, do you think so? I always feel...

Mr Hamilton   What the hell's going on here!? It says hotel outside—now, is this a hotel or isn't it?

Basil Well...within reason.

Mr Hamilton You know something, fella—if this was back in the States I wouldn't board my dog here.

Basil Fussy, is he? Poodle?

Mr Hamilton *(standing up and facing Basil)* Poodle! I'm not getting through to you, am I. You know, I stay in hotels all over the world and this is the first time I've had to bribe a chef to cook me a meal and then found out he doesn't have the basic goddam ingredients. Holy Cow, can't you see what a crummy dump this is?

Basil *(shouting towards the kitchen)* You're listening to this, are you, Terry?

Mr Hamilton I'm talking to *you*!

Basil *(to kitchen)* It's all right, Terry, you can get on with...

Mr Hamilton Shut up, will you, and listen to me. Can't you see this ain't good enough?

Basil Yes, I see what you mean.

from 'Waldorf Salad' in *The Complete Fawlty Towers*
by John Cleese and Connie Booth

Checking Out the Dinner

1 Explain why Basil is confused when Mr Hamilton orders a screwdriver?

2 Mr Hamilton reads from a tourist magazine: 'Relax in the carefree atmosphere of old English charm...' Why is this humorous?

3 'What the hell is that?' How does this line give us an indication of the character of Mr Hamilton? How would you describe him?

4 What is humorous about Sybil's answer to the question: 'How long have you been married, Mrs Fawlty?'

5 Why does Basil try to interest the Hamiltons in a Ritz salad instead of a Waldorf?

6 What does Basil do to try to avoid Mr Hamilton's anger toward the end? How successfully does this tactic work?

7 How would you describe the character of Basil as it is shown in this extract?

8 What would be needed to bring out the humour of this extract in the television production?

9 Mr Hamilton seems to be a stereotype of the American tourist. How would you want him to dress if you were directing the television production?

10 Why do you think the *Fawlty Towers* series has been so popular with Australian viewers?

11 What are three of the important qualities in a successful comedy television series?

12 What are two ways in which humour can be created in a television show?

TELEVISION ADVERTISING

Some television commercials are government-sponsored. They are usually directed at warning about an issue of social concern, or at providing general community information. The following storyboard shows the planning stage of a television commercial that was developed by the government-funded 'QUIT. For life' program. It is a powerful commercial directed at warning young people of the dangers of smoking. Study the storyboard and then answer the questions.

General chatter, music.

Questions

1 What impression is being created by the first two scenes?

2 How is this impression being aided by the background noise and music?

3 What two things first indicate that something is not right?

4 How is the tension built up?

5 How is horror created visually in the commercial?

6 What changes do we see in each girl's face from the beginning to the end of this commercial?

7 What is the impact of the scream?

8 What effect does the complete silence at the end have on the viewer?

9 How would you rate the effectiveness of this commercial? Why?

10 What effect does this ad have on you? Why?

Now the music has turned sinister . . .

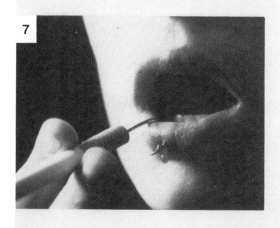

'QUIT. FOR LIFE' STORYBOARD

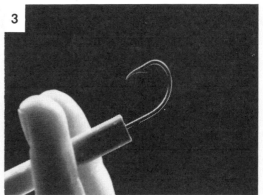

Music turns momentarily weird.

and the tension begins to build.

Sustained chord drowns music and chatter.

SCREAMS

NICOTINE'S A DRUG. BEFORE YOU KNOW IT, YOU'RE HOOKED.

QUIT. For life.

THE DRUG OFFENSIVE

Abrupt silence.

6
OUT OF THE PAST

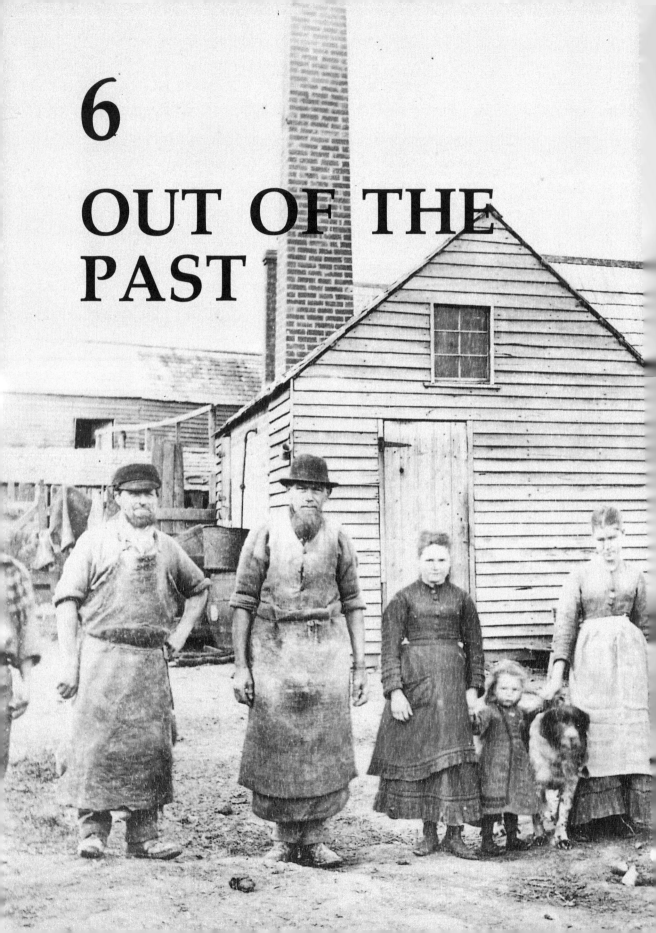

NOVELS

The Dragon's Revenge

Angered because Bilbo the Hobbit has stolen some of his treasure, Smaug the dragon launches an attack on a nearby town of lake-dwellers. He believes these people must have aided the thief. A lookout is the first to warn of the dragon's attack.

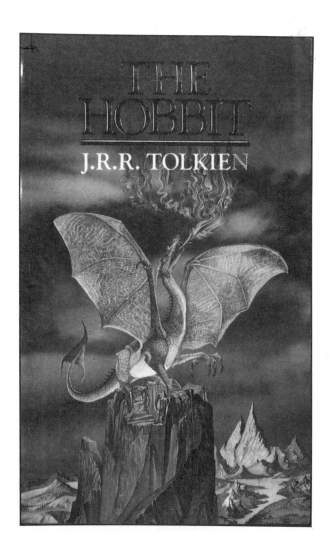

The dragon is coming or I am a fool!' he cried. 'Cut the bridges! To arms! To arms!'

Then warning trumpets were suddenly sounded, and echoed along the rocky shores. The cheering stopped and the joy was turned to dread. So it was that the dragon did not find them quite unprepared.

Before long, so great was his speed, they could see him as a spark of fire rushing towards them and growing ever huger and more bright, and not the most foolish doubted that the prophecies had gone rather wrong. Still they had a little time. Every vessel in the town was filled with water, every warrior was armed, every arrow and dart was ready, and the bridge to the land was thrown down and destroyed, before the roar of Smaug's terrible approach grew loud, and the lake rippled red as fire beneath the awful beating of his wings.

Amid shrieks and wailing and the shouts of men he came over them, swept towards the bridges and was foiled! The bridge was gone, and his enemies were on an island in deep water—too deep and dark and cool for his liking. If he plunged into it, a vapour and a steam would rise enough to cover all the land with a mist for days; but the lake was mightier than he, it would quench him before he could pass through.

Roaring he swept back over the town. A hail of dark arrows leaped up and snapped and rattled on his scales and jewels, and their shafts fell back kindled by his breath burning and hissing into the lake. No fireworks you ever imagined equalled the sights that night. At the twanging of the bows and the shrilling of the trumpets the dragon's wrath blazed to its height, till he was blind and mad with it. No one had dared to give battle to him for many an age; nor would they have dared now, if it had not been for the grim-voiced man (Bard was his name), who ran to and fro cheering on the archers and urging the Master to order them to fight to the last arrow.

Fire leaped from the dragon's jaws. He circled for a while high in the air above them lighting all the lake; the trees by the shores shone like copper and like blood with leaping shadows of dense black at their feet. Then down he swooped straight through the arrow-storm, reckless in his rage, taking no heed to turn his scaly sides towards his foes, seeking only to set their town ablaze.

Fire leaped from thatched roofs and wooden beam-ends as he hurtled down and past and round again, though all had been drenched with water before he came. Once more water was flung by a hundred hands wherever a spark appeared. Back swirled the dragon. A sweep of his tail and the roof

of the Great House crumbled and smashed down. Flames (unquenchable) sprang high into the night. Another swoop and another, and another house and then another sprang afire and fell; and still no arrow hindered Smaug or hurt him more than a fly from the marshes.

Already men were jumping into the water on every side. Women and children were being huddled into laden boats in the market-pool. Weapons were flung down. There was mourning and weeping, where but a little time ago the old songs of mirth to come had been sung about the dwarves. Now men cursed their names. The Master himself was turning to his great gilded boat, hoping to row away in the confusion and save himself. Soon all the town would be deserted and burned down to the surface of the lake.

That was the dragon's hope. They could all get into boats for all he cared. There he could have fine sport hunting them, or they could stop till they starved. Let them try to get to land and he would be ready. Soon he would set all the shoreland woods ablaze and wither every field and pasture. Just now he was enjoying the sport of town-baiting more than he had enjoyed anything for years.

But there was still a company of archers that held their ground among the burning houses. Their captain was Bard, grim-voiced and grim-faced, whose friends had accused him of prophesying floods and poisoned fish, though they knew his worth and courage. He was a descendant in long line of Girion, Lord of Dale, whose wife and child had escaped down the Running River from the ruin long ago. Now he shot with a great yew bow, till all his arrows but one were spent. The flames were near him. His companions were leaving him. He bent his bow for the last time.

Suddenly out of the dark something fluttered to his shoulder. He started—but it was only an old thrush. Unafraid it perched by his ear and it brought him news. Marvelling he found he could understand its tongue, for he was of the race of Dale.

'Wait! Wait!' it said to him. 'The moon is rising. Look for the hollow of the left breast as he flies and turns above you!' And while Bard paused in wonder it told him of tidings up in the Mountain and of all that it had heard.

Then Bard drew his bow-string to his ear. The dragon was circling back, flying low, and as he came the moon rose above the eastern shore and silvered his great wings.

'Arrow!' said the bowman. 'Black arrow! I have saved you to the last. You have never failed me and always I have recovered you. I had you from my father and he from of old. If ever you came from the forges of the true king under the Mountain, go now and speed well!'

The dragon swooped once more lower than ever, and as he turned and dived down his belly glittered white with sparkling fires of gems in the moon—but not in one place. The great bow twanged. The black arrow sped straight from the string, straight for the hollow by the left breast where the foreleg was flung wide. In it smote and vanished, barb, shaft and feather, so fierce was its flight. With a shriek that deafened men, felled trees and split stone, Smaug shot spouting into the air, turned over and crashed down from on high in ruin.

Full on the town he fell. His last throes splintered it to sparks and gledes. The lake roared in. A vast steam leaped up, white in the sudden dark under the moon. There was a hiss, a gushing whirl, and then silence. And that was the end of Smaug.

from *The Hobbit* by J.R.R. Tolkein

Reading for Meaning

1 What is the purpose of sounding the trumpets? *To warn the people that the dragon's coming*

2 Why do you think the townspeople fill all the vessels with water?

3 Why does Smaug's approach seem 'terrible' when the townspeople first sight him?

4 Why was the dragon unable to cross to the island on the bridge?

5 What was the effect on Smaug of the twanging of the bows and the shrilling of the trumpets?

6 Who kept urging the townspeople to fight to the end?

7 How did the townspeople try to put out the fires on the house roofs?

8 How did the dragon knock down the roof of the Great House?

9 What is the first indication that the people are giving up the fight?

10 What do we learn about the Master from his attempt to escape? *He was a coward and only wanted 2 save his own life*

11 Why was the dragon pleased to have the people getting into boats and escaping into the river?

12 Why was Bard's position desperate as he tried to defend the town?

13 What creature offers advice to Bard?

14 Where did Bard's fatal shot hit Smaug?

15 What indication do we get of the loudness of Smaug's death cry?

16 What was Smaug's final act of destruction?

17 What do we learn about Bard's character from this passage? *Bard was a courageous character*

18 What atmosphere is created by the writer in this passage and how is it created? *Fear. When the dragon arrives, and it starts?*

The German Fighter

A lone German raider, looking to inflict some damage over England, runs into an unexpected welcome.

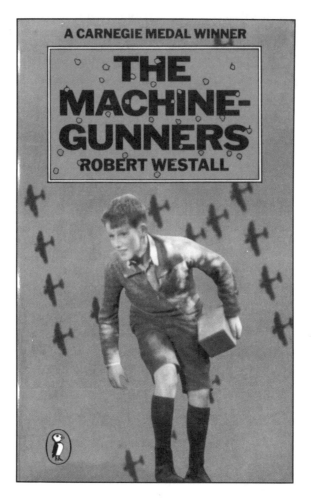

Frost lay on the branches, and froze Clogger's breath on the eyepiece of the telescope. He wiped it angrily with his glove. But it was impossible to be really unhappy on such an evening. The sky was a dimming blue from horizon to horizon. The January evenings were beginning to draw out. Clogger consulted the old watch-and-chain that the lookouts always carried in their top pockets. Five o'clock. Fifteen minutes more in the Crow's Nest. He scanned the horizon with the telescope again. He was shivering so much that the horizon jumped round like a kangaroo.

Then he sucked in his breath. There was a dot, low over the waves. He lost it, and couldn't find it again. A stream of frightful Glaswegian words escaped his lips. When he finally spotted it again, it was nearer. He could see it had two engines.

'Captain, sir?' Chas's head emerged from a loophole.

'Plane, sir. Twin-engined, flying low.'

'Scarper!' shouted Chas. 'Gun out!' They whipped the silver fabric off the gun, and pushed the muzzle past Clogger as he scrambled in.

'Ey, watch it. I don't want a hole where ma dinner is!'

Chas gripped the gun and peered down the gunsight.

'Lower the fence!' Cem undid the knotted rope and the section of fence fell away, revealing the view over the bay. There was nothing in sight.

'Oh, *no*! *Another* false alarm! Clogger, you been at your uncle's whisky again?'

'There *was* something. Ah tell ye. It's too far off to see wi'out the telescope yet. Wait.'

And soon, there it was: a British plane, a Blenheim? Chas's eyes watered with the strain of looking. It was very low for a British plane. But perhaps it was damaged?

No. The propellers had that same queer windmill look. It was gliding in, with its engines shut off. It was black. It was *him*. And, as before, it would pass right overhead.

He lined up the sights on it. It grew bigger and bigger. Wait, wait. Finger on the curving trigger.

'Go *on*!' said Cem, and nudged him.

There was a flash and a roar. Something hit Chas in the chest, much harder than Boddser Brown's fist. He fell over backwards, pulling the gun with him. He lay on the ground with the thing still punching away at his chest. Wood splinters and soil rained down. He stared aghast at a gaping

hole in the roof; through which he saw the German plane, crosses and all, pass as in a dream. It looked completely unharmed.

The tremendous banging of the gun ceased. Cem stared at the enormous hole in the roof.

'Cor blimey.'

The stream of bullets from the machine-gun missed the German fighter by miles. But it startled the pilot so much he put the plane into a near-vertical climb and nearly stalled. While he was battling to regain control, he was spotted by a lone pom-pom [anti-aircraft] gunner on the Bank Top, who had been seeing to his gunsight. Long lines of red stitching followed the fighter up the sky.

More pom-poms opened up. One blew off the fighter's wing-tip and that seemed to drive the pilot mad. Far from trying to escape, he started a personal vendetta against the pom-poms. Once he came so low, he curved round the lighthouse on the Bank Top at zero feet, causing a fat woman with a pram to faint at the entrance to Chapel Street.

The end to such mad behaviour was inevitable. Three Spitfires from Acklington got between him and the sea. But the pilot seemed beyond caring. He headed straight for the Spitfires, guns blazing. They were still blazing when he blew up over the harbour mouth. You could hear people cheering on both sides of the river.

What with the explosion and the cheering, nobody had noticed a small dark mass that had detached itself from the Messerschmidt at the last possible moment. It fell nearly to the ground before a parachute opened, and it still hit the ground rather hard.

Sergeant Rudi Gerlath, of the victorious Luftwaffe tried to stand up, but his ankle was agony. So he crawled instead, gathering the tell-tale folds of parachute as he went, into a clumsy bundle. He was in some sort of garden. Apart from the forest of brussels sprouts around him, the only cover was some little wooden sheds.

He crawled to the first shed, and opened the door, only to be greeted by a frantic clucking and fluttering. Hens! And where there were hens, people came to feed them. No go. He shut the door and crawled on.

The next hut contained one big fat rabbit, who regarded Rudi thoughtfully while chewing his way up a long dandelion leaf.

'Rabbit, I envy you,' said Rudi. 'Rabbits live longer than rear gunners.'

The next hut was empty, except for spades and sacks. Rudi climbed in painfully, pulling the muddy parachute after him. He looked at his ankle. It wasn't broken or even bleeding. Just sprained so he couldn't walk.

Might as well surrender, he thought. Might be a hot meal before interrogation. I'd reveal all the secrets of the Third Reich for a glass of schnapps and a lump of sausage.

He opened the hut door and shouted loudly. Nobody came. Eventually he got tired of shouting and fell asleep.

from *The Machine Gunners* by Robert Westall

Reading for Meaning

1 What is it about Clogger's breath that indicates how cold it is?

2 Why is it 'impossible to be really unhappy' on such an evening?

3 At what time is Clogger's shift in the Crow's Nest supposed to finish?

4 What causes the horizon to jump 'round like a kangaroo'?

5 Why does Clogger swear?

6 Who is the leader of the gun crew?

7 Why can't the gun crew see the plane at first?

8 What three features of the plane enable the gun crew to identify it as the German raider?

9 What causes Chas to fall backwards?

10 Why does the pilot have to fight to regain control of his plane?

11 What does the pilot focus his attack on?

12 Why don't the people notice that the pilot has parachuted out?

13 Why does the pilot gather up his parachute before he goes to hide?

14 Why doesn't he try to hide in the henhouse?

15 What benefits encourage the pilot to consider surrendering?

16 What does this passage show us about the character of the pilot?

The Giant Boar

A huge, savage boar is trapped and the King's hunting party moves in for the kill.

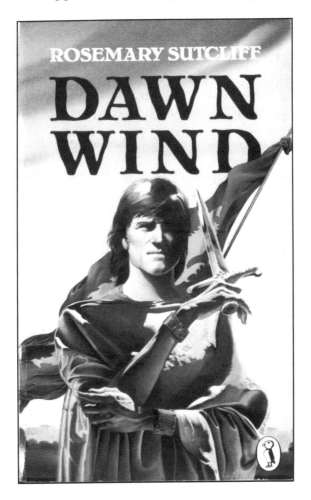

The Black Wood stood like an island in the sea of marshes, black as its name even now in the light of the winter's morning; and within sight of it they checked to set on the hounds. Even as they did so a boy came running, glancing back as he ran, and shouting his story even before he reached them. 'He's still there! He would not have taken to the marshes, and the birds have been quiet all the while in the neck of the woods, so he can't have gone that way!'

There was a long wait, while the King's hunters with the great hounds still in leash went questing to and fro. And then, far over towards the neck of scrub that joined the Black Wood to the forest, a hound gave tongue. 'Sa! Garm has him,' said the King. 'I'd know that bell note of his anywhere.'

And now the other hounds had taken up the cry, and the notes of the hunting horn were blowing thin through the tangled wild-wood and scaring up the plover from the marshes. The pace of the hunt had quickened from the steady lope that it had been before, and suddenly they were all running.

They were among the trees now; the low-hanging branches lashed at their faces and tangled the spears, snags of rotten wood tripped them up, and brambles clawed at them like living enemies wherever the trees fell back a little—and always the belling of the hounds and the thin song of the hunting horn sounded through the woods ahead of them. Now the beaters were drawing close; Owain could hear their shouting, a great circle of uproar, beginning to narrow in on itself, as he ran, head down, behind the slight racing figure of Bryni.

And then, as it seemed between one gasping breath and the next, the whole pattern had changed, and they had come to the very heart of the day's work. They were on the edge of a clearing where a great yew tree had come down in the winter gales and brought others with it in its fall; and on the far side of the open space, backed against the mass of the fallen bole, stood as though waiting for them, a gigantic black boar.

He scarcely looked a thing of flesh and blood at all, but as though he belonged to the dark earth of the wood itself, and the dark elemental spirit of the wood. He stood with lowered head, swinging a little from side to side; his eyes were red like the sullen gleeds of a burnt out fire, and the great curved tushes gleamed against the blackness of his narrow wicked face. Yellowish froth dripped from his jaws, and where it fell on the snow, it steamed.

The hounds, yelling in rage and hate, sprang forward as they were slipped from the leash; from the darkness of the woods beyond, the yelling and crashing of the beaters was still closing in, and all round the clearing the hunters crouched, each man with the butt of his spear braced under his instep. Owain was just behind Bryni in the second line, his spear braced like the rest, in case the boar should break through, but having made sure that his knife was loose in his belt, for the more likely task of a man in the second line would be to help dispatch the beast if the man in front—in this case Bryni—ran into trouble.

The hounds were all about the boar now, yelling into his black devil's mask as he swung his head from side to side. Across Bryni's braced shoulder Owain saw the coarse black bristles along his back and the redness of his wicked little eyes, and caught the sharp stink of him on the wintry air. He trundled forward a few steps, then Garm, the greatest of the King's boarhounds, leapt raving at his throat, and instantly the whole scene burst into roaring chaos. The hounds were all on to their quarry now, baying and belling as they sprang for a hold and were shaken off and sprang again. They were no longer hunting-dogs around a boar, but one confused mass of boar and hounds that rolled slowly forward across the clearing.

But the boar was shaking free of the hounds as he came. Garm lost his grip, and springing in once more, missed the throat-hold, hung for a moment tearing at the huge black shoulder, and was flung off again; a big brindled hound lay kicking his life out in a patch of reddening snow, and the demon of the woods, scattering the enemies that clung to him and dragged him back, was quickening into a grotesque trundling charge that seemed to the waiting spearmen as elemental as a landslip roaring towards them. He was heading for the centre of the great curve of men, where the King and his closest hearth-companions waited, crouching on their spears. But he never reached them, for as the dogs scattered, young Bryni straightened a little behind his braced spear, flung up his arm with a whooping yell '*Hi-ya-ya-aiee!*' and flourished it above his head, like a boy trying to attract the attention of a friend three fields away.

Among all that uproar, the shout might have had little effect, but the sudden movement caught the great brute's eye, and his anger, which until that moment had been for the whole hunt, gathered itself and centred upon it. He swerved in his charge and came straight for Bryni.

Owain felt for one instant as though an icy hand had clenched itself on his stomach, and the next, the great brute was on to Bryni's spear-point. It drove on, carried by the weight of its own charge, until brought up by the cross-guard at the neck of the spear; but it seemed that the deep-driven blade had not found the life; not yet, at any rate. For one sharp splinter of time, Owain saw the boy's shoulder brace and twist and strain, as he fought to keep the spearbutt under his instep; then it was wrenched free, and still clinging to the shaft he was being shaken and battered to and fro as a dog shakes a rat.

'Hold on, Bryni!' Owain shouted. 'For God's sake *hold on!*' He was springing forward, expecting even in that instant to see the boy's hold broken and the black devil upon him. He dived in low among the raving hounds, his spear shortened to stab; other men were with him, other blades caught the wintry light, as he heaved aside the body of a hound and drove in his spear. Now he too was being shaken to and fro, the shaft twisting like a live thing in his hands; the breath was battered from his body, and the stink of the boar and its hot blood were thick in his throat, choking him as the world spun and rocked before his eyes. And then suddenly it was over. Whether it was his own blade or that of one of the other men that had found the life, he never knew, or whether at the last Bryni's spear had taken effect after all; the great brute shuddered, gathered itself together for one last convulsive moment of hate, and crashed down on to its side, seeming to shake the whole forest with its fall.

from *Dawn Wind* by Rosemary Sutcliff

Reading for Meaning

1 Why does the King's hunting party stop briefly within sight of the Black Wood?

2 How do they know that the boar has not gone into the neck of the woods?

3 What is the first sound to indicate that the boar has been located?

4 What other sounds quickly follow this sound?

5 Identify three hazards that face the King's hunters as they race through the trees?

6 What has created the clearing where the boar is found?

7 When they first sight the boar, what suggests it is ready to fight?

8 What is the task of the men in the second line of hunters?

9 What starts the attack?

10 What does Bryni do that causes the boar to change the direction of its attack?

11 What stops Bryni's spear from penetrating any further?

12 What comparison does the writer make to show the boar's great strength as it shakes Bryni about?

13 Why does Owain adjust his grip on his spear as he dives in to help?

14 Why does Owain heave aside a hound as he moves into the attack?

15 What three possibilities exist concerning the final cause of the boar's death?

16 What do we learn about the character of Bryni from this extract?

POETRY

GLIMPSES OF THE PAST

The Witches' Chant

Round about the cauldron go;
In the poisoned entrails throw.
Toad, that under cold stone
Days and nights has thirty-one
Sweltered venom sleeping got
Boil thou first i' th' charméd pot!

Double, double toil and trouble,
Fire burn and cauldron bubble.
Fillet of a fenny snake,
In the cauldron boil and bake;
Eye of newt and toe of frog,
Wool of bat and tongue of dog,
Adder's fork and blind-worm's sting,
Lizard's leg and howlet's wing,
For a charm of powerful trouble,
Like a hell-broth boil and bubble.

Double, double toil and trouble;
Fire burn and cauldron bubble.
Cool it with a baboon's blood,
Then the charm is firm and good.

William Shakespeare

Going Through the Old Photos

Me, my dad
and my brother
we were looking through the old photos.
Pictures of my dad with a broken leg
and my mum with big flappy shorts on
and me on a tricycle
when we got to one of my mum
with a baby on her knee,
and I go,
'Is that me or Brian?'
And my dad says,
'Let's have a look.
It isn't you or Brian,' he says.
'It's Alan.
He died.
He would have been
two years younger than Brian
and two years older than you.
He was a lovely baby.'

'How did he die?'
'Whooping cough.
I was away at the time.
He coughed himself to death in Connie's arms.
The terrible thing is,
it wouldn't happen today,
but it was during the war, you see,
and they didn't have the medicines.
That must be the only photo
of him we've got.'

Me and Brian
looked at the photo.
We couldn't say anything.
It was the first time we had ever heard about Alan.
For a moment I felt ashamed
like as if I had done something wrong.

I looked at the baby trying to work out
who he looked like.
I wanted to know what another brother
would have been like.
No way of saying.
And Mum looked so happy.
Of course she didn't know
when they took the photo
that he would die, did she?

Funny thing is,
though my father mentioned it every now and then
over the years,
Mum — never.
And he never said anything in front of her
about it
and we never let on that we knew.
What I've never figured out
was whether
her silence was because
she was more upset about it
than my dad —
or less.

Michael Rosen

Questions

1 What three photos are mentioned at the beginning of the poem?

2 What sort of mood or atmosphere is there at the start of the poem?

3 How does the mood change after they start talking about the photo of Alan?

4 Why couldn't Alan's life be saved?

5 'For a moment I felt ashamed'. Why do you think the boy felt this way?

6 Why does he study the photo of Alan?

7 'And Mum looked so happy'. What reason is suggested for this?

8 How do the parents differ in the way they handle their grief for Alan?

9 Why don't the boys ever tell their mother that they know about Alan?

10 What question does the boy have about his mother's silence? What do you think is the explanation for her silence?

11 What feelings does this poem stir in you?

12 Why do you think the poet wrote this poem?

The Film

Clearing the house we found
Your old box camera,
Put away long before
You left for hospital,
And in it an exposed film.
A red roll on a black spool,
What could chemistry's kiss
Awaken from this chrysalis
of time?

It unrolled to a back garden,
A son and daughter's visit,
A grandchild skipping on the grass,
And you sitting, content, in the last
Sunshine of your last Summer,
So close, so intimate,
So special as to be
Without point to others, yet
In its very ordinariness
Saying everything.

John Cotton

Questions

1 When do they find the old film?

2 Why are they 'clearing the house'? What has happened?

3 What is there about the camera that suggests its owner was elderly?

4 What is meant by 'chemistry's kiss'?

5 The old film is a 'chrysalis of time'. What does this mean?

6 What are some of the memories contained on the film?

7 What word describes the elderly person in the photos as having lived a fulfilling life?

8 The photos would be 'without point to others'. Why?

9 What do you think the poet means by: 'In its very ordinariness/Saying everything'?

10 How would you describe the relationship the poet seems to have had with the person who has died?

Throwing a Tree

The two executioners stalk along over the knolls,
Bearing two axes with heavy heads shining and wide,
And a long limp two-handled saw toothed for cutting great
    boles,
And so they approach the proud tree that bears the
    death-mark on its side.

Jackets doffed they swing axes and chop away just above
    ground,
And the chips fly about and lie white on the moss and fallen
    leaves;
Till a broad deep gash in the bark is hewn all the way round,
And one of them tries to hook upward a rope, which at last
    he achieves.

The saw then begins, till the top of the tall giant shivers:
The shivers are seen to grow greater each cut than before:
They edge out the saw, tug the rope; but the tree only
    quivers,
And kneeling and sawing again, they step back to try pulling
    once more.

Then, lastly, the living mast sways, further sways: with a
    shout
Job and Ike rush aside. Reached the end of its long staying
    powers
The tree crashes downward: it shakes all its neighbours
    throughout,
And two hundred years' steady growth has been ended in
    less than two hours.

Thomas Hardy

Questions

1 Why are the two men called 'executioners'?

2 Why is the word 'stalk' an appropriate one to describe the way they walk?

3 What are the axes used for?

4 After the men start using the saw, what is the first sign that the tree is weakening?

5 Why do you think Job and Ike shout as the tree comes down?

6 What indication is there of the size of this tree when it comes down?

7 What contrast does the poet give us at the end of the poem? What do you think his purpose is?

8 How effective is this poem in helping you to appreciate the death of this tree? What are your feelings about such an action?

The Night-Ride

Gas flaring on the yellow platform; voices running up and down;
Milk-tins in cold dented silver; half-awake I stare,
Pull up the blind, blink out — all sounds are drugged;
The slow blowing of passengers asleep;
Engines yawning; water in heavy drips;
Black, sinister travellers, lumbering up the station,
One moment in the window, hooked over bags;
Hurrying, unknown faces — boxes with strange labels —
All groping clumsily to mysterious ends,
Out of the gaslight, dragged by private Fates.
Their echoes die. The dark train shakes and plunges;
Bells cry out; the night-ride starts again.
Soon I shall look out into nothing but blackness,
Pale, windy fields. The old roar and knock of the rails
Melts in dull fury. Pull down the blind. Sleep. Sleep.
Nothing but grey, rushing rivers of bush outside.
Gaslight and milk-cans. Of Rapptown I recall nothing else.

Kenneth Slessor

Poem to be Buried in a Time Capsule

My poem is in itself
a kind of time capsule.
It contains my essence,
my native speech,
my choice of words,
my thought, my laughter
and my very breath.

You can swallow it
like a vitamin pill—
one that you absorb
through eyes and ears,
until your own lungs,
throat, tongue and lips
reconstitute its voice.

Through its lines you hear
my own voice speaking
across the centuries.
Though I have long been dead,
this poem is a living thing
from secret sources
that are living still.

Be careful as you
unearth my mystery; and
unwind my age-old wrappings
tenderly, with understanding
of my fragility, that hides
an unsuspected toughness
preserving precious seeds.

—Because a time capsule poem
is also a kind of time bomb
whose delayed-action meanings
can only be safely defused
by those who learn to read
between the lines.—Otherwise
I self-destruct! So mind what you do.

James Kirkup

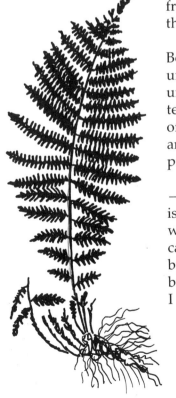

Questions

1 Explain why the poem is similar to a time capsule.

[handwritten: essence]
[handwritten: Because it contains the poets, native speech, choice of words thoughts laught and his very own breath]

2 How can you 'absorb' a poem 'through eyes and ears'?

3 'Through its lines you hear/my own voice speaking/across the centuries.' What does the poet mean?

[handwritten: The poet means to say that in the poem he talks about the diff ages the was]

4 In what way is the poem 'a living thing'?

[handwritten: The poem in a way is a ↓. ↓ as it contains secrets of things that r still living.]

5 Why is 'unearth my mystery' a better choice of words than, say, 'learn about my mystery'?

6 What is the 'time-capsule poem' compared to in the last verse?

[handwritten: a bomb]

7 'So mind what you do.' Why does the poet give this warning?

8 This poem is based on a clever comparison between a poem and a time capsule. Did you enjoy the poem? Why?

[handwritten: Yes, I ↓ was something different and based on something that is highly unusual. because.]

[handwritten: A4) Being read and felt by the people eventhough he has died.]

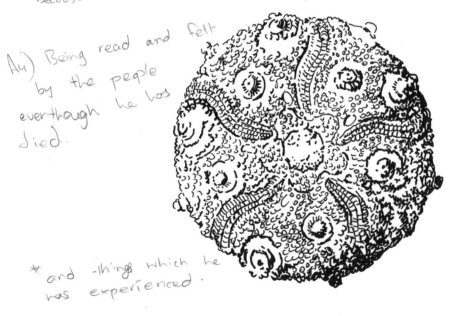

*[handwritten: * and things which he has experienced.]*

[handwritten: A3 Others will learn about the poets feeling]

[handwritten: A8) We r enjoying the poem. It is an historic event.]

WRITING

WRITING A STORY

There are three important elements in any story:

- **setting** (*where* the action takes place)
- **characters** (*who* is involved in the action)
- **plot** (*what* takes place, the storyline)

A successful story weaves these elements together in such a way that our interest is aroused and our attention held.

When writing stories we have to begin in such a way that the reader becomes interested. A boring, slow-moving start will often mean that the reader gives up before he or she gets involved with the characters or plot. It is often effective to begin a story with a fast-moving piece of action. Then, once the reader is involved, details of the plot can be added, characters can be developed and the setting can be filled out.

Read through the following passage and notice how interest is high because we are quickly involved in the action. The setting is Coober Pedy, an isolated opal-mining town in South Australia, where the countryside is dotted with old mine shafts. Ernie is re-working one of these shafts because he has previously discovered some quality pieces of opal there. As the plot unfolds we begin to get glimpses of Ernie's character. For example, notice how tidy and careful his actions are as he exits from the chute at the end of the second last paragraph. This detail gives us a picture of the kind of person that he is.

Robbed!

It was a pleasant walk to the mine. After the recent heat it looked as if the temperature would be bearable for a day or two at least. Ernie carried an old canvas gelignite bag with him this time. It held a fresh supply of candles and matches, a water-bottle, a scraper, some string, a bit of lunch, and a few other odds and ends; but he was hoping that he would need it for a different purpose on the way back.

As soon as he reached the mine he slung the bag from shoulder to armpit with the piece of string, took a good look around, and started to descend the shaft. Nobody appeared to have noticed him. At the twenty-foot level he almost lost his hold for a second and it occurred to him that he was stupid for going off secretly like this on his own without letting anybody know; if he fell and hurt himself nobody would have any hope of finding him and he would be left to starve miserably to death. He dismissed the thought.

Once down, he crouched on his knee, lit one of the candles, and started crawling forward towards his chute. He moved eagerly now, all the excitement coming back to him as he neared the spot again. Near the intersection of the main tunnel with his own drive he found his water-bag lying on the floor in a wet patch of mullock where most of the water had leaked out slowly past the cork. He picked it up angrily, shaking it near his ear to gauge the amount that was still left. He found the old wire spider on which he had left it lying nearby; evidently in his haste he hadn't hammered in the spike properly and the weight of the bag had pulled it out. He replaced it as best he could and continued on. Now that he was nearing the end of his own drive he was desperately anxious to explore the hole that had yielded his opal; he was willing to spend all day widening and deepening it, digging all round it if necessary, to see whether there was any more colour to be found. Perhaps he had only scratched the surface;

perhaps a stone like the *Olympic Australis*, as big as a loaf of bread, was still hidden there waiting to be prised out of its matrix.

The tunnel was getting lower and he realised that he hadn't been clearing the mullock back as far as he should have. He was panting and wheezing, as much from excitement as from exertion, when he finally reached the end of the drive. He held up the candle to get a good look at the working face and the corner where he'd been digging. Then he stopped short. There was a huge hole in front of him. For an instant he was convinced that he'd followed the wrong tunnel, and he half turned to go back. Then he looked again, carefully. No, this was his chute all right, his pick lying nearby, his shovel, his water-bag back there. He held up the candle in bewilderment and looked around again. Suddenly, with a rush that almost made him shout aloud, the meaning of it all flooded in on him. 'I've been robbed!' 'I've been robbed!' He crawled to the edge of the hole and held the candle closely against the sides. It was ragged and uneven, about three feet across and perhaps a little more than two feet deep. Whoever had done it had obviously been in a hurry because a lot of the mullock had just been thrown back on to the floor of the tunnel, leaving very little room to manoeuvre.

Pushing and scrabbling forward, Ernie crawled right down into the hole itself, then heaved himself up until he sat on the rim, with his feet in the hollow. He stood the candle on the mullock nearby and began sifting through all the loose stuff methodically. Most of it was rock and worthless potch but here and there he found traces of colour. A few chips even gleamed with real depth, but on the whole they looked like what they were—pitiful leftovers, remnants and accidental bits broken off from the big ones that were gone.

Ernie took the gouge and picked steadily around the edge, probed the sides, dug out and enlarged the bottom. There was nothing

more to find. The slide he had been following for days which had led him to his treasure had petered out. The thing he didn't know was whether he had left a great deal behind last time, and whether the thieves who had bandicooted his claim had made a rich haul or not.

He felt sure they had. The stuff that was at home in his biscuit tin was almost certainly the beginning of bigger things. He felt suddenly very angry; angry with himself for not having stayed on to finish his find, for not having brought spare candles or at least a torch, for not having returned yesterday despite dust-storms and heat. Now it was too late. If he had allowed a fortune to slip through his fingers he would never know — and even if he did he would never be able to get it back.

His anger was followed by despondency.

He collected the few bits of colour he had found and put them in his pocket. Then he took his gouge and shovel, his canvas bag and candle, his water-bottle and other odds and ends, picked up his old water-bag on the way, and retreated slowly back to the main shaft. Despite the brightness of the day his climb up the shaft was slow and gloomy.

The more Ernie thought about it the more he seethed. It was monstrous. He had registered the claim — and paid ten dollars to do it. He had taken out a Miner's Right. And, having found opal, he'd had it ratted out in front of his nose. No wonder some miners guarded their mines with rifles; no wonder they threatened to drop sticks of gelignite on top of poachers' heads. It was all they deserved.

from *The Fire in the Stone* by Colin Thiele

YOUR TURN TO WRITE

Select one of the following topics and write a story about it. Try to capture interest by involving the reader in some fast-moving action, right from the beginning. As your story develops make sure that you weave in sufficient description so that the setting and its importance are clear, and let the words and/or actions reveal something about the characters of the people involved.

Topics

- New pet disrupts family
- Lonely birthday
- More money than I'd ever seen before
- Fishing trip disaster
- Fun at the supermarket
- Everything suddenly went dark!
- Help! My house is on fire!

- So I set out to become rich
- To the top of the mountain
- Rock concert rage
- Lost in the bush
- A true friend
- Rescued
- Long-distance runner

LANGUAGE

FORMS OF COMMUNICATION

There are many different ways of communicating a message to other people. We call these **forms of communication**. For example, we may communicate our message in the form of a letter, a poem, a short story, a novel, a play, a cartoon, a diary extract or a report. Each of these, and others, can be considered forms of communication.

Why do people choose one form rather than another? Here are three reasons:

1 Sometimes the form is already pre-chosen, because that is the way people in our society usually communicate a particular type of message. For example, a letter is the appropriate form to use when applying for a job. We would not normally write a poem to a potential employer!
2 Sometimes the form is chosen because it best suits the skills and talents of the communicator. For example, Cobb's cartoon on page 211 communicates a message by making use of a form or medium that matches his artistic talents as a cartoonist. He would probably not have communicated nearly so well by writing a play.
3 Sometimes the form is chosen because it is the most suitable medium for communicating the desired message. For example, an advertisement with visual impact and persuasive language is a better medium by which to sell a product than an essay on the product's virtues.

Let's look closely at three different forms of communication: a diary, a poem and a cartoon. Each focuses on an aspect of education.

DIARY

Dog at School

Write the summary

Wednesday   March 11th

Dragged myself to school after doing paper round and housework. My mother wouldn't give me a note excusing me from Games so I left my PE kit at home. I just couldn't face running about in the cold wind.

That sadist Mr Jones made me run all the way home to fetch my PE kit. The dog must have followed me out of the house because when I got to the school gate it was there before me. I tried to shut the dog out but it squeezed through the railings and followed me into the playground. I ran into the changing rooms and left the dog outside but I could hear its loud bark echoing around the school. I tried to sneak into the playing fields but the dog saw me and followed behind, then it saw the football and joined in the lesson! The dog is dead good at football, even Mr Jones was laughing until the dog punctured the ball.

Mr Scruton, the pop-eyed headmaster, saw everything from his window. He ordered me to take the dog home. I told him I would miss my sitting for school dinners but he said it would teach me not to bring pets to school.

from *The Secret Diary of Adrian Mole Aged 13¾* by Sue Townsend

Diary Questions

1 'Dragged myself to school after doing paper round and housework.' What common feature of diary writing does this sentence demonstrate?

2 How does Adrian feel at the start of this incident?

3 How does Adrian feel about Mr Jones? What evidence is there for his opinion?

4 'The dog is dead good at football...' How formal or 'correct' does the language in a diary need to be? Why?

5 What stopped Mr Jones from laughing?

6 What was Adrian most concerned about when he was ordered to take the dog home?

7 What is there in this extract to show that diary entries are normally not for public reading?

8 What purpose is served by keeping a diary?

POEM

Dear Examiner

Thank you so much for your questions
I've read them most carefully through
But there isn't a single one of them
That I know the answer to.

I've written my name as instructed
Put the year, the month and the day
But after I'd finished doing that
I had nothing further to say.

So I thought I'd write you a letter
Fairly informally
About what I can see from my desk here
And what it's like to be me.

Mandy has written ten pages
But it's probably frightful guff
And Angela Smythe is copying
The answers off her cuff.

Miss Quinlan is marking our homework
The clock keeps ticking away
I suppose for anyone outside
It's just another day.

There'll be mothers going on errands
Grandmothers sipping tea
Unemployed men doing crosswords
or watching 'Crown Court' on TV.

The rain has finally stopped here
The sun has started to shine
And in a back garden in Sefton Drive
A housewife hangs shirts on a line.

A class files past to play tennis
The cathedral clock has just pealed
A mower chugs backwards and forwards
Up on the hockey field.

Miss Quinlan's just read what I've written
Her face is an absolute mask
Before she collects the papers in
I've a sort of favour to ask.

I thought your questions were lovely
I've only myself to blame
But couldn't you give me some marks
For writing the date and my name.

Gareth Owen

Examining 'Dear Examiner'

1 Why does the student decide not to attempt the exam questions?

2 What has the student been able to do in response to the exam paper?

3 What does the student intend to write about to the examiner?

4 Why do you think Miss Quinlan's 'face is an absolute mask' when she reads what the student has written?

5 What favour does the student ask of the examiner at the end of the poem?

6 How would you describe the mood of the poem? Is it light-hearted or serious, or both? What makes you think so?

7 What two forms of communication are combined in 'Dear Examiner'?

8 In a sentence or two, explain what you think is the main point of this poem.

9 Why do you think Gareth Owen has chosen the form of a poem for his message?

10 How effective is this form of communication?

CARTOON

Cartoon Questions

1 How would you describe the mood of Cobb's cartoon? What evidence is there to support your answer?

2 In a sentence or two explain what you think Cobb's message about exams is. Could this message be conveyed in a poem? Why or why not?

3 What is Cobb communicating by depicting the person's brain the way he does?

4 What is Cobb communicating by drawing such a robot-like person?

5 Why do you think Cobb has used the form of a cartoon to communicate his message?

6 What do you see as the qualities of a good cartoon 'with a message'?

GETTING IT RIGHT

Remember that a **noun** is a naming word, while a **verb** is a doing word. For example:

nouns: cat, health, Australia, anger
verbs: sang, enjoy, described

The following words are correctly spelt with a 'c' when they are nouns, and with an 's' when they are verbs.

Nouns	Verbs
advice	advise
practice	practise
device	devise
prophecy	prophesy
licence	license

Choosing the Noun or Verb

Choose the correct word from the brackets to complete each of the following sentences.

1 My . . . . to you would be to go ahead.   (advice/advise)

2 Gazing into the cloudy crystal ball she began to . . . .   (prophecy/prophesy)

3 We usually . . . . a plan to win each match.   (device/devise)

4 The golfer put in extra . . . . on his putting.   (practice/practise)

5 The driver opened his wallet and produced his . . . .   (licence/license)

6 We . . . . hockey on Tuesday afternoons.   (practice/practise)

7 The witch's . . . . was very clear and very frightening.
(prophecy/prophesy)

8 A strange . . . . was fastened to the chariot wheel.   (device/devise)

9 To follow up on the new law, the police will . . . . all street musicians.
(license/licence)

10 What did they . . . . you to do?   (advise/advice)

DRAMA

The Mummy's Purse

by Robert Hood

This humorous play is about the search for the tomb of a famous, but fictitious, king.

CHARACTERS

Sir Reginald Bore, famous archeologist
Edna, his mother
Professor Fanny Finkle, Sir Reginald's associate
Terry Slime, a guide
Gerald, Reginald's father
Bonyelbows, a tomb guard
Nefertrustaman, a serving girl
King Tut-Tut-Tisk-Tisk-Who's-A-Naughty-Boy-Then
Queen Wotzamatta, King Tut's mother

There is a spotlight on Sir Reginald Bore, who is giving a lecture. He is standing behind a lectern.

Reginald   My friends and academic enemies...I mean, colleagues! We all know that significant archeological discoveries can be made by accident. An eminent example is that of Professor Gooseliver of Muckabout University, who discovered the lost civilisation of the Stinkite people when he clumsily flushed himself down the outside loo. But it is the mark of a true archeological genius to be able to gather information from the most obscure of clues and from that information to piece together the fact that we live upon the ruins of an ancient city, whose ruler, King Tut-Tut-Tisk-Tisk-Who's-A-Naughty-Boy-Then, is buried at our very feet. Such a clue has come into my possession, and with it I, Sir Reginald Bore, plan to revolutionise...

Edna   *(from the darkness)*   Reggie, sit down and finish your breakfast!

Reginald   ...I plan to revolutionise...

Edna   Breakfast, Reggie!

Reginald   ...plan to revolutionise breakfast!   *(Pause)*   Oh, no! Mother! You've ruined my speech!

(Lights come up. We are now in the kitchen of Sir Reginald Bore and his mother, Edna. There is a formica table set for breakfast, and three chairs.)

Reginald *(leaving the lectern)*   Mother, really! I was practising my speech!

Edna   That's nice, dear. I've always said you need to improve the way you speak. Sometimes you sound like your mouth's full of old bricks!

Reginald   Not my speech! My *speech*! I'm giving a talk to the Archeological Society tonight!

Edna   You're not hobnobbing with riffraff again! Really, Reggie, I would have thought you'd have more respect for your father, dear Gerald — God rest his soul!

Reginald   He's not dead, mother! He ran away from home, that's all! He hated it when you cheated at Monopoly.

Edna   He didn't run away from home! How can you say such a thing, Reggie? He went on an extended holiday to Barbados. For his liver!

Reginald   A twenty-year holiday?

Edna   He has a very bad liver.

Reginald   The point is, mother, I'm speaking to the Archeological Society tonight because I'm a world-famous archeologist and I've made a startling discovery!

Edna   World-famous archeologist! Really, Reggie! I do wish you wouldn't persist with these silly ideas of yours!

Reginald   I've had twenty-three papers published in *The Archeological Weekly* alone! And I've got doctorates from ten universities world-wide.

Edna   Good grief, Reggie! All you do is grub around in the dirt and vandalise derelict buildings with your friends! You come home with cracked crockery!

Reginald   They're ancient artifacts!! That's what archeologists look for, for heaven's sake!

Edna   I just wish you'd get a decent job. Here's your porridge.

(She puts a big plate of porridge in front of him at the table. The porridge is green and lumpy.)

Reginald Oh, yuck! You know I hate porridge. And *your* porridge is always so foul!

Edna Fowl? It is not. My *chicken soup* is fowl.

Reginald Your porridge and your chicken soup are both foul! They're green and lumpy and they make me sick.

Edna Sit down and eat your porridge, or you can go to your room right now, young man!

Reginald I'm 35 years old and a leading scientist, mother!

Edna You're a very naughty boy!

(Edna hits Reginald and reluctantly he eats his porridge. Edna stands over him while he eats. After the first sickening mouthful there is a knock.)

Reginald *(under his breath)* Saved!

Edna Oh, dear. Now who can that be?

Reginald I'll get it! *(He goes out.)*

Edna If it's not one thing, it's another. It's probably one of Reggie's filthy old friends.

(Reginald re-enters with Fanny. She is beautiful and dressed in a glamorous dress.)

Reginald It's Professor *Harry* Finkle, mother! He's here to go over some important archeological business with me.

Edna *(coldly)* Oh, yes. *(aside, to audience)* I've never trusted that Harry Finkle. He's one of the strangest men I've ever seen! Reggie and he go off on long holidays together. They call them 'expeditions', but I reckon they just hang around down the pub!

Fanny Ah, breakfast! I'm famished.

Reginald *(aside to her)* I'd avoid the porridge.

Edna *(to Reginald)* I thought I told you your friends could only come over after breakfast, Reggie.

Reginald That's right. That's why Harry's here. He's after breakfast. *(he grins stupidly)* Anyway, we need to work on the kitchen table. Don't we, Fanny.

Fanny Yes, my dearest!

Edna Fanny? You called him Fanny.

Reginald No, no, I said Danny. It's his middle name.

Edna *(to Fanny)* And you called Reggie 'my dearest'!

Fanny No, no, not at all. I didn't say 'my dearest', I said 'I'll have *my beer first*!'

Reginald Really, mother, I think you're going deaf. We can't waste our time repeating everything, you know!

Edna *(getting up)* Well, I'm sure I wouldn't want to disturb you. I'll be out in the garden. I've got to dig a hole to bury the leftover porridge!

(She goes out, taking the pot of porridge with her.)

Fanny Reginald, my love! Alone at last!

Reginald Yes, my dearest Fanny! But we must be careful. She nearly caught us out that time.

Fanny I don't think I can take this much longer, Reggie. When can we tell everyone we got married last week?

Reginald   We have our careers to think of, Fanny. We're both important archeologists, on temporary grants from Muckabout University. You know what the Vice-Chancellor thinks of his staff marrying each other. He'll cut off our funds!

Fanny   But why must we pretend I'm a man in front of your mother?

Reginald   She's very jealous! If she thought I spent so much time alone with a woman, she'd report me to the University. They'd cut off our funds, and she'd cut off our arms.

Fanny   This makes it all the more important that your new discovery is proven correct. If we can find the mummy of King Tut-Tut-Tisk-Tisk-Who's-A-Naughty-Boy-Then, we will have nothing to fear. Our careers will be safe! Have you got the evidence?

Reginald   Right here!   *(he produces a fancy purse)*

Fanny   *(suspicious)*   It looks like a woman's purse! Have you been seeing someone else, Reggie?

Reginald   No, of course not! This isn't just a woman's purse. It's the purse of Queen Wotzamatta.

Fanny   King Tut-Tut-Tisk-Tisk-Who's-A-Naughty-Boy-Then's mother! Where did you get it?

Reginald   In the second-hand knick-knack store down the road. It only cost me $10.50.

Fanny   You were robbed! I saw a much better one at Grace Bros for $5.99.

Reginald   No, no, you miss the point: This is Queen Wotzamatta's purse—the only one of its kind—and in it I found this...   *(he takes a piece of paper from the purse)*

Fanny   What is it?

Reginald   It's the plans for a tomb—the tomb of her son, King Tut-Tut-Tisk-Tisk-Who's-A-Naughty-Boy-Then!

Fanny   He died young, didn't he?

Reginald   An inscription found on the back of an old cornflake packet said he was struck down at the breakfast table.

Fanny   Breakfast table?

Reginald   Yes. Apparently he refused to eat his porridge.

Fanny   Queen Wotzamatta must have been very vicious.

Reginald   Yes. And a terrible cook!

Fanny   Does this plan for the tomb show where they built it, Reggie?

Reginald   Yes, and it's somewhere close by. I've hired a guide—a fellow called Terry Slime—and he assures me he can take us straight there. He knows a sewer outlet we can crawl through. In fact he's the world's greatest expert on finding his way through sewers.

Fanny   He's gone through the motions, has he?

Reginald   Often. He's worth every scent.

(Lights out. The curtain closes. During the blackout the set can be changed. Noise doesn't matter. Slime comes on, in front of the closed curtain, holding a flashlight.)

Slime   It's this way. Come on, you two! It's only mud.   *(aside)*   Well, twenty per cent of it is mud.

(Reginald and Fanny enter.)

Fanny   This is the filthiest sewer I've ever been in. It hasn't been cleaned in months, I'd say.

Reginald   They never clean sewers, my love.

Fanny   No? Why not? No civic pride?

Slime   Sewers aren't meant to be clean. They're damp, dark, dirty places, where people like me come to really enjoy themselves.

Reginald   Yes, Fanny, sewers are full of excrement.

Fanny   Oh, dear. What's excrement?

Slime   Look under 'E' in the dictionary. If you can't find it there, just look under your shoe.

Fanny   *(looking under her shoe)*   Yuck!

(Slime laughs sinisterly.)

Reginald   *(indicating the sound of the set being changed behind the curtain)*   What's all that noise?

Slime   Rats!

Reginald   Rats! What are they doing?

Slime   Changing the set for the next scene, I think.

Reginald   Oh, good. Then we can get out of this horrible mess.

(There is a loud crash.)

Slime   And into another horrible mess!   *(he laughs)*

(They exit on the opposite side of the stage. The curtain opens. We are in a tomb. There are two mummy-cases, a lounge chair and a TV set. It is very messy. Gerald is sitting on the lounge, watching the TV and drinking a can of Coke. He is being fanned by Nefertrustaman, who is dressed like an Egyptian serving-girl. Bonyelbows stands to one side, his arms crossed. He looks fierce. In fact he is guarding the doorway. He has a big sword. Gerald gets up and turns off the TV.)

Gerald   Boring! Utterly boring! *The Curse of the Mummy's Tomb*! What rubbish! The worst movie I've ever seen.

Nefer   I didn't think it was too bad.

Gerald   Really, Nefertrustaman, I would've thought you'd been in this place far too long to find a film set in a mummy's tomb even remotely interesting!

Nefer   It was exciting.

Gerald   I've spent twenty years in this tomb and I don't think there's anything at all exciting about it.

Nefer   I've spent three thousand and twenty years here! You get used to it after a while.

Gerald   *(taking her aside)*   Look, Nefertrustaman, let's get out of here, eh? We can take a trip to Barbados.

Nefer   You know we can't. Bonyelbows over there wouldn't let us. We're cursed to spend eternity as death-companions to King Tut-Tut-Tisk-Tisk-Who's-A-Naughty-Boy-Then and his mother. . .

Gerald   There's two of us and only one of him. If we rush him he couldn't stop us.

Bony   Yes, I could! I've got superhuman strength. Queen Wotzamatta asked the gods to give me these amazing powers, and they always gave her what she asked for.

Gerald   Why?

Bony   She threatened to send them a few tonnes of her homemade porridge as a sacred offering if they didn't.

Gerald   If I'd known I'd have to stay here forever, I never would've tried to escape from my wife by hiding in this tomb. I'd have gone straight to Barbados instead.

Nefer   Everyone who enters this tomb, must stay here and serve the mummified remains of King Tut-Tut-Tisk-Tisk-Who's-A-Naughty-Boy-Then until the world ends!

Gerald   I know, I know. I've heard it all before!

(Suddenly there is a knocking sound.)

Gerald   What was that?

Nefer   Rats?

Gerald   No, I think we're about to have some visitors!

Slime   *(off)*   See? I told you I'd find the place.

Reginald   *(off)*   Wow! What a fantastic antechamber! Look at all the nice rubble!

Fanny   *(off)*   We've done it, Reggie. I bet the mummy of King Tut-Tut-Tisk-Tisk-Who's-A-Naughty-Boy-Then is through this doorway. We'll be the first living people ever to enter this tomb!

(They enter from behind Bonyelbows.)

Fanny   *(pushing past Bony calmly)*   Excuse me!

Gerald   Greetings, folks!

Fanny   There's people here! Alive!

Reginald   Good grief! We weren't the first then!

(Bonyelbows gets behind them so they can't exit again.)

Gerald No, no. Sorry, I'm afraid you weren't the first. I was! Twenty years ago. And these other two have been in here for over three thousand years.

Slime Who are you? The caretaker?

Gerald Doctor Gerald Bore at your service. I'm pleased to meet you. At last there'll be someone else I can play Monopoly with. *(he indicates Nefertrustaman.)* *She* cheats!

Reginald Doctor Gerald Bore! Surely not! You went on a holiday to Barbados.

Gerald Didn't make it, I'm afraid. Got stuck in here.

Reginald But I'm your son — Reggie!

Gerald Reggie! Good heavens! How you've grown!

Reginald But *you* haven't changed a bit.

Gerald No, well...it's all part of the curse. We have to live in here forever, you see!

Fanny What? Live in here forever? Why?

Nefer King Tut-Tut-Tisk-Tisk-Who's-A-Naughty-Boy-Then and his mother Queen Wotzamatta wanted it that way.

Slime What's to stop us just leaving the way we came?

Nefer *(pointing at Bonyelbows)* Him! He's got superhuman strength.

(They look at Bonyelbows. He grins.)

Bony Hi! Nice to meet you.

Reginald But you wouldn't stop us from leaving, would you?

Bony Oh, yes. And I'd be forced to beat you up a bit too.

Reginald Why?

Bony I need the exercise.

Slime A supernatural guardian! That's hardly a convincing argument! Anyway, I'm not scared of some three-thousand-year-old wimp! I'm leaving right now.

(Slime tries to walk past Bonyelbows. Bonyelbows just flicks him casually and Slime goes staggering across the tomb, crashing into one of the mummy-cases.)

Fanny   Wow!
Reginald   Now that's what I call a convincing argument.
Nefer   I told you he had superhuman strength.

(Suddenly Slime screams out.)

Slime   The mummy-case! It's opening!   *(he faints)*
Gerald   That's what I've dreaded all these years. The mummy of King Tut-Tut-Tisk-Tisk-Who's-A-Naughty-Boy-Then has come alive!

(The mummy-case opens, revealing a reasonably tatty mummy, wrapped in bandages. Its eyes open. The others cower in terror, except for Nefertrustaman and Bonyelbows, who bow low to the ground.)

Tut   What's all the racket! I'm trying to get a good millenium's sleep. Is it time to get up yet?
Reginald   It's him! King Tut-Tut-Tisk-Tisk-Who's-...
Tut   Yes, yes. All right! There's no need for the whole thing. Just call me Louie.
Fanny   Louie? Is that your real name?
Tut   Of course not. My real name's completely unpronounceable.   *(he comes closer and whispers confidentially)*   Tell me, is my mother still around?
Reginald   Well, your mother's mummy is over there!   *(He points to the other mummy-case)*
Tut   My mummy's mummy!
Fanny   Yes.
Tut   Then she's dead?
Gerald   As dead as you were, anyway.
Tut   But she hasn't been walking around? Or making porridge?
Reginald   No.
Tut   Good.   *(he unwraps his bandages)*   Then it's time I made myself scarce. How long have I been in here?
Fanny   Over three thousand years!
Tut   That should have been long enough. At last I'll be free. I'll never have to eat my mummy's porridge again.

(Nefertrustaman comes over to him on her knees.)

Nefer   What about me, O Great King?
Tut   Ah, Nefertrustaman. You're here!
Nefer   You promised that if I'd wait for you you'd lay the world at my feet.
Tut   Yes, of course I did. Our love had to remain secret while my mother was alive—for she was too jealous and would have slaughtered us both. Or worse. She would have made us eat her porridge!
Nefer   *(standing)*   But now we can be together!
Tut   Yes. Forever. But we'd better get out of here first!

(He and Nefertrustaman head for the exit, but Bonyelbows stands in the way.)

Tut   Out of my way, vassal! I am your King.

Bony   Sorry. I serve Queen Wotzamatta. She said no one leaves and as far as I'm concerned that means you too.

Tut   How dare you!

(Suddenly there is a crashing sound.)

Fanny   What was that? Rats?

Tut   Rats? I hate rats! Bonyelbows, though you won't let us out, the least you could do for your King is to go and check up on that noise!

Nefer   Please, Bony.

Bony   Oh, all right then!

(He turns and goes out. There is a horrible squishy sound and he screams, off. Then he comes staggering back in, his head covered in oozing, green porridge.)

Bony   Something attacked me from above! It's horrible! Help me somebody! Help!   *(he collapses unconscious)*

Reginald   That looks like mother's porridge.

Gerald   You're right, son! I remember it from twenty years ago. In fact I still have nightmares about it.

Tut   Well, whatever it is, it's put Bonyelbows' superhuman powers out of action and given us a chance to escape. Come on, Nefertrustaman!

(They start to leave. Suddenly the other mummy-case swings open and Queen Wotzamatta jumps out.)

Queen Tut-Tut-Tisk-Tisk-Who's-A-Naughty-Boy-Then! Stop where you are! You're not going off with that woman! You haven't even had any breakfast, you wicked lout!

Tut Mummy's alive! Oh, no! Come on, Nefer! Let's go!

(Tut and Nefertrustaman rush out, followed by Queen Wotzamatta yelling.)

Queen Stop! Come back here, you naughty, naughty boy!

(She exits. Suddenly we hear a tremendous crash.)

Fanny What's happened now?

Reginald I'll go look! *(he exits; in a moment he re-enters)*

Fanny Well? What is it?

Reginald It's mother! She fell through the roof of the antechamber right on top of Queen Wotzamatta. King Tut and Nefertrustaman have escaped.

Gerald Your mother! Don't tell me Edna's here!

Edna *(entering)* I am indeed! One minute I'm burying the porridge leftovers in the garden and the next I'm sitting on someone's mummy. And what do I find down in this dim, dark hole? My son and my long-lost husband!

Gerald Yes, Edna! It's me! I've been trapped in this tomb for twenty years! I've missed you, Edna!

Edna   Have you? That's nice   *(she gives him a hug)*

Gerald   It's wonderful! I've got my family back again. My loving Edna, my son and his splendid wife?

Edna   Wife? What wife? Not that woman I squashed out there?

Gerald   No. This lady here, Edna.   *(to Fanny)*   What was the name again?

Edna   That's Harry...Professor Harry Finkle. Oh, Reggie, you haven't married a man, have you?

Fanny   My name's Fanny, Mrs Bore...Professor Fanny Finkle. I'm a woman.

Edna   Really? Well, that explains a lot! I must say it's a great relief to me.

Reginald   We were married last week during that conference on the lost civilisations of Marrickville. I hope you don't mind.

Edna   Of course not. Not now that I've got my Gerald back.   *(to Gerald)*   I promise I won't cheat at Monopoly any more, Gerrie.

Reginald   *(to Fanny)*   Then we can be together at last, my dearest Fanny.

Fanny   *(as they fall into each other's arms)*   Oh, Reggie!

Edna   Now there's only one thing left to do.

Gerald   What's that, Edna?

Edna   Go back upstairs and have a nice bowl of porridge! But I fear the fall I took has made me forget how to make it.

Others   Hurrah!

Queen   *(staggering in)*   Wait a minute! I've got a super recipe you can use!

(The others groan, while Edna and the Queen start to compare notes.)

Questions

1   What is the connection between Sir Reginald Bore's name and the first speech we hear him make?

2   What kind of a person is Edna, Reginald's mother?

3   Why did Reginald's father leave home?

4   What are two of Reginald's outstanding qualifications as an archeologist?

5   Where does Reginald find the map showing the location of King Tut-Tut-Tisk-Tisk-Who's-A-Naughty-Boy-Then's tomb?

6   How did Bonyelbows get his superhuman strength?

7   Why hasn't Gerald grown older?

8   How does Bonyelbows lose his strength?

9   What evidence is there that Edna has changed at the end of the play?

10   How would you dress to play the part of (a) Sir Reginald (b) Terry Slime (c) Bonyelbows?

11   Which character in the play did you find the most amusing? Why?

12   Which incident did you like best in the play? Why?

7
RELATIONSHIPS

NOVELS

The First Meeting

Selina, a blind girl whose time is spent threading beads, is allowed for the first time to work sitting in the park.

I settled back against the trunk of the tree. I would just sit awhile.

I heard a million small sounds I had never heard before: magic teasing sounds. The dearest sound I heard was made by a leaf — it fell on top of my head — ff-t-

I put up my hand to see what it was, because I had not known that it was a leaf. Good little leaf to fall from your branch in summer instead of waiting for the autumn. Falling just to make me happy.

I felt along the curving centre vein of the leaf — my first leaf.

I counted the uneven scallops. Eleven, and one ungrown, little scallop.

The centre vein was like a great river, with little rivers branching out. On the back of my leaf, the centre vein was raised, like the backbone of a fish.

I found out later that my leaf fell from an oak tree. I would've loved it no matter where it came from.

That morning in the park, every bird sang, like mad.

Crazy, cool little winds danced over the grass and carried the loveliest smells I had ever smelt.

It was hard to sit still. I wanted to jump up, pull off my shoes. I wanted to climb to the very tip top of my tree. Roll on the grass. Hunt for the flowers that I knew must be somewhere near. But as Rose-ann is always saying: 'The milk has been spilt. You're blind, Sleena. No use crying.'

So I sat, as Ole Pa had told me, but you can take a long shot on the fact that my heart and mind were dancing like mad.

I knew I should be doing beads. But how could I?

I just sat.

My conscience but jumped when I heard a far-away clock striking eleven. I couldn't believe I had been in the park for more than two hours!

I threaded my needle.

In the room I had always been able to thread without knowing I was threading. Out here in the park it was different. So many things to take my mind away from my hands.

Something else, not a leaf, fell from the tree, down the neck of my blouse. I felt it creeping down, down. Horrible! I tried to reach it with my hand and knocked over one of the bead boxes.

There was a slope where I was sitting.

That was that!

I would not be able to come to the park any more. I could never find all those beads in the grass. I hadn't even one thread completed. Not even one thread. It was too sad — more than sad.

I felt finished. The milk — no, the beads had been spilt — for sure.

No use to say 'no use to cry.' I sat and cried.

When Gordon asked me, 'Can I do anything to help you?' I stopped crying.

I covered my face with my hands and listened with all of me.

'Are you all right?' asked Gordon.

I found out later that Gordon had been sitting on a bench when Ole Pa and I had arrived at the tree. He'd been watching me for more than two hours. Just watching.

See how bad it is to be unable to see!

He had watched me play with my oak leaf, listen to the sounds around me, begin my work, knock over the box — watched me cry.

Gordon's voice was so deep that although it came from above me it seemed to come from all about me. Almost I thought it was the tree saying, 'ARE-YOU-ALL-RIGHT?'

I took away my hands. I knew that the owner of the voice would not mind my unsightly face. I knew I should've said, this being a stranger, 'Thank you. Nothing is wrong.'

But I felt free to say: 'Yes. Something is wrong. I've spilt a box of beads. I'm blind. I can't do my work without I find every one.'

'I thought you were blind,' said Gordon. 'I've been watching you. Now let me see — beads, beads, ah — yap! Dozens of the little devils.'

I heard them dropping into the box.

It was hard to believe my luck. 'I thank you from the depths of my heart,' I said. I spoke in my deepest voice.

For the first time I heard Gordon laugh. I never heard anyone laugh like that before — warm. Comforting.

'You are a honey,' said Gordon. 'There! Every bead back in the box ma'm — what happens now?'

'Now?' I asked.

'Yes. What do you do with the beads?' He was picking them up, letting them rain back — pak, pak, pak — into the box.

'Grade and thread them on these.' I showed him the threads.

'Does it take long? How clever you are. Do you ever make mistakes?'

'Clever! Even a fool couldn't make a mistake.'

'So easy even a blind person can do it, huh?'

The way Gordon said 'blind' made it sound like something not to be hidden away.

'Yes,' I said. I laughed, and I liked the sound of my laugh, so I laughed again.

'Do you come here often?' he asked. 'I come here every day. I've never seen you before.'

'Because I've come for the first time today. That's why you've never seen me.' Then I asked him, 'Why do you come here every day? Sir,' I added politely.

'I work at night. I work for a newspaper. Usually I don't come to the park until much later. Something got into me this morning. Go to the park early, this 'thing' said. I was quite angry — having to get up earlier, rushing down to the park. Now I know that I came because you would need me to find your beads. Wonderful, isn't it, the way things work out!'

It took him a long time to say all that because he spoke each word clear; each word had a beginning and an end, not like Rose-ann, Ole Pa and me. We speak so fast each word trips over the next.

'And,' he went on speaking, 'you must not call me Sir. My name is Gordon Ralfe — I'm a man just six feet tall, aged thirty — I served in the Navy. I—'

'Excuse me, Mr Ralfe,' I interrupted. 'I'm not used to meeting new people. I am sure pleased to meet you. You are telling me so much all at once. May I ask how much taller than me six feet is?'

'How tall *are* you? Hmmm! I should say you would be five feet, yes, and perhaps four inches, so I must be just about eight inches taller than you. Next question, please?'

No one had ever allowed me the freedom

of asking questions—allowed me, *asked* me to ask! I thought deeply. The thing about my face being unsightly was uppermost, so I asked:

'Would you kindly tell me. Is my face— I know I have a loused-up face—I know that, Mr Ralfe, but is it—does it make you...?' I wished I had not asked about myself. He, I supposed, was disappointed that my question was not about him, for he did not seem to want to answer me. Then he said:

'Loused up? Your face! Loused up? If you wore dark glasses—if you did—you'd be one of the prettiest girls in the world. I know this because I've been all over the world.'

'All over the world?' I gasped. I couldn't believe it.

Gordon laughed again. 'I see one has to be careful talking to you. Not exactly all over the world, but places, I've been places, have surely seen, as I was saying when so rudely interrupted'—I knew he was smiling—'a mighty lot of pretty girls. You, with dark glasses, would be one of them.'

from *A Patch of Blue* by Elizabeth Kata

Reading for Meaning

1 How do the 'million small sounds' affect Selina?

2 How does Selina feel after she discovers the leaf?

3 As Selina counts the scallops on the leaf she finds that there are 'eleven, and one ungrown, little scallop'. What does this incident reveal to you about Selina?

4 'I knew I should be doing beads.' Why isn't she?

5 'I sat and cried.' Selina cries because she has knocked over a box of beads, but what is the deeper reason for her tears?

6 Explain why Gordon's voice seems to 'come from all about me'.

7 How does Selina feel when Gordon laughs?

8 How does she feel when Gordon first speaks of her blindness?

9 What conclusion does Gordon draw about the reason he felt he had to come early to the park on this day?

10 How does Gordon's way of speaking differ from Selina's?

11 Why does Gordon not want her to call him 'Sir'?

12 How does Gordon's invitation to ask more questions affect Selina?

13 Why does Selina ask about her face?

14 How is Selina able to tell he is smiling during his last speech?

15 What do you learn about the character of Gordon from this passage? Give some evidence.

16 What feelings does this passage arouse in you? Why?

Fight in the Gym

In this tough inner-city school, the attitude of a new teacher, Mr Bell, creates problems, especially with one class member.

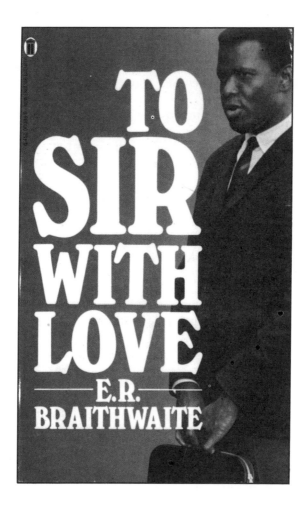

The least athletic member of the class was Richard Buckley, a short, fat boy, amiable and rather dim, who could read and write after a fashion, and could never be provoked to any semblance of anger or heat. He was pleasant and jolly and a favourite with the others, who, though they themselves chivvied him unmercifully, were ever ready in his defence against outsiders.

Buckley was no good at PT or games; he just was not built for such pursuits. Yet, such is the perversity of human nature, he strenuously resisted any efforts to leave him out or overlook him when games were being arranged. His attempts at accomplishing such simple gymnastic performances as the 'forward roll' and 'star jump' reduced the rest of the PT class to helpless hilarity, but he persisted with a singleness of purpose which, though unproductive, was nothing short of heroic.

Buckley was Bell's special whipping boy.

Fully aware of the lad's physical limitations, he would encourage him to try other and more difficult exercises, with apparently the sole purpose of obtaining some amusement from the pitiably ridiculous results. Sometimes the rest of the class would protest; and then Bell would turn on them the full flood of his invective. The boys mentioned this in their 'Weekly Review', and Mr Florian decided to discuss it at a Staff Meeting.

'The boys seem to be a bit bothered by remarks you make to them during PT, Mr Bell.'

'To which remarks do you refer, Mr Florian?' Bell never used the term 'Sir', seeming to think it 'infra dig'. Even when he granted him the 'Mr Florian' he gave to this form of address the suggestion of a sneer.

'From their review it would seem that you are unnecessarily critical of their persons.'

'Do you mean their smell?'

'Well, yes, that and the state of their clothing.'

'I've advised them to wash.'

'These are the words which appear in one review.' The Headmaster produced a notebook, Fernman's, and read: '"Some of you stink like old garbage."'

His tone was cool, detached, judicial.

'I was referring to their feet. Many of them never seem to wash their feet, and when they take their shoes off the stink is dreadful.'

'Many of them live in homes where there are very few facilities for washing, Mr Bell.'

'Surely enough water is available for washing their feet if they really wanted to.'

'Then they'd put on the same smelly socks and shoes to which you also object.'

'I've got to be in contact with them and it isn't very pleasant.'

'Have you ever lived in this area, Mr Bell?'

'No fear.'

'Then you know nothing about the conditions prevailing. The water you so casually speak of is often to be found in the walls and on the floors than in the convenient wash basin or bath to which you are accustomed. I've visited homes of some of

these children where water for a family in an upstairs flat had to be fetched by bucket or pail from the single back-yard tap which served five or six families. You may see, therefore, that so elementary a function as washing the feet might present many difficulties.'

Bell was silent at this.

'I've no wish to interfere, or tell you how to do your work; you're an experienced teacher and know more about PT than I'll ever do,' — the Old Man was again patient, encouraging — 'but try to be a little more understanding about their difficulties.' He then turned to other matters, but it was clear that Bell was considerably put out by the rebuke.

Matters came to a head that Monday afternoon. I was not present in the gym, but was able to reconstruct the sequence of events with reasonable accuracy from the boys' reports and Bell's subsequent admissions.

During the PT session he had been putting them through their paces in the 'astride vault' over the buck, all except Buckley, who was somewhat under the weather and wisely stood down from attempting the rather difficult jump, but without reference to or permission from Bell, who was not long in discovering the absence of his favourite diversion.

'Buckley,' he roared.

'Yes, Sir.'

'Come on, boy, I'm waiting.' He was standing in his usual position beside the buck in readiness to arrest the fall of any lad who might be thrown off balance by an awkward approach or incorrect execution of the movement. But the boy did not move, and the master stared at him amazed and angry at this unexpected show of defiance by the one generally considered to be the most timid and tractable in the whole class.

'Fatty can't do it, Sir, it's too high for him.' Denham interposed.

'Shut up, Denham,' Bell roared. 'If I want your opinion I will ask for it.' He left his station by the buck and walked to where Buckley was standing. The boy watched his threatening approach, fear apparent in his eyes.

'Well, Buckley,' Bell towered over the unhappy youth, 'are you going to do as you're told?'

'Yes, Sir.' Buckley's capitulation was as sudden as his refusal.

The others stopped to watch as he stood looking at the buck, licking his lips nervously while waiting for the instructor to resume his position. It may have been fear or determination or a combination of both, but Buckley launched himself at the buck in furious assault, and in spite of Bell's restraining arms, boy and buck crashed on the floor with a sickening sound as one leg of the buck snapped off with the sound of a pistol shot. The class stood in shocked silence watching Buckley, who remained as he fell, inert and pale; then they rushed to his assistance. All except Potter; big, good-natured Potter seemed to have lost his reason. He snatched up the broken metal-bound leg and advanced on Bell, screaming:

'You bloody bastard, you f—ing bloody bastard.'

'Put that thing down, Potter, don't be a fool,' Bell spluttered, backing away from the hysterical boy.

'You made him do it; he didn't want to and you made him,' Potter yelled.

'Don't be a fool, Potter, put it down,' Bell appealed.

'I'll do you in, you bloody murderer.' Bell was big, but in his anger Potter seemed bigger, his improvised club a fearsome extension of his thick forearm.

That was where I rushed in. Tich Jackson, frightened by the sight of Buckley, limp and white on the floor, and the enraged Potter, slobbering at the instructor in murderous fury, had dashed upstairs to my classroom shouting: 'Sir, quick, they're fighting in the gym.' I followed his disappearing figure in time to see Bell backed against a wall, with Potter advancing on him.

'Hold it, Potter,' I called. He turned at the sound of my voice and I quickly placed myself between them. 'Let's have that, Potter.' I held out my hand towards the boy, but he stared past me at Bell, whimpering in his emotion. Anger had completely taken hold of him, and he looked very dangerous.

'Come on, Potter,' I repeated, 'hand it

over and go lend a hand with Buckley.'

He turned to look towards his prostrate friend and I quickly moved up to him and seized the improvised club; he released it to me without any resistance and went back to join the group around Buckley. Bell then walked away and out of the room, and I went up to the boys. Denham rose and faced me, his face white with rage.

'Potts should have done the bastard like he did Fatty, just 'cos he wouldn't do the bloody jump.'

I let that pass; they were angry and at such times quickly reverted to the old things, the words, the discourtesies. I stooped down beside Buckley, who was now sitting weakly on the floor, supported by Sapiano and Seales, and smiling up at them as if ashamed of himself for having been the cause of so much fuss.

'How do you feel, old man?' I enquired.

'Cor, Sir,' he cried, smiling, 'me tum does hurt.'

'He fell on to the buck. You should have seen 'im, Sir.'

'Gosh, you should've heard the noise when the leg smashed.'

'Mr Bell couldn't catch Fatty, Sir, you should've seen him.'

Most of them were trying to talk all at once, eager to give me all the details.

from *To Sir with Love* by E.R. Braithwaite

Reading for Meaning

1 How does the class treat Buckley?

2 Even though Buckley is the least athletic person in the class, he always has a go at whatever is asked. What quality of character does this show?

3 Why does Bell encourage Buckley to try difficult gymnastic exercises?

4 What 'system' enables Mr Florian (the Headmaster) to obtain information on how the students feel about their teachers.

5 What is noticeable about the way Mr Bell addresses the Headmaster?

6 What tone does the Headmaster use when he confronts Bell with the student's complaints?

7 Having reprimanded Bell, the Headmaster attempts to encourage him. How does Bell take all of this?

8 Why on this particular Monday afternoon, does Buckley not attempt the 'astride vault'?

9 Why is Bell surprised when Buckley does not obey him at first?

10 Why do you think Denham speaks up on Buckley's behalf?

11 How does Buckley feel when Bell comes over to him?

12 Why does Buckley run at the buck in 'furious assault'?

13 How does the class react after Buckley's fall?

14 What emotion controls Potter, and what effect does it have on him?

15 How does the teacher telling the story manage to distract Potter?

16 Why does the teacher ignore the swear words?

17 What does this passage show about the character of Bell?

18 What does this passage show about the loyalties the class members feel for each other?

The Mistake

A German lad, Günther, discovers just how serious the leaders of the Hitler Youth Movement are when he makes the mistake of talking out of turn. This incident occurred in 1937.

The sky was a uniform grey. It had been drizzling for the last half-hour. Small puddles were beginning to form, and the ground was sodden beneath our feet.

Our uniforms soaked up the rain. We were chilly. Together with two other *Fähnleins*, we stood in an open square and listened to the speech of our *Oberjungstammführer*.

Our region's youth leader talked and talked and talked. He spoke of the *Führer*, the ordinary corporal of World War I, of the German armed forces and the work of the *Führer*. He spoke about us members of the *Jungvolk* and our duty to mature into first-class soldiers.

We had stopped listening. The boys in the first rank were absent-mindedly staring at the overcast sky. In the ranks toward the rear, boys were playing with their fingers or cleaning out their pockets. The restiveness spread through the audience.

The *Oberjungstammführer* seemed to feel the growing discomfort. His eyes wandered from right to left; he was trying to discover who was causing the disturbance.

'You know,' Günther whispered, nudging Heinz in his side, 'he wants to turn us all into soldiers.'

Heinz nodded.

The speaker had stopped speaking.

No one moved. Everyone was alert, looked across at our corner if they could. All were waiting.

'Who spoke just now?' snarled the youth leader.

Silence.

Günther and Heinz pretended to look around, then looked innocently at the official. Those of us sitting next to them tried to look as unconcerned as possible.

'Who was it who talked?' the voice asked again. The leader was approaching our platoon.

Those who were uninvolved followed what was happening as if it was a play.

We were beginning to feel more uncomfortable.

The *Oberjungstammführer* turned red.

'This platoon only,' he said, pointing at us. 'At attention!'

Our heels cracked together as one. All tried to stand perfectly: hands pressed flat against trouser seams, elbows angled slightly forward, chests out, heads straight, eyes fixed. We suspected everything mattered now.

'I want to know which of you has been babbling?' the party official demanded. 'Step forward, whoever it is!'

The platoon stood motionless; not a single eyelid twitched.

'I will count until three and the blabbermouth will speak up! One—two—three! Well? So you don't want to? Platoon leader!'

With five firm steps Heinz had stepped to the front. In perfect form, he stopped in front of the official.

'Who in your unit has blabbed?'

Heinz stood even straighter. 'I do not know, sir. I heard nothing!'

His superior's neck began to swell. His head turned even redder. He gestured wildly. 'What? You cover for the dirty swine in your platoon! And you want to be a leader!' His voice broke. 'You are nothing, nothing at all!' he screeched. 'I will—'

'I was the one who spoke, sir!' said Günther, lifting his arm.

The *Oberjungstammführer* broke off, disconcerted. He looked at Heinz and Günther in turn. 'We will talk later!' he shouted at Heinz. 'Fall into line!'

Heinz walked, pale and serious, back to his position.

All at once the leader's voice turned very soft. Smiling kindly, he said to Günther, 'Step forward!' Günther pushed his way out of the ranks backward, ran around the unit, and positioned himself three steps in front of the *Oberjungstammführer*.

'So it was you, eh?' said the leader in a near-whisper.

We were straining to hear every word, no longer felt the cold and the dampness.

What did you say?' the official asked Günther.

Günther said nothing.

The official moved closer to him. 'What did you say?'

Günther pressed his lips together.

'Answer!' roared the *Oberjungstammführer* in a voice so loud we recoiled in fear.

But Günther did not answer.

Resolutely the leader turned around. Facing us all, he declared: 'I will now give you a taste of how the German *Wehrmacht* handles such deceitful and obstinate people, how they make them break.' He raised his voice. 'The following orders are meant only for this one!' he said, pointing at Günther.

'Lie down!'

Günther threw himself to the ground.

'Up! Quick-march!'

Günther picked himself up and ran forward.

In front of a large puddle: 'Lie down!'

Günther let himself fall beside the puddle.

'What? You refuse to execute orders? Up!' Günther leapt up. His pants and tunic showed muddy patches.

'Two steps to the right!'

Günther followed the order. Now he stood exactly in front of the puddle.

'Down!'

The water splashed high.

'Slide!'

Günther pushed himself on his stomach through the slimy water.

'Turn about!'

In the middle of the puddle, at its deepest spot, Günther turned around and, still on his stomach, slid to the edge.

'Up! Quick-march!'

Dripping, soiled from face to shoes, Günther ran through the square. Mud flew from his clothes as he ran.

'Attention!'

Facing the *Oberjungstammführer*, Günther stood to attention.

'Knees, bend!'

Arms held out in front of him, Günther sank into the crouch.

'Hop!'

In the crouch, Günther hopped across the empty square. When he splashed through puddles, the water sprayed his face. A dark liquid dribbled from his hair. He was swaying as he moved.

'Attention!'

Again Günther pulled himself upright.

'About face!'

Günther turned to face us.

'Look at the dirty pig!' jeered the *Oberjungstammführer*.

'Take cover!'

Without looking around, Günther dropped down and pressed his face into the sludgy ground.

'Attention!'

Günther got up.

The *Oberjungstammführer* was grinning. 'Five steps forward!'

Günther obeyed. The last step brought

him once more to the edge of the large puddle.

'I must spare my voice. You will observe my thumb signs and follow them. This means "Lie down!" With closed fist the official pointed his stretched-out thumb downward. 'And this means "Up!"' He pointed toward the sky. 'Let's go!'

The thumb pointed down. Günther flung himself into the water.

The thumb was raised. Günther shot up.
Thumb down.
The water spurted high.
Thumb up.
The water streamed back into the puddle.
Down!
Up!
Down!
Up!
And we watched at attention.

from *I Was There* by Hans Peter Richter

Reading for Meaning

1 From your reading of this passage, what does *Oberjungstammführer* mean?

2 How long had it been raining prior to this incident?

3 Why do the boys gradually stop listening?

4 Identify two actions that show the growing restlessness of the boys?

5 Why does the *Oberjungstammführer* move his eyes from right to left across the group?

6 How does Günther get Heinz's attention?

7 Why does the speaker stop speaking?

8 What do Günther and Heinz do to pretend they are innocent?

9 What is the first change in the *Oberjungstammführer's* appearance that shows his increasing anger?

10 Why does everyone in the platoon try 'to stand perfectly'?

11 Why does Günther 'confess'?

12 What was the first effect that the 'confession' had on the *Oberjungstammführer*?

13 The *Oberjungstammführer's* voice turns very soft and he smiles. What do you think this indicates?

14 Why do the others no longer feel the cold or dampness?

15 What is the purpose behind the *Oberjungstammführer's* orders to Günther?

16 How do we know that Günther has considerable strength and courage?

17 What emotions do you think the other platoon members have as the officer tries to humiliate Günther?

18 What does this passage show about the character of the *Oberjungstammführer*?

POETRY

Advice to a Teenage Daughter

You have found a new war-game
called Love.
Here on your dressing-table
stand arrayed
brave ranks of lipsticks
brandishing
swords of cherry pink and flame.
Behold the miniature armies
of little jars,
packed with the scented
dynamite of flowers.
See the dreaded tweezers;
tiny pots
of manufactured moonlight,
stick-on-stars.
Beware my sweet;
conquest may seem easy
but you can't compete with football,
motor-cycles, cars,
cricket, computer-games,
or a plate of chips.

Isobel Thrilling

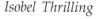

Questions

1 Why does the poet describe love as a 'war-game'?

2 'brave ranks of lipsticks'. Why is this an appropriate way of describing the lipsticks?

3 'packed with the scented/dynamite of flowers'. Why is 'dynamite' an unexpected word here? Is it a suitable word in this poem?

4 Why do you think the poet describes the tweezers as 'dreaded'?

5 What is the poet referring to when she writes of 'tiny pots/of manufactured moonlight,/stick-on-stars'?

6 What word in the poem first suggests a warning is being issued?

7 In the last four lines of the poem, which item in the list seems most shocking? Why?

8 In your own words, what is the 'advice to a teenage daughter'?

9 How would you describe the overall mood of this poem?

10 What do you see as the strengths of this poem?

Film Star

He was a rich pin-up boy—Mercedes, plane, etc.
His smile, like the winter sun, was bright,
But didn't warm you. One side of his face
Was handsome—the side that caught the light
   In front of the cameras.

And all the girls adored him.

His days were a whirlwind of wonders: he fell off
Mountains, jumped out of the sky, fought
With twenty at a time, went down with his ship
Smiling—it was all the bravest sport—
   In front of the cameras.

And all the girls adored him.

But was the smile his own? Yes, but never
The danger. That burning driver in the prairie race
Was another man. Where was the rich pin-up boy then?
Reading his newspaper in a safer place—
   Behind the cameras.

And all the girls adored him.

Weeks later, on his way to the studio, he crashed
His Mercedes, cut his face (the handsome side). O cruel blow!
Fifteen days he lay on his back, a little boy
Frightened of the dark, crying for mother. He wouldn't go
   In front of the cameras.

And all the girls forgot him.

Ian Serraillier

Guitarman

I play my Guild guitar like a sub-machine gun,
spraying out music while these fingers make their runs
across the hopscotch of a fretboard
in steps and turns,
a sword of a plectrum strokes the strings
and booming from the box's crater
a lava of sound oozes out.

I'm a guitarman,
I'm a magnetic island
which the strobe lights cling to.
And all I do is let loose from silence
a running stampede of notes
as my hair swings
with its strands of wire.
I feel tense in a punishing duel
between myself and the audience.
I lift my guitar like a railway signal,
unmoved; except my tremulous fingers,
always aiming steady as I fire.

Gordon Phillips

Questions

1 What brand of guitar does this guitarist play?

2 In the first line of the poem, to what kind of person does the guitarist seem to be comparing himself?

3 'a sword of a plectrum'. Why does the word 'sword' seem appropriate here?

4 '...booming from the box's crater/a lava of sound oozes out'. What is the emerging sound being compared to here?

5 Why is he able to describe himself as a 'magnetic island'?

6 'a running stampede of notes'. What does this line seem to suggest about the technical skill of the guitarist? Explain your answer.

7 How does the guitarist seem to think of the audience?

8 What kind of music do you think this guitarist plays? Why?

9 How would you imagine this guitarist's performance would appear to the audience? Why?

10 What do you see as the strengths of this poem?

My Gran

her forehead's finely crackled
like an old china cup
lips neatly pleated
and pin-tucked
blue eyes
like bright beads
peep out beneath white brows
her snowy hair
fits smoothly as a cap

living more in yesterday
she watches Time fly by
the present
is a minefield she mistrusts
her territory has slowly shrunk
to one small battered base
a fox-hole
where she sits and waits
a sanctuary of dreams.

Joan Poulson

Tich Miller

Tich Miller wore glasses
with elastoplast-pink frames
and had one foot three sizes larger than the other.

When they picked teams for outdoor games
she and I were always the last two
left standing by the wire-mesh fence.

We avoided one another's eyes,
stooping, perhaps, to re-tie a shoelace,
or affecting interest in the flight

of some fortunate bird, and pretended
not to hear the urgent conference:
'Have Tubby!' 'No, no, have Tich!'

Usually they chose me, the lesser dud,
and she lolloped, unselected,
to the back of the other team.

At eleven we went to different schools.
In time I learned to get my own back,
sneering at hockey-players who couldn't spell.

Tich died when she was twelve.

Wendy Cope

Questions

1 What does the name 'Tich' suggest about this girl's appearance?

2 Why do you think the poet recalls Tich Miller's glasses before anything else?

3 What experience did the poet and Tich share?

4 What are two 'tactics' the poet and Tich used so that they seemed not to care too much about being chosen on a team?

5 '...the flight/of some fortunate bird'. Why, in this poem, does the word 'fortunate' seem to have special meaning?

6 How did the poet, in time, learn to overcome her feelings of inferiority?

7 Why is the last line on its own? What effect does it have on the reader?

8 What does this poem seem to illustrate about how children behave to those who are different?

9 What emotions does this poem arouse in you?

10 'How would you describe the theme, or message, of this poem?

Remember Me?

Remember me?
I am the boy who sought friendship;
The boy you turned away.
I the boy who asked you
If I too might play.
I the face at the window
When your party was inside,
I the lonely figure
That walked away and cried.
I the one who hung around
A punchbag for your games.
Someone you could kick and beat,
Someone to call names.
But how strange is the change
After time has hurried by,
Four years have passed since then
Now I'm not so quick to cry.
I'm bigger and I'm stronger,
I've grown a foot in height,
Suddenly I'M popular
And YOU'RE left out the light.
I could, if I wanted,
Be so unkind to you.
I would only have to say
And the other boys would do.
But the memory of my pain
Holds back the revenge I'D planned
And instead, I feel much stronger
By offering you my hand.

Ray Mather

WRITING

VARYING SENTENCE LENGTH

The length of sentences serves as a useful tool to help the writer create an atmosphere or mood. Each of the passages in this section illustrates a different aspect of the importance of sentence length.

Writers often vary the length of their sentences in order to avoid monotony. However, sometimes they deliberately use sentences of similar length in order to *create* a mood of monotony. Read the following passage and notice how, in the first paragraph, all the sentences are of medium length. This helps us to become aware of how the night of waiting dragged on. But then a change occurs in the second paragraph. Notice that the writer has used short sentences to create an atmosphere of sudden tension. For example: 'The barn door had swung open. The pony had gone.' Longer sentences at this point would have worked against this atmosphere of tension.

THE DYING PONY

Billy Buck stood up from the box and surrendered the cotton swab. The pony still lay on his side and the wound in his throat bellowed in and out. When Jody saw how dry and dead the hair looked, he knew at last that there was no hope for the pony. He had seen the dead hair before on dogs and on cows, and it was a sure sign. He sat heavily on the box and let down the barrier of the box stall. For a long time he kept his eyes on the moving wound, and at last he dozed, and the afternoon passed quickly. Just before dark his mother brought a deep dish of stew and left it for him and went away. Jody ate a little of it, and when it was dark he set the lantern on the floor by the pony's head so he could watch the wound and keep it open. And he dozed again until the night chill awakened him. The wind was blowing fiercely, bringing the north cold with it. Jody brought a blanket from his bed in the hay and wrapped himself in it. Gabilan's breathing was quiet at last; the hole in his throat moved gently. The owls flew through the hayloft, shrieking and looking for mice. Jody put his hands down on his head and slept. In his sleep he was aware that the wind had increased. He heard it slamming about the barn.

It was daylight when he awakened. The barn door had swung open. The pony was gone. He sprang up and ran out into the morning light.

from The Red Pony by John Steinbeck

In the next passage a short sentence creates tension at the beginning of the description. Notice, also, that at the end of the passage we are given the outcome of the fight in a long sentence that keeps adding one piece of description to another.

SHOWDOWN

Wilson had it now. You could see him grasp the meaning. This quiet man was pushing him just as he had pushed Ernie Wright. As he measured Shane, it was not to his liking. Something that was not fear but a kind of wondering and baffled reluctance showed in his face. And then there was no escape, for that gentle voice was pegging him to the immediate and implacable moment.

'I'm waiting, Wilson. Do I have to crowd you into slapping leather?'

Time stopped and there was nothing in all the world but two men looking into eternity in each other's eyes. And the room rocked in the sudden blur of action indistinct in its incredible swiftness and the roar of their guns was a single sustained blast. And Shane stood, solid on his feet as a rooted oak, and Wilson swayed, his right arm hanging useless, blood beginning to show in a small stream from under the sleeve over the hand, the gun slipping from the numbing fingers.

from *Shane* by Jack Schaefer

In the following passage the writer uses long, rambling sentences to create a light-hearted mood of day-dreaming about a memory from the past. Towards the end of the passage some short sentences are used as he is about to reveal what was written on the piece of paper.

MESSAGE

I was walking, one afternoon in August, along a river-bank, thinking the same thoughts that I always think when I walk along a river-bank in August. As I was walking, I was thinking—now it is August and I am walking along a river-bank. I do not think I was thinking of anything else. I should have been thinking of what I should have been doing, but I was thinking only of what I was doing then and it was all right: it was good, and ordinary, and slow, and idle, and old, and sure, and what I was doing I could have been doing a thousand years before, had I been alive then...

And I was walking and thinking that I was walking, and for August it was not such a cold day. And then I saw, drifting along the water, a piece of paper, and I thought: Something wonderful may be written on this paper. I was alone on the gooseberry earth, or alone for two green miles, and a message drifted towards me on that tabby-coloured water that ran through the middle of the cow-patched, mooing fields. It was a message from multitudinous nowhere to my solitary self. I put out my stick and caught the piece of paper and held it close to the river-bank. It was a page torn from a very old periodical. That I could see. I leant over and read, through water, the message on the rippling page. I made out, with difficulty, only one sentence: it commemorated the fact that, over a hundred years ago, a man in Worcester had, for a bet, eaten, at one sitting, fifty-two pounds of plums.

from *Quite Early One Morning* by Dylan Thomas

In the final passage, which is a detailed description of an old sailor, long, rhythmic sentences appear to be the most appropriate.

OLD SEA-DOG

I remember him as if it were yesterday, as he came plodding to the inn door, his sea-chest following behind him in a hand-barrow; a tall, strong, heavy, nut-brown man; his tarry pigtail falling over the shoulders of his soiled blue coat; his hands ragged and scarred, with black, broken nails; and the sabre cut across one cheek, a dirty, livid white. I remember him looking round the cove and whistling to himself as he did so, and then breaking out in that old sea-song that he sang so often afterwards:

'Fifteen men on the dead man's chest —
Yo-ho-ho, and a bottle of rum!'

in the high old tottering voice that seemed to have been tuned and broken at the capstan bars. Then he rapped on the door with a bit of stick like a handspike that he carried, and when my father appeared, called roughly for a glass of rum. This, when it was brought to him, he drank slowly, like a connoisseur, lingering on the taste, and still looking about him at the cliffs and up at our signboard.

from *Treasure Island* by Robert Louis Stevenson

VARYING THE LENGTH OF YOUR SENTENCES

Choose several of the following topics and write two or three paragraphs on each. Pay attention to the length of your sentences as a means of helping to create an appropriate atmosphere.

- The mysterious phone call
- Speech Day seemed to go on forever
- My first attempt at being a disc jockey
- A great sporting achievement
- Breaking up
- An incident illustrating prejudice
- My safe place
- Riot at school
- Visitor from outer space
- Death of a pet
- Water-bomb fight
- Rock concert crowds
- Fight!
- Lonely old lady
- Christmas morning at our place
- Why did it have to happen to me?
- I have never been so sick

12.4.09. — Cow

LANGUAGE

WORD ORIGINS

Prefixes

A prefix is a word-part used at the beginning of a word to change the meaning, or to create a new word. The prefixes in these examples are in heavy type.

- **dis**enchantment
- **pro**ject
- **trans**mit

Select one prefix from the box to add to the word or word-parts in each of the eight groups below — that is, use one prefix per group. The meaning of each prefix is given in brackets in the box.

auto (self)	**trans** (across)	**inter** (between)	**pro** (forward)
sub (below)	**photo** (light)	**circum** (around)	**ex** (out of)

1 .pro posal   2 circum navigate
   .pro jection inter   circum ference
   pro . ceed ex   circum stances
   pro. nounce   circum scribe

3 photo graph
  photo synthesis
  photo meter
  photo genic

4 inter pretation
  inter vene
  inter cept
  inter mediate

5 auto matic
  auto mobile
  auto graph
  auto biography

6 sub terranean
  sub marine
  sub standard
  sub ject

7 ex pands
  ex ile
  ex cavation
  ex claim

8 trans plant
  trans port
  trans fusion
  trans lation

Creating Words

Using the Latin word in heavy type, complete each of the following sentences correctly. The first one has been done to help you.

1 The members of the advance party began to formulate their plans. **forma** (shape)

2 An audible cry for help came from the ditch. **audio** (I hear)

3 We are planning a family holiday overseas this year. **familia** (people of the household)

4 Andrews was nominated to be the leader of the group. **nomen** (name)

5 Kay Cottee's solo journey around the world is one of the noted ...sporting achievements of recent times. **nota** (mark)

6 The new relay station enabled the television signal to be transmitted much more clearly. **mitto** (I send)

7 He was given 'out', but it was a dubious decision. **dubito** (I am in two minds)

8 This is the smallest, most portable computer currently available. **porto** (I carry)

9 The location of the treasure was clearly marked on the map. **locus** (place)

10 The driver pressed his foot hard on the accelerater and sped past the truck. **celer** (swift)

11 The audience burst into applause after the orchestra's brilliant performance. **applaudo** (I clap)

12 When the marriage had reached the point of disaster, there seemed to be no alternative to getting a divorce. **divorto** (I turn away)

Latin Links

For each of the following clues find an English word that is linked to the Latin word shown in heavy type at the head of the group. The first one has been done for you.

1 navis (a ship, boat)
  a a country's ocean-going fighting force ..navy..
  b to sail a boat right around navigate
  c able to be sailed through safely navigable
  d to chart a course through water naugation

2 aqua (water)
  a a water tank for live fish and plants aquarium
  b the zodiac sign of the water-carrier aquarius
  c a bluish-green colour like seawater aqua marine
  d having to do with water aquebus

3 herba (grass, plant)
  a a plant whose leaves are used for medicine or flavour herbs
  b a chemical spray used to kill plants herbicide
  c to do with herbs herbac
  d grass-eating (animal) herbivors

Number Origins

Each of the prefixes in the box has its numerical meaning in brackets alongside. Use the prefixes to create English words for each of the meanings listed below.

unus (one)	**bi** (two)	**tri** (three)	**quad** (four)
quin (five)	**octo** (eight)	**decem** (ten)	**centum** (one hundred)

1 a score of one hundred runs   century

2 a sea creature with eight arms   octopus

3 a four-sided geometric figure   quadrilateral

4 a stand with three legs   tripod

5 to cut into two   bisect

6 a state of oneness   union

7 a one-hundred-year celebration   centenary

8 field-glasses with two lenses   binocular

9 a three-sided geometric figure   triangle...

10 an eight-sided geometric figure   octogan..

11 to bring together into one   unite....

12 a four-sided playing area in a school   quadtrangle

13 a two-wheeled pedal vehicle   bicycle.

14 five babies born at the same time   quadluplets

15 Roman soldier commanding one hundred men   centurion.

16 type of currency based on ten   dime....

The Source of Words

Alligator

Roman soldiers and travellers became familiar with most of the big lizards of their world, and one of the biggest was approximately the size of the male upper arm, so 'lacertus' (arm) was commonly used to name this lizard. This word was then borrowed and adapted into the Spanish language and became 'lagarto'. Spanish explorers in the New World were surprised to find a reptile there so large that they called it *the* lizard, 'el lagarto'. This term was then used in the English language and gradually changed to the present-day 'alligator'.

1 What was the original Latin word for a big lizard and what did it mean?
2 Why was the Latin word for 'arm' used as the term for a large lizard? *It*
3 Why did Spanish explorers call the alligator 'el lagarto'?

Cold shoulder

To 'give someone the cold shoulder' means to treat them as unwelcome, or to refuse to treat them well. In medieval England, good manners required that people offer food to weary travellers, but not all such visitors were equally welcome. A priest, or someone important, might be entertained very well but a poor traveller would probably be given the most ordinary meal that took no effort to put together—a cold shoulder of mutton.

1 What is the meaning of 'to give someone the cold shoulder'?   *to ignore a person*
2 Why did people feed travellers in Medieval times? *it was good manners*
3 What meal would commonly be given to an unwelcome guest?
    an ordinary meal

GETTING IT RIGHT

PROBLEMS WITH NOUNS AND VERBS

Lend/loan

The words 'lend' and 'loan' are frequently confused in speech and writing. 'Lend' is an action word, a verb. 'Loan' is a naming word, a noun. For example:

- I **lend** my possessions.   (correct)
- I **loan** my possessions.   (incorrect)
- I gave him a **lend** of some money.   (incorrect)
- I gave him a **loan** of some money.   (correct)

Put the correct word ('lend' or 'loan') in the sentences below.

1 She gave him a . .loan. . of her bike.

2 'Did your friend .lend.. you her evening dress?'

3 '. .lend.. me that umbrella, please. It's raining!'

4 We frequently .lend.. our car to our neighbour.

5 The young boy asked for a . .loan. . of the skateboard.

Taught/learned

'Taught' is the verb to use when a person *gave* a lesson. 'Learned' is the verb to use when a person *received* a lesson. For example:

- I **learned** him some good lessons.   (incorrect)
- I **taught** him some good lessons.   (correct)
- I **learned** a lot of valuable lessons from him.   (correct)

Choose the correct verb (taught or learned) to complete each sentence below.

1 Mr Frazer .taught. me all I know about computers.

2 The new instructor . .taught.. the drivers well.

3 The new recruits ..learned.. how to care for their horses properly.

4 Few cashiers have . learned. how to work as accurately as Tim.

5 The old farmer . .taught..me how to ride a horse.

DRAMA

WHODUNIT?

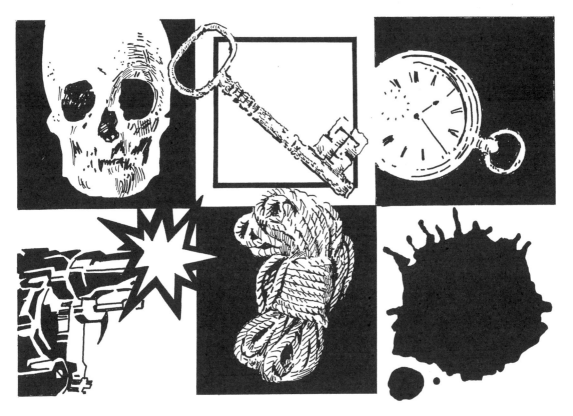

Over the years, people who produce plays, films and television shows have re-cognised the potential for viewer interest that is associated with courtroom scenes. What television shows can you recall that have featured courtroom battles?

Suspense can be developed in court-room scenes because cases take time to develop, new pieces of evidence can be revealed progressively, and emotions usually run high. Somehow we all seem to want to be able to solve the crime *before* the actual verdict is reached!

Your task is to develop a drama script that presents sufficient **evidence** or **clues** so that the jury can determine whether the accused is guilty or not guilty. But first, to help you get the idea, read the following script and see if you can find the evidence that enables you to solve the crime.

The Case of the Lost Diamond Brooch

CHARACTERS

Sheriff of the Court
Mrs Olivia Engels
Sarah Bronsky
Lucien Standish
Prosecuting Lawyer
Defence Lawyer

Sheriff   Ladies and Gentlemen, it is my task to bring you the details of the Case of the Lost Diamond Brooch, and to see that the court-room proceedings are undertaken in an orderly manner prior to your making a judgement about this case. Let me explain the background.

   Mr Lucien Standish is before you this day accused of stealing a valuable diamond brooch from Mrs Olivia Engels. Mr Standish will take the stand and counsel representing him will have him present evidence relevant to this case. Let me swear the defendant in.   *(To Lucien)*— Do you swear to tell the truth, so help you God?

Lucien   I do.

Defence Lawyer   Mr Standish, you are accused of having broken into the home of Mrs Engels and stealing this diamond brooch. Are you aware of the charges?

Lucien   Yes.

Defence Lawyer   Would you tell the jury how the brooch came into your possession.

Lucien   Well, I had been to the movies. I like to sit and watch the credits at the end, so I was one of the last to leave. As I was walking out of the theatre I noticed something shiny on the carpet. I picked it up and it was the brooch. I wasn't sure what to do with it so I took it with me.

Defence Lawyer   What happened then?

Lucien   A few days later I noticed an ad in the newspaper about a missing diamond brooch, offering a reward. So I took the brooch to the Engels' home and they recognised it as the lost brooch. I was about to get the reward when the police arrived and charged me with stealing the brooch.

Defence Lawyer   Do you have any evidence that you attended the film that night?

Lucien   Well, I was able to produce a ticket stub later for the police.

Defence Lawyer   Did you steal the brooch?

Lucien   No.

Defence Lawyer   No further questions.

Sheriff   The Prosecuting Lawyer will now have the opportunity to cross-examine Mr Standish.

Prosecuting Lawyer   Mr Standish, what is your occupation?

Lucien   I am presently unemployed.

Prosecuting Lawyer   What was the name of the film you saw that night?

Lucien   It was *Lost Empires* starring Andrew Lachlan.

Prosecuting Lawyer Who played the role of the schoolteacher in the film?
Lucien Evelyn Krantz.
Prosecuting Lawyer You claim that you found the brooch in the theatre. Don't you think it strange that no one saw it before you?
Lucien Perhaps. But those things happen.
Prosecuting Lawyer Why didn't you hand it in to the theatre manager or the police?
Lucien Well, I wasn't sure if it was of any value?
Prosecuting Lawyer No further questions.
Sheriff I now call a witness for the prosecution, Miss Sarah Bronsky.
(*To Sarah*) Do you swear to tell the truth, so help you God?
Sarah I do.
Prosecuting Lawyer Miss Bronsky, will you please tell the court what you were doing on the night these events took place.
Sarah Well, I board with the Engels. I had been doing some study in my upstairs room when I heard some strange noises downstairs. By the time I came down the house was quiet but, looking through the window, I saw a man running away. I had a good view of him under the street light.
Prosecuting Lawyer And can you identify this man?
Sarah Yes. It was Mr Standish.
Prosecuting Lawyer Did you know Mr Standish before this?
Sarah No.
Prosecuting Lawyer When did you next meet him?
Sarah I was there when he came to the house to claim the reward three days later. I recognised him and had Mr Engels call the police.
Prosecuting Lawyer No further questions.
Sheriff The Defence Lawyer may cross-examine.
Defence Lawyer Miss Bronsky, it was night when you looked out through the windows, was it not?
Sarah Yes.
Defence Lawyer Yet you claim that you saw the defendant sufficiently clearly to identify him. Did you see his face?

Sarah Well, not full on. He was running away.

Defence Lawyer So you cannot be sure if it was him?

Sarah I am reasonably sure. Even though it was night, I had a reasonably clear side-view at first.

Defence Lawyer But you cannot be *absolutely* sure?

Sarah No, I suppose not.

Defence Lawyer No further questions.

Sheriff I call another witness for the prosecution, Mrs Olivia Engels.
   (*To Olivia*) Do you swear to tell the truth, so help you God?

Olivia I do.

Prosecuting Lawyer Mrs Engels, when did you first notice that the brooch was missing?

Olivia When I came home from the movies on the night in question.

Prosecuting Lawyer Did you think you had lost it at the movies?

Olivia I did at first, but when I called them no jewellery had been handed in, and when we went down and searched the theatre we didn't find the brooch.

Prosecuting Lawyer When did you begin to suspect it might have been stolen?

Olivia Well, Sarah told us about the noises, and the man running away, but we didn't find anything else missing, so we didn't make too much of it. It wasn't until Mr Standish arrived to claim the reward and Sarah identified him that I really began to believe that I had left the brooch at home.

Prosecuting Lawyer You advertised in the paper?

Olivia Yes, I still believed it had been lost at the theatre so the next day I put an ad in the newspaper offering a reward and giving our post box number. It was two days later that Mr Standish arrived to claim the reward.

Prosecuting Lawyer No further questions.

Sheriff Your witness, Counsel for the Defence.

Defence Lawyer Mrs Engels, you believed you had worn the brooch to the theatre right up until Miss Bronsky identified my client as the intruder, is that right?

Olivia Well, yes, but I had begun to wonder. Neither my husband nor I could definitely remember me wearing it.

Defence Lawyer Mrs Engels, you offered a substantial reward for the brooch, did you not?

Olivia Yes, we were prepared to pay $1000.00.

Defence Lawyer Mrs Engels, I put it to you that you actually did wear the brooch to the theatre and that you and your husband and Miss Bronsky organised this whole farce to discredit my client, in order to save paying the reward. That is correct, is it not?

Olivia No, it is not!

Sheriff Members of the jury, although more evidence could be given, there is sufficient here for your verdict. Discuss, and then consider your verdict. Is Mr Standish guilty?

At this point a secret ballot vote should be taken by passing out slips of paper so that each class member can record either 'guilty' or 'not guilty'. Class members can then be invited to argue their case for or against before a decision is reached. (The solution is on page 288)

Now that you have the idea, proceed with the following steps:

1 Divide the class into small groups of five or six students. Each group chooses one of the following cases.

2 Develop your case into a drama script that is centred on a court-room scene and that contains enough evidence or clues for a verdict to be reached.

3 Present your drama to the class.

4 The class then becomes the jury and should vote, discuss and reach a verdict in the same way as for 'The Case of the Lost Diamond Brooch'.

CASES

1 The Case of the Murdered Millionaire
Sir Horace Grant was a sick man at the time of his death, but it has now been established that he was poisoned in his last meal. Characters could include his wife, from whom he was separated, two or three children, a nurse and a servant.

2 The Case of the Burnt-out Car
An expensive imported car belonging to a businessman, Stan Brucksworth, was mysteriously burnt-out. Mr Brucksworth has two business competitors, one of whom had threatened to get even with him after Mr Brucksworth had beaten him on a deal. It has been reported that Mr Brucksworth was in financial trouble, and the insurance company suspects that the car may have been deliberately burned to collect the insurance money.

3 The Case of the Dumped Chemicals
Toxic wastes have been found seeping from an illegal land dump into a nearby creek. The chemicals involved are used by three different companies in the area but each denies responsibility. Neighbours report that unmarked trucks came at night to dump the chemicals so it is unclear who is responsible.

4 The Case of the Wrecked Letter Box
The Fabian family has had their letter box vandalised. Sue Fabian's ex-boyfriend, Gus Benham, is a prime suspect. He is known to have made threats to pay back Mr Fabian after Mr Fabian forced Sue to break up with him. However, Gus claims he has an unshakeable alibi.

5 The Case of the Stolen Video
An alert policeman who had just booked Alex Stanwell for speeding noticed a video recorder on the back seat of the car. On checking out its number, he found that it had been stolen. Mr Stanwell claimed that he had bought it from a man whom he had met at the pub. The police believe Mr Stanwell was the thief.

8

CREATURES OF
THE WILD

NOVELS

Hawk

Some of the excitement of training a creature of the wild is captured in the following passage. Note that a 'lure' is used to exercise the hawk. It is a long cord with meat and a weight tied to the end. As it is swung around, the hawk swoops for the meat.

The hawk was waiting for him. As he unlocked the door she screamed and pressed her face to the bars. He selected the largest piece of beef, then, holding it firmly between finger and thumb with most of it concealed in his palm, he eased the door open and shoved his glove through the space. The hawk jumped on to his glove and attacked the meat. Billy swiftly followed his fist into the hut, secured the door behind him, and while the hawk was tearing at the fringe of beef, he attached her swivel and leash.

As soon as they got outside she looked up and tensed, feathers flat, eyes threatening. Billy stood still, whistling softly, waiting for her to relax and resume her feeding. Then he walked round the back of the hut and held her high over his head as he climbed carefully over the fence. A tall hawthorn hedge bordered one side of the field, and the wind was strong and constant in the branches, but in the field it had been strained to a whisper. He reached the centre and unwound the leash from his glove, pulled it free of the swivel, then removed the swivel from the jesses and raised his fist. The hawk flapped her wings and fanned her tail, her claws still gripping the glove. Billy cast her off by nudging his glove upwards, and she banked away, completed a wide circuit then gained height rapidly, while he took the lure from his bag and unwound the line from the stick.

'Come on, Kes! Come on then!'

He whistled and swung the lure short-lined on a vertical plane. The hawk turned, saw it, and stooped...

'Casper!'

He glanced involuntarily across the field. Mr Farthing was climbing the fence and waving to him. The hawk grabbed the lure and Billy allowed her to take it to the ground.

'Bloody hell fire.'

He pegged the stick into the soil and stood up. Mr Farthing was tiptoeing towards him, concentrating on his passage through the grass. With his overcoat on, and his trousers pinched up, he looked like a day-tripper paddling at the seaside. Billy allowed him to get within thirty yards, then stopped him by raising one hand.

'You'll have to stop there, Sir.'

'I hope I'm not too late.'

'No, Sir, but you'll have to watch from there.'

'That's all right. If you think I'm too near I can go back to the fence.'

'No, you'll be all right there, as long as you stand still.'

'I won't breathe.'

He smiled and put his hands in his overcoat pockets. Billy crouched down and made in towards the hawk along the lure line. He offered her a scrap of beef, and she stepped off the lure on to his glove. He allowed her to take the beef, then he stood up and cast her off again. She wheeled away, high round the field. Billy plucked the stick from the ground and began to swing the lure. The hawk turned and stooped at it. Billy watched her as she descended, waiting for the right moment as she accelerated rapidly towards him. Now. He straightened his arm and lengthened the line, throwing the lure into her path and sweeping it before her in a downward arc, then twitching it up too steep for her attack, making her throw up, her impetus carrying her high into the air. She turned and stooped again. Billy presented the lure again. And again. Each time smoothly before her, an inch before her so that the next wing-beat must catch it, or the next. Working the lure like a top matador his cape. Encouraging the hawk, making her stoop faster and harder, making Mr Farthing hold his breath at each stoop and near miss. Each time she made off Billy called her continually, then stopped in concentration as he timed his throw and leaned into the long drawing of the lure and the hawk in its wake, her eyes fixed, beak open, angling her body and adjusting her flight to any slight shift in speed or direction.

She tried a new tactic, and came in low, seeming to flit within a pocket of silence close to the ground. Billy flexed at the knees and flattened the plane of the swing, allowing the lengthening line to pay out before her.

'Come on, this time, Kes! This time!'

She shortened her stoop, and counter stoop, which increased the frequency of her attacks, and made Billy pivot, and whirl, and watch, but never lose control of the lure or its pursuer. Until finally the hawk sheered away and began to ring up high over the hawthorn hedge.

'Come on then, Kes! Once more! Last time!'

And she came, head first, wings closed, swooping down, hurtling down towards Billy, who waited, then lured her—WHOOSH—up, throwing up, ringing up, turning; and as she stooped again Billy twirled the lure and threw it high into her path. She caught it, and clutched it down to the ground.

He allowed her to take the remaining beef scrap from the lure, then took her up and attached the swivel and leash. She looked up sharply at a series of claps. Mr Farthing was applauding softly. Billy started towards him and they met half-way, the hawk fixing the stranger every second of their approach.

'Marvellous, Casper! Brilliant! That's one of the most exciting things I've ever seen!'

from *A Kestrel for a Knave* by Barry Hines

Reading for Meaning

1 In the opening sentences, what is there to suggest that the hawk is wild?

2 Why does Billy wear a glove?

3 Explain why Billy is so careful entering the hut.

4 What movements of the hawk show that she tensed up outside the hut?

5 How does Billy relax the hawk after they come out of the hut?

6 What distracts Billy so that the hawk gets the lure the first time?

7 Why does Mr Farthing look like 'a day-tripper paddling at the seaside'?

8 How does Billy get the hawk to let go of the lure?

9 How do we know that Billy is highly skilled in using the lure to train the hawk?

10 How do we know that Mr Farthing is enthralled by the training?

11 What evidence is there that the hawk learns as it continues to try to take the lure?

12 Why does Billy let the hawk have the lure at the end?

13 What feelings does Mr Farthing have about the training session? What evidence is there for your answer?

14 What qualities of Billy's character are revealed in the passage?

15 What qualities of the hawk are revealed in the passage?

Bear

An attack by a huge bear threatens to take the lives of two people in an isolated hut.

WILLIAM MAYNE

DRIFT

'Probably our most original living writer for the young' — *Observer*

There was wind and snow outside, and he could not see far at all. Everything was white, or white with shadows under it.

The shadows were blue and grey, and now and then they were so dark he could not tell the colour at all.

One shadow seemed to stay where it was but grow bigger. It was difficult to tell. The glass in the window was of a rough sort to start with, and there was snow outside and steam inside. Rafe's head got very warm up in the top of the hut.

The shadow he was watching grew bigger still. It seemed to spread in the glass.

It was a brown shadow. It was not a shadow at all. It was the bear coming closer and closer, sometimes roving on all fours, sometimes rising on its hind legs, seeking, sniffing.

'Bear,' he said.

Tawena hissed at him, just reminding him to keep as quiet as he could. She went on licking her fingers. She silently took a billet of wood and put it on the stove.

'If it wasn't for the bear,' Rafe thought, 'we should be warm and comfortable, and we've had a good meal.'

The bear went out of sight, round the hut. It went out of Rafe's mind too, and he jumped off the table with a thump. As he jumped he despairingly remembered that he should not have done it. The girl was too cross with him to hiss. She looked and looked.

Rafe began to look too. He naturally looked at the door, which was where he had seen the bear, and where he himself would have come in. But Tawena listened all round.

They both heard. They heard the bear snuffling and sniffing along the bottom of the hut wall, down behind the stove. Perhaps the smell was strongest there.

The bear huffed and breathed and blew. It began to scrape at the snow and ice outside. Claws hit the wooden wall of the hut, like nails being driven in.

Then it stopped snuffing at one place and went all along the wall, from corner to corner. It began to bite the corners of the hut, high up the wall, and right down at the bottom.

Inside, Tawena and Rafe listened and watched. The wood was planks, not logs, nailed at the corners to an upright post. The bear was pulling at the lowest planks, easing the nails out, and digging under the angle.

The floor began to give way, because there was a hole outside. Cold wind came in. The bear's claw showed. Tawena went to stand quite close to the place. Rafe went to the far corner. He could feel his heart clattering inside him.

The bear stopped digging at the corner. It came breathing round outside the hut, pawing at the walls. It had a particularly long look at the door, where there was a crack between the door and the frame. It breathed up so much air that Rafe thought it must take it all from the hut. It knocked on the door three times, like a person. Rafe thought he should open it, because it must be a person come to rescue them, but Tawena glared at him and he stood still.

The bear did not knock on the door again. Rafe began to think it had gone away. He moved towards the table and the girl hissed gently. Rafe thought the bear would have come anyway, even if he had not jumped off the table; but he would not jump down next time.

He got up once more, and looked from the window. He thought it must be near nightfall, because the hut was getting darker quite quickly.

Then he saw that the darkness at the window was the bear's shoulder and back. As he stood and watched the bear turned the back and the shoulder, and there was his head, and his eye looking in, looking back at Rafe's eye, with his head turning from side to side.

The bear could not see into the darkness

of the hut. But it could still smell that something was in there. It dropped down from the window.

Rafe climbed down from the table. The girl watched him.

'I think it's going away,' said Rafe, standing by the table, speaking in a whisper.

'Bear stay,' said Tawena. 'I know bear. Bear my people, my...' and there she waved her hands from side to side, because she did not know the English word. Rafe thought she meant something like God, but he did not think there would be claws and a smell like bear. Tawena must feel like that about the bear, because she was not frightened, only quiet. But, he remembered, she had been frightened once, out on the headland.

Now there was quiet for a time. Rafe sat on the table. The girl licked her fingers.

Outside the bear began to run, or perhaps it was digging deep and quick. Whatever it was doing it suddenly hit the back of the hut, behind the stove, hitting so hard that wood cracked, the stove tipped, the chimney split, and there was fire over the floor and smoke everywhere.

The fire was all they had to stop them dying in the night. At once they lifted the stove back, burning their hands, not caring. In the north countries fire is the first friend in the frost. They picked up the fire itself and heaped it back into the hearth. Rafe jammed the chimney back as near as he could get it, but the hut was full of smoke, and smoke came in more and more.

The bear came to the door again. Here it found it could sniff underneath much better than along the walls, and it found it could dig better too. It sniffed and dug. Inside the hut Rafe sneezed with the smoke. The hut swayed on the moving ice. There was a smart crack as the floe broke somewhere not far away.

Rafe thought, quite clearly, that when the fire went out they would die of cold, but before that the ice would break under them and the lake would drown them. So there was no need to worry about the bear.

He was wrong. At that moment the bear

decided to rear up and knock the whole door down, so suddenly that Rafe had to jump aside.

When he looked the door was on the floor, smoke was flying out through the doorway and cold air coming in. The bear was standing half in and half out, having a look round, deciding what to do next, quite certain it would be able to do it.

The bear licked its lips. It showed yellow teeth. It dribbled stringy dribble.

Rafe watched it. His mouth was too dry to move, his tongue was like leather. The bear was very close, the length of the door away from him. If it took a few bear's paces it would be touching him.

The bear thought about things, still deciding what to do next. It had its front feet on the fallen door, and now it moved its paws like a cat. It did not like the way the door shook under its weight, and was not sure whether it was safe to walk on. It brought its back legs further forward. Rafe thought it might jump right along the length of the door, and be in the middle of the hut.

The bear had been thinking about the door lying loose on the floor and perhaps being a trap. It had also been looking round. What it saw, and smelt, and wanted, and

had come in for, was the bacon hanging from the roof. That was where it looked.

It gathered its back feet together again. Rafe was sure it would jump now.

Tawena had been standing the other side of the stove, watching. Rafe turned his head and looked at her. He wanted to say something, but the words would not unswallow themselves. Tawena was standing there doing nothing. Rafe had the feeling that she was not properly afraid, and he thought she should be, because he was. Then he saw that her yellowish face was paler than it had been. He saw that she was breathing fast. He saw that her mouth was very tight shut, but her chin shook a little bit. He saw that she was frightened. Rafe did not want her to be frightened, because that was disagreeable for her, and made him more frightened than he had been.

Even the bear was still worried by the way the door rattled on the ice. It was still making up its mind, but the girl had made hers up. She left her place by the stove and walked to the doorway.

She walked on the door lying there. The bear said something in its throat, and lifted a front paw. The door twisted, and the girl went on walking along it, taking short steps.

She walked right up to the bear. Rafe felt that was all wrong, that she should not do such a thing, that the bear would hit her. He wanted to say that they should give the bear the bacon.

He did not have time. Something more frightening happened, and then something so strange that he could not have expected it, and neither could the bear or the girl.

The bear rose up on its hind legs, filling the doorway. It was actually standing just outside, where its back legs already were. It had not gone away from Tawena. Rafe could tell it was getting its paws ready to crush Tawena. First Tawena, then him, then the bacon, Rafe thought.

A strange thing was happening to the bear. It stood quite still, watching Tawena. But it began to grow smaller, and to go away. It was not walking. It filled less and less doorway, and was not so near.

'Gone away bear,' said Tawena, as if nothing odd was going on. 'Put door.' And she stepped off the door and began to lift it up.

'But what is it?' said Rafe. 'What is happening?'

'Ice break,' said Tawena, not thinking anything odd had occurred. 'Bear float away.'

Rafe felt that he was floating away too, as if his senses were not much good any more. But the piece of ice the bear had stood on, close to the door of the hut, had broken away and carried the bear off. The bear was now the far side of some ripply water, and back on all fours again, sniffing the ice, wondering what had happened to the bacon it had seen. Rafe understood how it felt.

from *Drift* by William Mayne

Reading for Meaning

1 Why is it difficult to see outside?

2 What sound does Tawena use to warn Rafe to be quiet?

3 What gives away their presence to the searching bear?

4 When the bear begins to bite the corners of the hut we get some idea of its size. How do we know it is huge?

5 Why does Rafe almost think the bear is a rescuer when it stands outside the door?

6 What causes it to get darker quite quickly as Rafe looks out of the window for the second time?

7 Why don't they care about burnt fingers when they lift the stove back?

8 What is the first indication that the ice is breaking up?

9 What is the bear doing when they first see it in the doorway?

10 What is the bear really after?

11 Why does Rafe think that Tawena should be 'properly afraid'?

12 What shows him that she is afraid?

13 Why doesn't the bear simply walk into the hut?

14 What is the 'strange thing' that happens to the bear when it rises up to attack Tawena? What has caused this to happen?

15 Why does Rafe understand how the bear feels at the end?

16 What differences do you notice between the characters of Rafe and Tawena?

Rats

In this extract, a rat plague arouses fear in the Rideout family. They are not sure how to cope with the dangerous intruders.

The day the rats came, Lettice saw the news on television. (The news was about rats, rats, nothing but rats: a whole world of rats. Earlier, she had watched the rats in the garden. She had seen them eat her guinea-pigs, overturn the dustbins form heaving knots and rings of grey bodies fringed with writhing, naked tails) Nobody had dared leave the house, for only in the house could you feel safe. Sickened and silent, Lettice made her way upstairs to the safety and isolation of her bedroom. She would go to bed and stay there.

She opened the bedroom door, unzipped her dress and screamed.

There were rats on her bed, three of them. They were eating a piece of chocolate she had put on her bedside table. One rat was sitting up like a squirrel, its yellow-brown teeth industriously nibbling through the paper wrapper and the silver paper beneath.

Lettice kept screaming. Lucas was the first

to reach her. He saw the rats and felt a great bubble of nausea inside his chest. The sickness turned to a sort of trembling hate. He took his shoes off and flung them, one after the other, at the rats.

The first shoe missed and sent the bedside table lamp smashing across the room. With his other shoe, he hit a rat so hard that it was knocked off the bed. It squeaked loudly when it was hit and fell to the other side of the bed.

Lettice still screamed and Lucas yelled curses while he looked for something else to attack the rats with. He picked up Lettice's hockey stick, seized it and went towards the two rats still on the bed. With unwinking red eyes, they watched him come. Their backs were humped. Their long naked tails twitched. The rat holding the chocolate did not drop it.

'Get out!' shouted Lucas. Or tried to shout: his voice would not work properly. He knew why. He was afraid – afraid of the two rats on the bed, terrified of the third rat that he could not see. Where was it?

Lettice was gone now. He heard her run down the stairs, screaming and sobbing, and his parents' voices. He wished his father would come upstairs. Where was the third rat? He was too frightened to approach the bed while the third rat could not be seen. He knew how rats attacked: the sudden darting run, the bunched, coil-sprung leap, the snap of the two long, fang-like front teeth...he had plenty of time to learn about their habits during the day. Particularly when they had got to the guinea-pigs.

Where was the third rat?

There! By the edge of the bed! Despite himself, Lucas let out a yelp of fear and backed away, terrified of the sudden spring and the fastening of the hideous teeth in his ankle.

But the rat had nothing of the sort in mind. It looked at Lucas for a long moment, then scrambled busily up the bedspread to join the other two. It reached out its obscene front paws for the chocolate bar, snatched it away and started to nibble and crunch, tearing at the wrapping.

When its mouth was full, it paused. All three rats stared straight at Lucas. Lucas felt his face reddening. His first thought was that he was embarrassed – embarrassed, if you please! – by the staring eyes. His second thought was, 'I am ashamed. Ashamed of being afraid. But I *am* afraid, sick afraid...'

These thoughts took only split seconds – and then his father was in the room, pushing past him and gasping, 'Get out of the

way, I'll *kill*—I'll *kill*—' He was carrying a few yards of nylon garden netting, strong, light stuff. He opened out the net and threw it over the rats. Immediately they began to scream and fight and scramble. Mr Rideout gathered the net together until he was holding a dangling bundle that writhed and heaved and squeaked and gibbered and thrust out jerking grey-pink limbs.

He clattered down the stairs, Lucas after him, making for the kitchen back door. 'In the garden', he muttered. 'Kill them outside.'

His wife stopped him. 'Don't open the door! You'll let more of them in!'

'Boiler room,' said Mr Rideout and opened the little door leading from the kitchen. Lucas made to follow him into the small, bare room but his father said, 'Keep out! Out!'

So they kept outside and listened to the swinging thumps. At first there were squeaks and screams as well. But long after these were over, the swinging thumps went on.

When he came out, Mr Rideout's face was pasty and sweating and his nostrils were white. He was trembling and panting so much that he could barely speak. 'Filth!' he said. 'Filth! And the whole place could be full of them.'

from *On the Flipside* by Nicholas Fisk

Reading for Meaning

1 How do we know that the plague is widespread?

2 What had Lettice seen the rats do outside?

3 Why was everyone afraid to leave the house?

4 Where had the three rats found the chocolate?

5 What happens when Lucas throws his second shoe?

6 How do the rats convey an absence of fear to Lucas as he prepares to attack them?

7 What reveals that Lucas is frightened when he tries to shout at the rats?

8 What prevents Lucas from approaching the two rats on the bed?

9 What does Lucas know about how rats attack?

10 What two thoughts occur to Lucas as his face reddens?

11 What feelings does Lucas's father have when he enters the bedroom? What evidence is there?

12 What reaction do the rats have to the net that is thrown over them?

13 What does Mr Rideout first intend to do with the rats?

14 Why does Mrs Rideout warn her husband not to go outside?

15 What evidence is there that Mr Rideout is *very* angry as he kills the rats?

16 What differences in character do you notice between Mr Rideout and Lucas in this incident? Support your answer with evidence from the passage.

POETRY

CREATURES GREAT AND SMALL

Kestrel

He lay on his breast against the house wall
The brass rings of his eyes still polished.
He must have arrowed full-tilt
Into the first floor windowglass
Making just one mistake
About space.

Handsomely banded sweeping wings,
Half-folded, hunched his shoulders
Like the pinions of a tabby angel.
His face narrowed wisely
To the small beak like a single horn
Delicately designed to hinge apart
And rend flesh.

After a week he's nothing.
Only his hard legs are fierce,
Stretching out talons
Hollow, flexible, smooth,
The colour of polished lava.
He lies on his back now, wings fallen apart,
Head like a wet pebble,
Ribcage small as a child's fist
Arching under a drenched grey vest.
His underfeathers flattened and swirled by rain
Look like a map
Of the world's winds.

Pamela Gillilan

Questions

1 How is the bird lying when the poet first notices it?

2 'The brass rings of his eyes still polished'. Why do you think the poet notices this straight away?

3 What is the 'one mistake/About space' that the kestrel made?

4 What do the 'sweeping wings' and 'shoulders' of the bird remind the poet of?

5 'Delicately designed to...rend flesh'. Why is the word 'delicately' unexpected here?

6 What part of the dead bird is least affected by the passing of time?

7 How is the bird lying after a week?

8 What do the bird's underfeathers remind the poet of at the end of the poem?

9 What strikes you as the outstanding quality of this poem? Why?

10 Did you enjoy this poem? Why, or why not?

Polar Bear

Hugging the wall, down
there in his open pit,
he ambles absently,
fitting his whole body
to the wide curve
of dingy cement.

Backwards and forwards
loping, big head weaving,
pressing one matted flank
and then the other
to the sun-scorched cliff
of his lonely prison.

His coat is far
from white—rather
a drab cream, with
yellow or brownish stains.
—He looks unhappy in the heat.
No wonder he never

turns to growl at
us, begging for attention.

James Kirkup

Praise of a Collie

She was a small dog, neat and fluid—
Even her conversation was tiny:
She greeted you with *bow* never *bow-wow*.

Her sons stood monumentally over her
But did what she told them. Each grew grizzled
Till it seemed he was his own mother's grandfather.

Once, gathering sheep on a showery day,
I remarked how dry she was. Pollochan said, 'Ah,
It would take a very accurate drop to hit Lassie.'

And her tact—and tactics! When the sheep bolted
In an unforeseen direction, over the skyline
Came—who but Lassie, and not even panting.

She sailed in the dinghy like a proper sea-dog.
Where's a burn?—she's first on the other side.
She flowed through fences like a piece of black wind.

But suddenly she was old and sick and crippled...
I grieved for Pollochan when he took her a stroll
And put his gun to the back of her head.

Norman MacCaig

Questions

1 'She was a small dog, neat and fluid'. Why is the word 'fluid' unusual here? What does it suggest about Lassie?

2 'She greeted you with *bow* never *bow-wow*'. Why does the poet say this about Lassie?

3 What would strike an observer as unusual about Lassie standing with her sons?

4 What struck the poet as remarkable about Lassie on the 'showery day' he mentions?

5 Who was Lassie's owner?

6 When the sheep bolted, Lassie would bring them back. What was unusual about her appearance as she brought them?

7 What colour was Lassie? What evidence is there for your conclusion?

8 'But suddenly she was old and sick and crippled...' Why do you think this comes to the poet's awareness 'suddenly'?

9 How does the poet feel for Lassie's owner at the end? Why?

10 What do you like best about this poem? Refer to one or two lines of the poem in your answer.

Gulls

The grey-white gulls all stand together;
Facing the gusty, salt-damp weather,
Toes turned in, webbed feet on sand,
Tails all pointing to the land.
Sometimes one will fly to sea,
More will follow, one, two, three,
As if warming up against the chill.
There! One swoops to make a kill!
Now the squabble and chase is on,
Bird after bird they rise, are gone
Over the rippling brink of spray.
Off they go, away, away
In linking circles across the tide,
Wider still and side by side.
The little fish glints in the sun,
Falls from the red beak, one by one
The boomerang wings dip down after
(Are those mewing cries their laughter?)
Ah! It is lost, far out of reach.
Tired birds fly back to the beach.
And grey-white gulls all stand together
Facing the gusty, salt-damp weather,
Toes turned in, webbed feet on sand,
Tails all pointing to the land.

Jean Laidlaw

Questions

1 What word in the opening lines tells us that it is a windy day?

2 Which direction are the gulls all *facing*?

3 When a few gulls suddenly fly out to sea what does it seem as if they are doing?

4 'One swoops to make a kill!' What is the poet describing here?

5 What word tells us that a noisy argument occurs after a fish has been caught?

6 Why do the gulls fly 'side by side'?

7 What feelings does the poet suggest the gulls might be experiencing as they enter into the chase for the little fish?

8 Why do the birds return to the beach?

9 The poem begins and ends with virtually the same four lines. Why does the poet do this?

10 What do you think the poet tried to achieve in this poem? Do you think she was successful? Why?

Lion

Poor prisoner in a cage,
I understand your rage
And why you loudly roar
Walking that stony floor.

Your forest eyes are sad
As wearily you pad
A few yards up and down,
A king without a crown.

Up and down all day.
A wild beast for display,
Or lying in the heat
With sawdust, smells and meat,

Remembering how you chased
Your jungle prey, and raced,
Leaping upon their backs
Along the grassy tracks.

But you are here instead,
Better, perhaps, be dead
Than locked in this dark den;
Forgive us, lion, then,
Who did not ever choose,
Our circuses and zoos.

Leonard Clark

WRITING

WRITING FOR A PURPOSE

People have all sorts of different purposes for writing. A school essay may be written to convince a teacher that you know your work and can argue well in writing. A job application has the purpose of presenting the writer's abilities and skills so that he or she has the best chance of getting the job. A letter to a newspaper usually aims to persuade other readers of a particular point of view about some issue. A poem may be written to try to capture the sights, sounds and feelings associated with a particular event. Letters to friends usually attempt to 'fill them in' on what you've been doing lately.

As the purpose of the writing changes, so does the way we write. For example, a letter to a newspaper will usually be written in a formal style, with careful attention to using the 'correct' words, spelling and punctuation. A letter to a friend will usually be far more relaxed and informal. In this kind of writing, using slang words or untidy handwriting are not considered important to the writer's purpose.

Read through the following guidelines and carry out the writing task. Remember to ask yourself, 'What is my purpose?' and 'How should I write this in order to best achieve my purpose?'

SCHOOL CANTEEN REPORT

Canteen Vocabulary

students	appetite	ingredients	margarine	inedible
delicious	beverages	nutritious	important	lukewarm
vitamins	flavour	prefects	noisy	chocolate

1 Use at least eight of the above words as you write a two-page report on the service and quality of the food at the school canteen. Imagine you are writing the report to be presented to the Students' Council so that they can make some recommendations to the school principal.

2 Include in your report the following:

- **a title page**, which lists (a) the topic of the report, (b) the writer, (c) whom the report is for and (d) the date.
- **an introduction**, which states why the report is being written and why this purpose is an important one.
- **the main part** of the report, which gives the 'facts and figures' and any other information relevant to the purpose. Each point should be presented logically. Divide this section into two parts—one on 'Quality of Food' and another on 'Service'.
- **a list of the conclusions** you have drawn from the information you have presented.

3 Write an initial draft of the report so that you will not be too worried about neatness, correct spelling, etc. Then go carefully through the draft, making corrections and alterations. Write out, or type up, your final copy.

4 Imagine that the report has been discussed by the Students' Council. Write out, under the heading 'Recommendations', a list of five recommendations that the Students' Council would like to make to the school principal about changes to the food and the service at the canteen.

LANGUAGE

FORMAL AND INFORMAL LANGUAGE

The language we use to communicate varies according to the situation we are in. An analogy can be drawn from the way we dress. For example, if we are attending a wedding we don't wear a T-shirt, thongs and our oldest shorts. If we are going to school we don't dress in a dinner suit or evening gown. We dress to suit the occasion. In the same way we use language to suit the occasion.

Formal language is often considered to be 'correct' language. It is the level of language we tend to use for serious, formal occasions such as writing a letter to a prospective employer, writing a letter to a Member of Parliament, writing a technical report, speaking before an important public gathering, and so on. Here is an example of formal language.

FEELING ACCEPTABLE

Whether a child feels that *he as a person* is unaccepted will be determined by how many of his behaviours are unacceptable. Parents who find unacceptable a great many things that their children do or say will inevitably foster in these children a deep feeling that they are unacceptable as persons. Conversely, parents who are accepting of a great many things their children do or say will produce children who are more likely to feel acceptable as persons.

from *Parent Effectiveness Training* by Thomas Gordon

Informal language is sometimes also called <u>colloquial</u> language. It is the level of language we use in everyday conversation, where we are not so concerned about formal 'correctness'. It is the kind of language we might use in writing a <u>personal diary</u> or a letter to a friend. It is not really less 'correct'; it is simply a different level of language appropriate to different situations. Read through the following example, noting the informal level of language used.

LOUISE

His sister Louise was bound to be prowling about somewhere. Then there came a blast of sound from her room as she turned the telly on, so he reckoned he was safe. He crept out.

Unfortunately, she had ears like a bat's.

'Where you going? she yelled.

He sighed, and opened her door. She was slumped in a bean bag guzzling crisps. He was ashamed to have to look at her.

'You ain't watching *Street Noise*? That's terrible,' he said, gazing at the screen.

'Mum said you wasn't to go out till you'd done your homework,' she said.

'I done it. Anyway, I gotta get some exercise, ain't I? People like *die* if they don't get any exercise,' he said, looking meaningfully at the bean bag and the crisps.

But she didn't understand sarcasm. 'I'll tell Mum,' she said, without taking her eyes off the telly, where some blonde girl was bouncing about enthusiastically.

'Get lost,' he said, and shut the door again.

from *How to Be Cool* by Philip Pullman

Changing Informal to Formal Language

Rewrite the following sentences in more formal language. Here is an example to show you what to do.

Informal: Small businesses everywhere are battling to make a go of it.

Formal: Small businesses everywhere are finding it difficult to continue making a profit.

1 It was a whacko thing to do but the whole class decided to be in it.

2 When I was knee-high to a grasshopper I had to work like a horse.

3 The sponsors tried to drum up some support but the concert ended up a schemozzle.

4 The boy said he felt crook and then proceeded to chuck all over the back seat.

5 The young man was broke so he put the bite on his friends.

6 Don't have a bar of any business deal that's on the nose.

7 If you blow it this time you may not get a second bite at the cherry.

8 The big guy was really a wimp and couldn't fight his way out of a paper bag.

9 To impress the birds he'd done himself up like a sore toe.

10 The girl who was smashed got dobbed in by someone from another class.

Formal and Informal Language Match-up

Match the informal or colloquial expressions from the left-hand column with the
formal equivalent expression from the right-hand column.

Informal	**Formal**
go bush	free
lose one's block	reject
scarce as hen's teeth	car in a dangerously rusted condition
on the house	deteriorate
knuckle sandwich	leave for the country
knock back	have a look
take a squiz	become uncontrollably angry
snags	the city
the big smoke	very scarce
rustbucket	inform on someone
put someone in	a punch in the mouth
go to the pack	sausages

FIGURATIVE LANGUAGE

Proverbs and Situations

Proverbs are short sayings that contain some common sense or advice. They are an
example of **figurative language**, which is language that carries a vivid or picturesque
message but is not meant to be taken literally. For example:

Proverb: It's no use crying over spilt milk.

Meaning: It's no use becoming too upset over what is past.

Consider the following proverbs and then choose the most appropriate one for
each situation.

Proverbs

- Birds of a feather flock together
- A stitch in time saves nine
- Too many cooks spoil the broth
- Many hands make light work
- A fool and his money are soon parted
- The early bird catches the worm
- The proof of the pudding is in the eating
- One swallow does not make a summer
- A bad workman always blames his tools
- It never rains but it pours

Situations

1 The cricket team won their first game but the coach warned them that they would have to keep on winning if they wanted to be premiers. h

2 Our neighbour won the lottery three years ago. He and his family had a world trip then he invested in the Stock Exchange. The last thing I heard was that he had lost the rest of the money. e

3 A team of five hundred cleaners came in to pick up all the rubbish at the stadium after the big rock concert. They finished the whole job in two hours. d

4 The headmaster, the coach, the team captain and one of the parents were all trying to tell the team what to do. No wonder they lost. c

5 My closest friends and I all love playing netball, surfing and listening to rock music. a

6 Yesterday I bashed my knee on a chair, my pen broke, I found out I'd failed my test and I caught a cold. j

7 Peter used to wash the salt water out of his fishing reel after every fishing trip and the reel is still good after ten years. b

8 The advertisement claimed that the car would get thirty-six kilometres to each litre of petrol, but we never get over twenty-eight. g

9 I failed Maths again. We have a hopeless teacher and our textbooks are so boring. i

10 Leanne applied for a casual position before anyone else in the class, so it's not surprising that she got a holiday job straight away. f

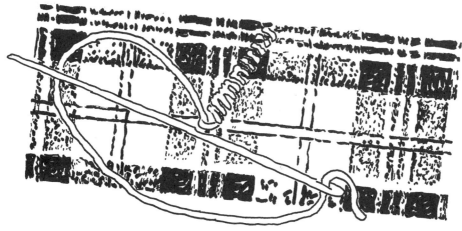

Idioms

Idioms are colourful expressions that we use in everyday language. Like proverbs, they are an example of figurative language and are not intended to be taken literally. Give the meaning of each of the idioms in heavy type in the following sentences.

told the secret

1 Mr Simpson **let the cat out of the bag** about the Christmas present he was buying for his daughter.

patch up *after a fight*

2 Someone had to **break the ice** so I went up and said 'hello'.

suspected *was suspicious*

3 The opening batsman **smelled a rat** as he looked at the green surface of the pitch.

ignored

4 Tammy gave Peter **the cold shoulder** after the school dance.

boastful

5 The new boy was unpopular because he was always **blowing his own trumpet**.

" " trouble

6 The little boy certainly knew how to **get into hot water**.

give up

7 The team was hopelessly outclassed but they wouldn't **throw in the towel**.

do my own work

8 After the way Jill let me down, I've decided to **paddle my own canoe**.

applause

9 The final performance of the play **brought the house down**.

end a quarrel

10 At last the two neighbours agreed to **bury the hatchet**.

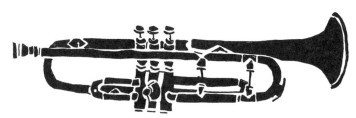

GETTING IT RIGHT

PROBLEMS WITH PRONOUNS

Subject pronouns (**I, he/she, we, they**) are used when someone is *doing* the action. For example:

- **I** hid the gift.
- **She** caught the ball.
- **They** ran for cover.

Object pronouns (**me, him, her, us, them**) are used when the action is *being done to* someone. For example:

- The bike hit **me**.
- The bird pecked **him**.
- The bull charged **them**.

Object pronouns are also used *after* prepositions such as 'by', 'with', 'from', 'to', 'for'. It is incorrect to use subject pronouns after prepositions. For example:

- The violinist played *for* Ed and **me**.   (correct)
- The violinist played *for* Ed and **I**.   (incorrect)

Choosing the Correct Pronoun

Complete the following sentences by choosing the correct form of the pronoun from the brackets.

1 ..I.... (I/me) walked slowly towards ..him. (he/him).

2 The play was written by ..me... (me/I) and my friends.

3 The amazing Miss Piggy suddenly smiled at .them. (them/they).

4 ..They. (They/Them) finally stopped smoking because they realised what it was doing to ..them. (they/them).

5 The team pledged their loyalty to ..me... (I/me).

6 .We... (We/Us) chose the tent that was big enough for all of .us.... (we/us).

7 After the emergency .she.... (she/her) collapsed, so they brought a cup of tea to .her... (she/her).

8 .They.. (They/Them) bought the computer from Tom and ..me... (I/me).

9 ..We... (We/Us) stood and applauded the artist after .he.... (he/him) had sung for .us..... (we/us).

10 ..I..... (I/Me) was angered by the advertising campaign because it was a subtle attack on my company and ..me... (I/me).

DRAMA

PROTEST

by Elsy Edwards

A public meeting about the issue of culling kangaroos raises many different viewpoints. Every member of the class can participate in reading this script. Allocate one number to each person. The odd numbers are in favour of culling kangaroos as a conservation measure; the even numbers are against it. The highest odd number is 29 and the highest even number is 34. If you act out the scene, stand near others who are on your side. Keep the reading rapid, to suggest the effect of a public meeting.

> **CAST**
>
> **People in a crowd**

Scene: A city square.

Person 1   Ladies and gentlemen. Friends.

Person 2   Friends! Call yourselves friends! Not friends of animals you aren't.

Person 3   Friends! Please listen. Listen before you judge. Let me give you the facts of the matter concerning the Kooribillie State Forest.

Person 4   The facts of the matter! The bloody facts of the matter were 700 dead kangaroos.

Person 3   We are not animal destroyers. We are animal conservationists.

Person 4   Try telling that to the kangaroos.

Person 6   Conservationists! How'd you like somebody pointing a rifle between your eyes and saying, 'This is for your own good.'

Person 1   Conservation of any species depends upon having sufficient territory for animals to live well.

Person 8   Live! You didn't give the kangas much chance to live. What makes us mad is that they were tame. They were used to people coming close to pat them. So they just stood to be shot.

Person 5 The kangaroos in the Kooribillie State Forest had become too numerous for their own well-being.

Person 10 They're not too numerous now, mate, unless you count the dead ones lying around.

Person 7 There are no dead ones lying around. The bodies were removed and burnt for reasons of hygiene.

Person 12 Yeah! Disposed of! Got rid of! Murderers!

Person 9 If you go to the reserve now...

Person 14 What's the point of going there now? There's nothing to show the kids any longer. Think it's worth the trip now all the roos are gone?

Person 9 There are now the right number left for the territory involved. The advice of expert naturalists gave us an estimate that the area could support 300 at most.

Person 11 And that's about the number that would have been around when the Aborigines were the only inhabitants.

Person 16 Three hundred! That's a laugh. We went there last week. We saw two roos! TWO roos! Every other time we've seen hundreds.

Person 13 Yes. Hundreds of underfed animals that had grazed the land almost bare. Hundreds of animals in distress, caught on the wire fence that surrounds the reserve, trying to get out for more feed.

Person 18 The ones that are left, if there are any left, will be so damned scared of humans you'll be lucky to see them again for years.

Person 15 Kangaroos don't breed when feed is scarce. Consequently there were no young joeys culled.

Person 20 If they don't breed, why were there supposed to be too many? Not that I agree there were too many, but if they don't breed if grass is a bit short, why couldn't you have left them alone and they would have sorted out their numbers for themselves?

Person 17 And while that was happening? With any animals, including humans, once they are starving, disease takes over. There could have been epidemic disease spread throughout the native kangaroo population of the entire eastern seaboard.

Person 22 Rubbish! Any fool, except maybe a so-called expert, knows sick animals keep away from the herd when they're dying. They're more considerate than some humans.

Person 19   How would you know.

Person 24   Pity somebody doesn't check some of you out for fleas and shoot you.

Person 21   Is there any sensible person present who wishes to ask an intelligent question so the real picture of the culling operation can be understood?

Person 26   Yes. I would like to know how long it is likely to be before the experts tell us the same thing has to happen again?

Person 21   About another twenty years, I would guess. Of course, there are many variable factors. For instance, the area of the state reserve may not always remain the same.

Person 28   So that's what it's all about! Some mangy donkey in parliament has decided to flog off the reserve to his mates and has to make it look useless as a park so he can pretend it doesn't matter.

Person 23   It does matter. Please friends, let me suggest this. If you know the park...

Person 30   I reckon most of us know it better than you do, sport.

Person 23   If you know the park, go back there after the next season, after the spring rains and see the difference. Now the paddocks are almost bare, brown and dusty...

Person 32   Of course they are. It's summer. Haven't you experts noticed?

Person 25   I've listened to your rubbish long enough. When I was a lad the whole area was green all year round.

Person 34   There, you see? And it was because there were no experts messing around with the roos then.

Person 25   No. They were in balance with the entire ecology.

Person 30   And nobody needed you interfering think-tanks to decide for the kangaroos whether they were breeding too often or not.

Person 29   If the farmlands hadn't taken over so much of the original forest we wouldn't have this problem today.

Person 27   You can't turn back the clock, Sir.

Person 29   And you can't talk to those who won't listen.

Person 34   Try talking to the kangaroos. Oh, sorry. I forgot. You can't explain to them. They're dead.

from *Play On!* by Elsy Edwards

Activity

Imagine you are a newspaper reporter covering this meeting. Write your article, summing up the viewpoints that were expressed.

ACKNOWLEDGEMENTS

The authors and publishers are grateful to the following for permission to reproduce copyright material:

Poetry and prose
John Agard c/o Caroline Sheldon Literary Agency for 'Hairstyle' © John Agard; Andre Deutsch Ltd for 'Going Through the Old Photos' from *Quick Let's Get Out of Here* by Michael Rosen, and for the extract from *Shane* by Jack Schaefer; The Bodley Head and E. R. Braithwaite for the extract from *To Sir with Love*; The Bodley Head and Paul Zindel for the extracts from *My Darling My Hamburger* and *The Pigman*; The Bodley Head and Phoebe Hesketh for 'Ward F4' by Phoebe Hesketh from *A Song of Sunlight*; Alan Bold for his poem 'The Boys of Winter'; Chatto & Windus/The Hogarth Press and Norman MacCaig for 'Praise of a Collie' by Norman MacCaig from *Collected Poems*; Collins Publishers for 'Old Mister Roberts' by Tony Charles and 'Dog-Gone' by Russell Adams both from *Toughie Toffee* chosen by David Orme; Collins/Angus & Robertson Publishers for 'The Night-Ride' by Kenneth Slessor from *Selected Poems* by Kenneth Slessor © Paul Slessor, 1944, for the extract from 'The Story of the World's Worst Whinger' from *The Yarns of Billy Borker* by Frank Hardy, and for the extract from *This School Is Driving Me Crazy* by Nat Hentoff; Bill Condon for 'Days of Joy and Heartbreak'; John Cotton for his poem 'The Film'; David Higham Associates Limited for the extract from *Drift* by William Mayne, and for the extract from *Quite Early One Morning* by Dylan Thomas; David Wilkinson Associates for 'Waldorf Salad' from *The Complete Fawlty Towers* by John Cleese and Connie Booth © Waterfall Productions Ltd and Connie Booth; Berlie Doherty for her poems 'The Face at the Window' and 'Race'; Faber and Faber Ltd for 'Tich Miller' reprinted from *Making Cocoa for Kingsley Amis* by Wendy Cope; Pamela Gillilan for her poem 'Kestrel'; Nigel Gray for his poem 'Adman'; David Harmer for his poem 'Dobbo's First Swimming Lesson'; Jonathan Cape Ltd and Gabrielle Lord for the extract from *Fortress* by Gabrielle Lord; Macmillan London and Basingstoke for the extract from *The Machine Gunners* by Robert Westall (1975), and for the extract from *Slake's Limbo* by Felice Holman; Wes Magee for 'Tracey's Tree' © Wes Magee; Margaret Gee Communications and Tortoiseshell Press for 'You Can't Love an Ostrich' by Kenneth Cook from *Frill-Necked Frenzy*; Mather Ray for his poems 'Remember Me' and 'Cross-Country', copyright Ray Mather 1987; Methuen London for the extract from *The Secret Diary of Adrian Mole Aged 13¾* by Sue Townsend; Michael Joseph Ltd for the extract from *The Day of the Triffids* by John Wydham © 1951 John Wyndham, for the extract from *A Kestrel for a Knave* by Barry Hines © 1968 by Barry Hines, and for the extract from *A Patch of Blue* by Elizabeth Kata, copyright © Elizabeth Kata 1961; Brian Moses for his poem 'The Way is Open'; Octopus Publishing Group for the extracts from *Ashes of Vietnam* by Stuart Rintoul; Oxford University Press for the extract from *Brother in the Land* by Robert Swindells (1984), © Robert Swindells 1984, and for the extract from *Dawn Wind* by Rosemary Sutcliff (1961), © Oxford University Press 1961; Penguin Books Ltd for 'The Children's Fall-Out Shelter', 'The Trouble with My Sister' and 'Billy Dreamer's Fantastic Friends' from *Gargling with Jelly* by Brian Patten, and for the extract from *On the Flip Side* by Nicholas Fisk; Peters Fraser & Dunlop Group Ltd for 'Money Moans' from *Sky in the Pie* by Roger McGough; Gordon Phillips for his poem 'Guitarman'; Robinson Publishing for 'Charles' by Shirley Jackson; Rogers, Coleridge & White Ltd for 'Cycling Down the Street to Meet My Friend John' from *Salford Road* (Kestrel, 1979) by Gareth Owen, and for 'Dear Examiner' from

Salford Road and Other Poems (Young Lions 1988) by Gareth Owen; Ian Serraillier for 'Film Star'; Solid Gold Publications for the video review 'Big' from *Video International Magazine*; Spike Milligan Productions for Spike Milligan's 'Beauty Without Cruelty' letters; Colin Thiele and Rigby Ltd for the extract from *The Fire in the Stone* (Rigby, 1973); Victor Gollancz Ltd for the extracts from *I am the Cheese* by Robert Cormier and *Rumble Fish* by S.E. Hinton.

Advertisements, photographs, book covers and cartoons
Auspac Media for the Frank & Ernest comic strip on p. 157, the Garfield comic strip on p. 169, and the Peanuts comic strip on p. 67, copyright United Feature Syndicate; Australian War Memorial for the photograph on p. 165; BBC for the photograph on p. 172; John Cardinal for the photographs on pp. 196 top, 197; Channel 10 for the photographs on pp. 155, 171; Coo-ee Historical Picture Library for the photograph on pp. 182–3; Malcolm Cross for the photograph on p. 247; The Directorate of the Drug Offensive (NSW) for the storyboard on p. 183; Gaffney International Licensing Pty Ltd for the Hagar comic strip on p. 37 © 1989 King Features Syndicate, for the BC comic strips on pp. 73, 248 © Field Enterprises 1982. Hodder & Stoughton for the cover on p. 230; Japan Airlines for the advertisement on p. 167; Lucasfilm Ltd for the photograph on p. 28; The Macmillan Company of Australia for the covers on pp. 13, 234; Macmillan Accounts and Administration Ltd for the cover on p. 120; Dale Mann/Retrospect for the photographs on pp. 143, 277; NASA for the illustration on p. 119; Northside Productions for the photographs on p. 81 top right, bottom left and bottom right; Pan Books (UK) for the cover on p. 84; Frank Park/ANT Photo Library for the photograph on p. 206; Penguin Books Australia for the cover on p. 124; Penguin Books Ltd for the covers on pp. 3, 128, 188, 191, 226, 260, 263, 268; Otto Rogge/ANT Photo Library for the photograph on p. 158; Silvestris/ANT Photo Library for the photograph on pp. 258–9; Stock Photos for the photographs on pp. 48–9, 80, 81 right centre, 83, 224–5; Transworld Publishers Ltd (Corgi Books) for the cover on p. 57; Wild and Woolley Pty Ltd for the Ron Cobb cartoon on p. 211; William Collins Pty Ltd for the covers on pp. 50, 54.

While every care has been taken to trace and acknowledge copyright, the publishers tender their apologies for any accidental infringement where copyright has proved untraceable. They would be pleased to come to a suitable arrangement with the rightful owner in each case.

Edited by Vivienne Perham
Illustrated by Carol Pelham-Thorman
Cover design and photograph by Jan Schmoeger

Solution to 'The Case of the Lost Diamond Brooch' (pages 254–6)
Lucien Standish is guilty. The advertisement only listed a post box number, yet he knew which house to go to.